Dr Arthur Janov is currently director of the Primal
Training Center in California. He lives part of
each year in France with his wife.

Also by Dr Arthur Janov:

The Primal Scream
Prisoners of Pain

The New
PRIMAL SCREAM

Primal Therapy Twenty Years Later

Dr Arthur Janov

ABACUS

First published in Great Britain by Abacus in 1991
Published in Cardinal by Sphere Books Ltd in 1992
This Abacus edition published in 1993
Reprinted 1993, 1999, 2001, 2003, 2004, 2009 (twice), 2010, 2011, 2012,
2013 (twice)

A CIP catalogue record for this book
is available from the British Library.

ISBN 978-0-349-10203-0

Typeset by Leaper & Gard Ltd, Bristol, England
Printed and bound in Great Britain by
Clays Ltd, St Ives plc

Papers used by Abacus are from well-managed forests
and other responsible sources.

MIX
Paper from
responsible sources
FSC® C104740

Abacus
An imprint of
Little, Brown Book Group
100 Victoria Embankment
London EC4Y 0DY

An Hachette UK Company
www.hachette.co.uk

www.littlebrown.co.uk

For France

For Ellie: Je t'aimerai à jamais

There are two ways to be fooled:
One is to believe what isn't so;
The other is to refuse to believe what is so.

Soren Kierkegaard

ACKNOWLEDGEMENTS

The production of a book always involves help by others. In my case, my wife France spent a good part of her life reading and correcting the text. She encouraged, offered suggestions, and was a continuous help to me. She was my daily sounding board.

An editor who was a real help was Dr David Lyon, a man with a wide ranging knowledge who was most helpful in the organization of the book, who saw where to cut and where to add, and above all to point out what was not clear and what required more precise explanation.

My secretary was Nadine Barner. Additional typing and organizational help was provided by Kerry and Diane Feltham, who often under time pressure never failed me. Thanks finally to my patients who over the years showed me the way, taught me more often than I could teach them, and who provided me with the insights into human behaviour that were my real education in the realm of psychology.

CONTENTS

Part Two – The Forms of Neurosis

Contents   xv

INTRODUCTION

Primal Therapy: Twenty Years Later

'Some years ago I heard something that was going to change the course of my professional life and the lives of my patients. What I heard was an eerie scream welling up from the depths of a young man lying on the floor during a therapy session. I can liken it only to what one might hear from a person about to be murdered.' (*The Primal Scream*, 1970.)

The scream that I described twenty years ago is the product of some unconscious, universal, intangible wounds that most of us carry around and which never seem to heal. My prophecy was indeed accurate. It did change my life and the lives of many thousands of patients. That scream has led me on a search for its sources, and that in turn has brought me to the depths of the unconscious. It has inspired individuals from thirty countries to come to my therapy, and given me a broader perspective on humanity. I believe that the discovery of the pain underlying that scream is an important discovery in the field of psychology, for it means, ultimately, the end to so much suffering in human beings. It means there is a way to stop the misery in which so many of us are mired every day of our lives.

After two decades of searching and researching, after dealing with thousands of patients with every imaginable psychological and physiological affliction, we have arrived at a precise, predictable therapy that reduces the amount of time one spends in treatment and eliminates all of the wasted motion. It is a therapy that has been investigated for over fifteen years by independent scientists, and the findings are consistent. Primal Therapy is able to reduce or eliminate a host of physical and psychic ailments in a relatively short period of time with lasting results. It can produce feeling human beings who can experience every aspect of themselves, whose brains are not compartmentalized so that one area no longer knows what another part is experiencing ... individuals whose bodies are no longer strangers to their minds.

A person who can feel can sense what lies within him, and no longer needs to deceive himself. Self-deception is a *sine qua non* of neurosis. It requires that we lie to ourselves. 'To thine own self be true' is hardly the neurotic's motto.

This book is not just about a psychotherapy. It is about the human condition. It is about how to detect neurosis and how we know what is normal. It is about weeping and its role in health for each of us. It is about anxiety and depression and what they really are. It is about despair and hope, and the silent scream known as illness. It is about the malignancy of hopelessless, tumourous depression, broken dreams, and ruptured relationships. It concerns the nature of love. And finally, it is about real intelligence, not about being cultured, educated and erudite. It is about being able to love and to give, to survive, and to lead a life which is intelligent, one that is neither self-destructive nor hurts others. How smart does anyone have to be to know that crying children should be picked up and soothed?

The pains we found underlying that scream I heard so long ago were what I call Primal Pains; they derive from any source early in life – surgery, physical abuse, or simple neglect. The central element of these pains comes from the lack of love. The key is that the event from which they arise contains more pain than could have been integrated at the time, making it necessary to repress a good part of it, and store it for future reference. Primal Pains arise not only from this lack of love but from those epiphanic moments or scenes when a child realizes he is not loved and will not be. They arise when he is shaken for a brief and forgotten moment by the understanding that he cannot be what he is and be loved, for that moment and for other moments of equally monumental hopelessness. He then struggles with all of his heart to be what parents want him to be. He puts away the pain, or rather it is automatically put away from him by our miraculous system of repression.

This repression effectively produces two selves at war with each other more: the real self, loaded with needs and pain, and the unreal self, the self out of touch with the other self that was still able to deal with the outside world. The function of the unreal self is to keep the real self from showing its face. Its role is to make the body perform despite the turmoil going on below. The best way to do this, it seems, is for the unreal self to remain ignorant of its own history. That is why I think neurotics are ahistoric beings. They have been robbed of their past by pain.

The major source of this pain is prolonged unfulfilled need early in life. At a certain key juncture, unmet needs for love, shelter and protection turn into pain, which in turn requires repression. After the split, the unreal self continues to act out on the basis of these needs. I call this program 'symbolic acting out', trying to obtain fulfilment in symbolic ways. This is the essence of neurosis. Old pains are repressed, then acted out in ways which are unreal and merely symbolic.

We have found a way to reverse this process by having patients go back and relive the original overwhelming scene, feeling or need, bit by bit over time until it is finally resolved and out of the system. Patients can reverse the neurotic evolutionary process, and can, in effect, reverse a history that goes back even to their birth. What we have found is that it is possible to ride the vehicle of feeling back through the years to those traumatic way stations where our development was retarded.

When individuals do this, there are predictable changes that we can measure over the years. Brain function and brain structure change, blood pressure and heart rate drop, and there are changes in numerous hormones. More importantly, our recent research indicates a significant change in the immune system of those who relive pain. This may well have implications for the treatment of catastrophic diseases such as cancer.

We now know a great deal about pain and how pervasive it is, even among those who would never believe it exists inside of them. We know more, too, about the process of repression, how it works and where. Science has moved along in the past twenty years, and so has Primal Therapy. Thus we are able to see how recent discoveries in the field of brain science, immunology, pain, repression, endorphines, weeping, and cancer are related to our work. What used to be hypothesis is now established fact. What was supposition is now demonstrable. What was a rather general theory is now a detailed structure that allows us to deal with and predict with some accuracy the course of therapy in our patients.

It means that for many there is a way out of pain and neurosis, a way out of migraines, ulcers, colitis, phobias, and constant broken relationships. It means that neurosis and its treatment are measurable entities, that progress can be quantified, that psychotherapy can now be brought into the realm of strict scientific method. It is no longer just an art form. The techniques are there, irrespective of the therapist, for altering mental illness.

The number one killer in the world today is neither cancer nor heart disease. It is repression. Unconsciousness is the real danger, and neurosis the hidden killer. In my decades of practice I have become increasingly convinced of this fact. Repression, a stealthy, hidden, intangible force strikes many of us down. It does so in so many disguised forms – cancer, diabetes, colitis – that we never see it naked for what it is. That is its nature – diabolic, complex, recondite. It is all pervasive, yet everywhere denied because its mechanism is to hide the truth. Denial is the inevitable consequence of its structure.

There is almost no disease, mental or physical, without repression. One of the ways we know the truth of this statement is through reversing disease by leading patients to their pain and lifting the lid of repression. Later on, we shall see how, in research, many diseases can be reversed simply by injecting chemicals that reverse the repressive process. We can see repression's work in high blood pressure, for example. When we put patients back into their early pain, blood pressures rises enormously; when they finish reliving this pain, blood pressure drops significantly.

What is being repressed, by and large, are needs and feelings. That is why feeling early pain, by weakening repression, allows someone to become feeling again. This is what gives back meaning and allows one to finally experience joy, beauty and colouration of life. It means unifying the selves and making someone organic, integrated and whole. We shall learn in this book why feelings are paramount. They put an end, not only to symptoms, but to the struggle for symbolic fulfilment. The real self emerges, and the search for oneself ceases. The real self has been found inside the pain.

The principles regarding Primal Pain and Primal Therapy have not changed in more than twenty years. Everything else has. I think that what has changed the most is the predictability of the treatment. In the beginning we did not have enough experience with a wide variety of patients to know what was going to happen, except in a general way, when we attacked the pain. Now we know not only what will happen, but on what level of consciousness the patient is operating. This allows us to know what to expect in the sessions which follow. The levels of consciousness which I first discovered some years ago have also been verified by a number of research scientists. It is something we see all the time – three discreet levels of consciousness which determine what kind of symptoms the person will have and what kind of behaviour to expect. We shall see more about these levels and how they work in the chapter on the Mind.

Patients go more deeply into the unconscious than they

used to, and we know much more about that unconscious and how dangerous or friendly it is. We know which early pains are too dangerous to feel, and which are not. We know how to steer patients into areas that will not overwhelm them. Our techniques today are light years ahead of what they were decades ago. New information on endorphines has clarified much for us in the realm of pain, and I hope for the readers of this book as well.

When I started out we were told that it was impossible for a person to relive his birth because the nervous system was not sufficiently mature at the time to record usable memories. I discounted the event of birth for years due to that misinformation. We know now that the birth trauma is indeed coded and stored in the nervous system. A whole cottage industry of rebirthers has grown up around my discoveries, leading to the most dangerous kind of charlatanism.

We certainly know more today about how early events are actually imprinted in us, which is something I shall discuss in detail. For that early environment and the impact of the early event never leave us. They remain embedded in the system forever. Fortunately, we have perfected a method of altering those imprints – imprints which seriously dislocate the functioning of so many organ systems.

Having seen every kind of sexual deviation imaginable, I am now also able to discuss what lies behind sexual dysfunction. We shall see that profound sexual problems often predate sex education and mis-education, and that the resolution of these problems comes from dealing with these very early events that have nothing inherently to do with sex. That does not mean that bad sex education doesn't contribute. There are other forces, however, never before considered, that play a part.

Nearly every work on stress discusses the subject in terms of the present: marital stress, job stress, etc. What I shall discuss here is a stressor that is imprinted, never leaves, and constantly puts us under enormous pressure. No matter how calm the environment in which we live, this kind of stress wreaks its havoc. It will kill us far before our time, which is why it is so important for us to understand it. This is particularly true because few of us are aware of its existence or its power. It is a sledgehammer force that escapes our knowledge, precisely because of repression.

In summary, the four basic principles I outlined in the original work were:

1. Pain is at the core of mental and physical illness – pain that comes from trauma and unmet needs.
2. There are three distinct levels of consciousness dealing with this pain.
3. Early traumas leave a permanent imprint in the system.
4. It is possible to relive these imprinted memories and resolve neurosis and physical disease.

This book is about what happened to these original discoveries, sometimes in the words of my patients, sometimes in my own. I have said it before: neurosis is a disease of feeling. Feeling is the problem of today. Again and again we encounter people who cannot feel, can't get much out of life, and believe existence is all grey and dull. For them it is, for their repressed pain keeps them in search of magic, a belief system that will automatically transform their life into something meaningful. The best I can offer is to transform someone into himself. I do not think there is any more than that to get in this life. There is nothing more healing, nor preventive of disease, than feeling.

The following pages will take us on a journey to the unconscious. We will investigate those subterranean passages that lead us out of darkness and into wellness and health. We know there is a way to understand and prevent illness. Our approach is a radical departure from conventional psychotherapy, no more the fifty-minute hour. Feelings determine how long the therapy lasts. No longer is the power in the hands of the doctor. The patient who feels always knows more about himself and what is best for him therapeutically than the doctor. No more insights dominated by wise men. Those will arise from the patient who feels.

We are aware that neurosis is not caused by lack of insights, nor is it resolved by inculcating them. Our approach is not to strengthen defences or to build an 'ego'. Rather, therapy involves penetrating the defences. Too often we confuse a strong defence system with being normal. On the contrary, a strong defence system means a potent neurosis – well sequestered, but there, nevertheless.

The contradiction is that the strong, well-encased neurotic is often highly functional in this society. Until he has a coronary at the age of fifty-seven he seems 'well'. The hidden forces take time to do their damage. Those who unburden themselves of their early pain also produce, and produce well and efficiently. But they are no longer driven to it. Work for them is no longer a discharge of tension. It is something positive. The neurotic produces and keeps busy to keep his past from intruding into the present. The task for health, rather, is to plunge into our history rather than fleeing from it, travelling to the source of our problems rather than spending all of our lives palliating them.

Primal Therapy differs from other therapies in the sense that we are not in the business of strengthening the defences so that people can function. We see defences as abnormal, a sign of pathology. That is not to say that they serve no function. They do, and they are most important when early pain is so shattering as to threaten the integrity of the system. They are a bulwark against the real self, however. And we are striving to make people real, not according to our prejudices, but according to the reality residing inside each and every one of us. It is tears that help dissolve the boundaries of the unconscious. That is why I believe that a therapy without tears, a neurosis without feeling, in effect, can never be effective.

We know what lies in the unconscious. Having been down to its antipodes we see that it is not populated with id forces, demons, or mysterious shadow powers. Indeed, there is nothing mystical about it. It is the repository of the heavy traumas of our lives, no more no less. Making the unconscious conscious is our job. After that, there is little left to do. We no longer need a special patois and esoteric diagnostic categories to describe people who simply were not loved, who got very little in their lives, and who suffer. Better to describe how that suffering comes about, what basic needs have to be fulfilled. Above all, we want to learn how to alleviate suffering. All the rest, for me, is extraneous.

It takes a good deal of time to resolve neurosis. It was laid down in slow, steady increments over the years, and won't be undone by any magic seminars or weekend lectures. We slide into neurosis without a whimper, and develop symptoms which seem mysterious. Nothing dramatic seems to have happened, but suddenly we are sick. We have been stricken down by our own reality. Our pain has finally become palpable, our self-deception fatal.

Because Primal Therapy has changed my life and the lives of thousands of individuals, I hope that learning about it will make a difference in the lives of those who read this book. While scientists ponder about ultimate proofs for the cause of this disease or that, there are many who suffer untold agonies each and every day of their lives. Research is a necessity for scientists, but a luxury for suffering humanity who cannot wait for final statistical proofs. For them, waiting may be a fatal disease. We don't have to wait to feel. We have the means to help people become feeling human beings. Our feelings have waited a long time for their chance. Let us give ourselves that gift.

Arthur Janov

PART ONE
Why We Get Sick

1

The Basic Human Needs

The world is having a nervous breakdown. People are irritable, aggressive, tense, and anxious. Neurosis is on the march. It is galloping ahead at full speed and no one seems to know what is going on or why. Above all, no one seems to know how to stop this inexorable march to destruction. Year after year there is more illness, more suicide, more violence, more alcoholism and drug addiction. The world is coming apart at the seams. Valium is the glue holding it together.

In this book I shall address myself to this mass neurosis to see if we can find out why we and our friends are crumbling emotionally, why we are sick, unhappy and depressed, and why society seems so unfeeling and indifferent.

I'm going to build a case for what I believe is the cure for neurosis. In order to do that, we shall have to explore the building blocks which form the basic structure for neurosis. The substrate of neurosis will always return to the basic need. We shall trace unfulfilled need as it wends its way through the body labyrinth disguising and transforming itself, first into pain, and then, due to repression, into phobias, obsessions, depression, high blood pressure, tension, anxiety, and yes, even cancer. We shall travel along the hegira of deprived need as it metamorphoses itself from a simple childhood state to deformed adult function including perversions, misperceptions, and paranoid ideas. Our pursuit will be methodical, systematic, unrelenting, and finally, I hope, rewarding. We shall not abandon our investigation until the nature of neurosis is laid bare, and more importantly, until the nature of cure is understood. The pursuit of feeling need will ineluctably lead us to the graveyard of neurosis, where childhood pain is interred at last. Let us first look into basic needs.

It seems as though we are all missing something and scrambling to get what we think we've missed. What we seem to want is simply 'more'. So many of us are searching for a way out, and are lost and bewildered by the world. It seems that emotional deprivation has become a legacy transmitted from one generation to the next. The inheritance of emotional deprivation, for some reason, seems more certain and ineluctable than the inheritance of eye colour and the shape of our mouths.

One wonders why one generation cannot fulfil the emotional and physical needs of its offspring. Why is the deprivation which they themselves suffered visited anew onto their own children, part of a cycle which no doubt began before our grandparents' time? Our grandparents, many of whom were born in the last century, or the early years of this century, were not only emotionally deprived themselves, but had only a limited understanding of what children's needs were. It was not widely understood that young children needed to be held and caressed a lot, nor that children had feelings that needed to be expressed. Rather, children were expected to behave and obey. Feelings were the last thing to be understood or respected.

Our Needs and Their Fulfilment

Even today, there is confusion about our needs and how to go about seeking their fulfilment. The result of this confusion is unhappiness, frustration, and a growing pessimism. Too often we harbour a cynicism about one another until we become an aggressive group of misanthropes. Our needs have been neglected from early on, not only by a non-caring, every-man-for-himself society, but by parents who still don't know what children need to grow up properly. Parents seem to know only discipline and struggle. They want children of character, but what they get are neurotics. It is everybody's fault and nobody's fault. It seems to be part of the human condition. It is not. I think we need to understand more about need and the pain it leads to when it is not fulfilled.

We are all born into this world a mass of need. The beginnings of our lives are completely dominated by needs which are 'hard-wired' in the system.

Our first needs are solely physical ones for nourishment, safety and comfort. Later, we have emotional needs for affection, understanding and respect for our feelings. Finally, intellectual needs to know and to understand emerge. The role of love is critical. Love is an essential quality in the fulfilment of needs at every level of development, and is contained in the satisfaction of all needs. The fulfilment of needs by one human being for another should not be a mechanical exercise, but must be rooted in genuine feeling.

Love: A Basic Factor in All Needs

There is, above all, a pervasive need to be loved. When we are children each new need in our development must be fulfilled in order for us to feel loved. Love is not something that rides above the satisfaction of needs, but something which is contained in such satisfaction. That is what love means to a child. Love is not simply words we utter to a child when we say, 'You know we love you', while we deprive him of real love by failing to touch him. It means first understanding what those needs are, and then satisfying them.

Very early in life, while we are still in the womb, love means that the mother cares enough about her baby to feed herself properly, to make sure that she reduces the stress in her life, that she neither smokes nor drinks, and that she tries to lead a healthy life. Even before conceiving a child, love means that she prepares herself for the baby, that the birth of a child is truly something that she wants and plans for, not an accident that disappoints her. Her sense of disappointment, if it exists, will find its way into the baby's system and create havoc. Love means having a baby for the right reasons, that the baby is someone she can love and give to, not an object she is using to hold a marriage together, or something she produces for some other unreal reason.

Love means a proper birth, a birth without drugs whenever possible, a natural birth that will give the baby every chance in life. A mother cannot love a baby knowing how harmful anaesthetic is, and then load herself with drugs to make childbirth more comfortable. Nor is a baby going to be loved when he is not allowed to develop in a natural way, but is delivered according to a doctor's timetable by caesarean section.

Love means that the child is with her mother just after birth and not left alone to feel terrified, alone and alienated. Those minutes and hours after birth are crucial for normal development. The baby must have frequent physical contact with its parent. A major portion of the brain is given over to touch; clearly, it is important. One cannot imagine loving an infant and then turning it over to a nurse or maid immediately after birth. The touch it receives must be loving, caring and tender, not something done perfunctorily, harshly, and hurriedly by a paid employee. Touch is crucial in early life. Without enough of it the baby will suffer for the rest of its life from that lack. If the mother is tense, and has never understood just how needful a baby is, she will be impatient. If the father gets up several times a night with the baby and then has to go to work in the morning, he may become irritable. He is often unable to be the kind of parent the baby needs. A baby doesn't understand father's work; it understands only its own needs.

Emotional Needs of the Developing Child

As the child develops he must be allowed to be himself. That means going at a pace that is inherent to him and no one else. The child must walk and talk when appropriate and not when a parent, who needs a bright, advanced child, decides it should. The child cannot be loved when he is forced to learn way ahead of his time.

As time goes on, the child has a new set of emotional needs beyond the physical ones. He needs, not only to be touched, as he will for the rest of his life, but he needs to be allowed to express his feelings – to be angry, to be negative, to say 'no' and to not have to obey instantly when someone gives him an order. In short, his feelings must be respected. He must be allowed not only to receive affection, but just as importantly, to give it. He must be allowed to hug and kiss spontaneously without being brushed aside. A good birth and plenty of physical affection puts a child way ahead in terms of avoiding pain and being normal later on.

The emotional needs of a child include being able to talk about feelings to one's parents without fear of disapproval or condemnation. A child needs to be allowed to say, 'I'm afraid', without being shamed. He needs to be able to say, 'I don't like Uncle Harry', without being chastised for his feelings. When a child is not permitted these things he learns not to express himself, to keep everything inside until he loses track of how he really feels.

The young child is very sensitive to his surroundings. It doesn't take much to alter his natural tendencies. He learns before he speaks. He can understand that he cannot crawl on his father's lap or grab mother's legs any time he wants. It takes only one or two severe reprimands to divert these natural tendencies. He soon learns to give up on physical love in favour of some kind of approval from his parents. He learns that he cannot be loved when he wants it, only when his parents decide to bestow love upon him.

He also learns not to ask for what he wants. If a parent

needs to feel important or smart, it will be the child who will be pressed into service. Thus, the father who needs to know everything will not tolerate being challenged by his children. They will soon knuckle under. They will soon learn to talk only about him if he has needs to be talked to and listened to, needs which originated in his own childhood.

Children learn instinctively what they need to get by in life. It is an automatic response. The depressed mother makes the child into someone who must cheer her up because he needs a normal, happy, smiling mother. I must emphasize that whatever goes wrong, the child, with no other frame of reference, whose parents are the world to him, thinks it is his fault. He struggles to make his parents into what their own parents could not – loved human beings. He struggles to make them feel important, wanted, respected, attractive, liked or smart, whatever it is that they need. If the parent could never make friends as a child, then his own child will have to be his friend.

A child needs not only the obvious: shelter, proper nourishment and medical care, but also stability, routine and a calm environment. Clearly, two parents fighting all the time affects the fulfilment of these needs. Feeling for your child is not just feeding, clothing and providing shelter, which too many parents view as the *summum bonae* of child rearing. Rather, it is giving the child the feeling that he or she is wanted, adored, and accepted for himself. When a parent says he has worked hard, thus ignoring the family, in order to provide for them, he has probably done everything but provide that which is essential in child rearing – love. How many of us would have settled for a little less elegant shelter and fewer steaks on the table if we could have had a feeling of total affection in exchange?

The child also needs to be understood as a person. This means that his faults as well as his assets must be honestly recognized. If he has learning deficiencies, the parent must accept this and not push the child in order to reflect well on the parent. It means that the desires, interests and choices of the child must be respected. A frail child is not going to be a football player and a young girl cannot be the boy that daddy wanted. Love means to listen to the child and not rush off when he has something to say. It means supporting him in what he wants to do with his life. It means understanding his fears and apprehensions, his anger and his tantrums. It does not mean suppressing everything for appearances. It means having time for him, time to listen to his complaints, fears and hopes.

The Importance of Freedom

A child needs freedom, not only of expression, but of movement. A child needs to be allowed to explore, to use his curiosity without being stopped at every turn of the way. Too often, parents put children on a tight leash. Every move the child makes is controlled. Every avenue he explores is circumscribed. Children soon feel hedged in and, as a consequence, begin to hedge themselves in. They lose their natural, bounteous curiosity. They lose their enthusiasm and spontaneity. Parents who have had their spontaneity squeezed out of them have forgotten. The child who is shushed and reprimanded for her buoyancy time after time, will stop being emotional and spontaneous. Later on, she may have a very unhappy sex life when it is time to react.

A child needs to say, 'Hold me mommy', without hesitation and without feeling she will be rebuffed by a mother who cannot tolerate closeness. The child never knows mother has a problem with affection (having been deprived herself) and imagines something is wrong with herself. Then feelings of low self-esteem, and feelings of being unlovable set in. Parents have to be genuinely interested in the child and not distracted by their own lack of fulfilment.

The Free Flow of Love

Once there is genuine love and interest in the child as another human being, all interaction flows naturally. Then the child can say freely what is on his mind and be understood. He can express his ideas about the world, his friends, school or whatever, and be respected for his ideas, rather than being ignored. He needs to be listened to because he needs to express himself. He does not need a constant, 'Don't bother me now. Can't you see I'm busy?'

All of the above is not so difficult if it flows from someone who truly wants and loves his child and who isn't suffering from a mass of his or her own unfulfilled need. Unfulfilled needs will soon be transferred to the child. It is very difficult to fulfil a child's emotional needs when the child is not wanted. Too much of the parents' behaviour will be perceived by the child as pretence. Children are never fooled. From birth they are all feeling, and sense every nuance of their parents.

It may seem banal to say that children are human beings and need what we all need. But there are many parents who tell their children that they love them without ever showing that they do, and imagine that they have done their job. Imagine telling your boyfriend, husband, girlfriend or wife that you love them without ever touching them. It would be hard to expect them to actually perceive love in your attitude.

When love is there, the key antidote for neurosis is present. Its absence is the central ingredient around which neurosis grows. It is usually the subtleties that account for emotional illness, the small nuances of feelings, not the acts themselves. One can be held by a parent who is extremely tense. That touch makes the child feel uncomfortable. Or one can be held by a parent who is calm, relaxed and loving.

This is easy to understand through the analogy of a loving, adult sexual relationship. Obviously, the best experience is with someone who isn't a tense wreck. Without the sexual component, the principles with regard to loving children are the same ... full focus on the child, physical attention, lots of time, no other distractions, with the child becoming the whole universe for those moments.

When Needs Go Unfulfilled

When needs are not fulfilled the child suffers, not, unfortunately, for just the moment, but for the rest of his life. There is a timetable of need; certain needs can only be fulfilled at that time and no other. A newborn needs immediate closeness to his mother right after birth. Those first hours are critical. If this doesn't happen there will be pain forever after. And nothing the child or adult does later can undo that deprivation.

It will not do any good for a parent to apologize later for all the deprivation visited upon a child. The hurt is there and is never erased by a request to be pardoned. You don't erase need with an apology. That force is gigantic. The hurt is lodged in the storage tank. A self-centred parent who leaves a child early in his life cannot be forgiven, no matter how much both desire it later on. The lack of fulfilment is a reality. The divorced parent who hardly sees his child cannot come around in the child's teen years and expect to start afresh. There is a load of hurt the child must feel first. It isn't a matter of forgiveness. That is meaningless. Feeling the need, hurt and resentment, however, may clear out some of the debris so the parent and child may have some kind of relationship.

To feel means to go back and experience the exact needs of the infant and child. To feel the ache to be held as it happened. To feel the early resentments, the needs to be listened to, not criticized, to be taken along on trips, to feel part of, to belong, etc. It means to experience all of one's self, which means feeling the pain brought by the original deprivation.

The Reality of Need

What I am discussing are not just ideas. We have seen these needs in all of their full agony in patients who have been deprived. Certain so-called 'needs' are unreal, however. I have never seen a real need for prestige or fame in patients on the floor of my clinic, except as a substitute for other needs that were real.

The needs I have discussed are no more than the result of my observations, discovered among the pleas of human beings in touch with their childhoods and infancies. These needs are neither metaphorical nor conceptual. They are basic biologic realities. When they are felt, the biology from which they spring changes all the way down to the cellular level, including the nerve cells of the brain. Going through the motion of feeling, or sobbing in abreaction or catharsis will not affect those changes. Basic changes must always involve basic need. Fulfilment stabilizes the system.

What about poverty? Aren't proper surroundings a basic need? Yes and no. Love is always the priority in avoiding neurosis. But living in abject circumstances certainly affects development. There is a need to have clothes, housing, and the material comforts that others have. But when a patient lies on the floor on therapy and exposes his naked need, material comforts are rarely cried about. Living in poor surroundings will only make one feel inferior when the other emotional factors are missing. Poverty, in short, is a factor in illness, but in my experience, it is not paramount. I had always believed that poverty was more of a factor than it is. But it is the patient who decides what is crucial, not I.

In Primal Therapy we do not suggest needs to patients. In the beginning we never know exactly what they are. The patient feels them, and in these feelings needs are revealed.

The Rise of Substitute Needs

When needs are not fulfilled, substitute or secondary needs take their place. When a neurotic parent treats his child neurotically he creates in the child new needs that are not biologically based but derivative. A mother who must dominate her child, and who therefore renders the child passive and weak, creates a 'need' in the child either to dominate a partner in adult life or, depending on the rest of life's circumstances, to find another dominating woman to marry. One marries a controlling person in order to go on acting dependent. A child who was rejected or ignored may grow up with a need to be famous. This is obviously not a childhood biological need.

The so-called need for self-esteem, for example, is not basic. A loved child feels wanted and worthy. He isn't spending his adult life trying to boost his ego or to feel important. He was important to the only people who counted when he was a baby – his parents. To be unimportant to them means to have 'low self-esteem'.

Being unloved makes one feel unattractive, thus the feeling, 'I could not attract them'. The later struggle then is to attract everyone, regardless of whether or not they really matter to one's life. The neurotic need to be reassured constantly about one's looks happens when you don't feel good about yourself. The child bases his worth in every sense on the love of the parents. Feeling loved allows her to base her worth on yourself.

The treatment for low self-esteem is not about trying to feel worthy, nor of ego-boosting exercises. Quite the opposite. Treatment lies in letting oneself feel the devastating feeling of not being wanted or desired. This allows one to see that the inability to love was the parents' problems and was not due to some inherent flaw in the child. This can only happen when one stops struggling against needing constant reassurance, and feels to its depths the lack of love.

Substitute Needs Become Neurotic

A neurotic parent creates neurotic needs in his child. A child who is not responded to because his parents are lifeless grows into an adult who has a need to get an emotional response out of others. He needs a reaction. The feeling is, 'Look at me. Know I am alive. Know that I exist.'

Later, as an adult, the child who did not receive a response may try through acting dramatically to become a 'star'. Or he may talk incessantly in order to be the centre of attention. He exaggerates and dramatizes in order to provoke a response in others. Sometimes this kind of person goes to a psychologist and is diagnosed as suffering from 'primary narcissism'. It doesn't have to be that complicated. He just needed some basic attention so he could be himself. Nor is the situation resolved by present day fulfilment alone. If present day fulfilment could change one's feelings, the movie actors I see who have had more than their share of adulation wouldn't feel like totally worthless human beings.

A parent who treats his child without warmth may create a need in the person to later become involved with cold, icy kinds of people. There is now an instilled fear of warmth, and a new need not to get close to others. Or a pseudo-independence – 'I don't need anyone else. I'm happy in my isolation'. Now there is the 'need to be alone' because being with others (meaning the parents, early on) means pain. No normal person enjoys being alone all of the time.

Once someone is deprived in childhood they grow up confused about the difference between love and need. They tend to 'fall in love' with someone who can fulfil their needs. The woman who has been infantilized will 'fall in love' with a take-charge, controlling man so that she can go on being the baby her parents made her. The man whose parents were emotionless, and who has suppressed his feelings and warmth, will not seek an open, warm partner, but rather someone who is reserved like his parents. Then the struggle begins to try to make this partner warm and loving.

The woman who never had a father is going to 'fall in love' with an older man and make him into what she needs. She will expect him to be everything her father wasn't. She does not see the man for what he is just as she never saw her parents for what they were. This is a sure recipe for early divorce.

Does she need to learn different expectations? Not at all. Her expectations are real. The problem is that she must feel these needs in context, in terms of the real person she wants – her father. She will then see what she needs to see, that is, her needs. We never see beyond our needs no matter how smart we are. We can never be wiser than our unfelt needs, nor can we be more perceptive than our needs allow. Unfelt needs make us dumb in specific relevant areas. We don't perceive a person realistically because our unmet needs are immediately superimposed on the reality of the person. We always see our needs first. That is because they are our primary reality; all else is secondary.

The Resolution of Neurotic Needs

The basic need for the neurotic is resolution. The neurotic must resolve his early needs so that he is not stuck 'back there' for the rest of his days. If he doesn't get that resolution he will have exactly the same need at fifty that he had at five and with the same force. Nothing that happens in later life can weaken that force one iota. Once the old needs are felt, when the person can return to his childhood and experience his life back then, the derivative symbols, such as the need for power, prestige, and fame fade away. As long as symbolic needs remain, life's energy, what Freud called 'libido', will be channelled into them. The person will seek power (because he was totally controlled when young and had no power over himself) and will not be into sex. The energy that should go into relationships is now diverted into the pursuit of symbols.

Remember: first there is need and then 'the need for'. No

matter what 'the need for' is for – sex, money, power, beliefs – it is first and foremost a primary, pure need.

When someone can discuss his symbolic needs and begin to feel his real needs there is often an overwhelming sadness – a sadness at the waste of all that energy and time – at the waste of life. It is a sadness of resignation, 'I'm never going to please them no matter what I do.' Then the drive and the dream are over. It is time to get down to real life.

2

Primal Pain: The Great Hidden Secret

The Nature of Emotional Pain

When people's needs remain unfulfilled they are transformed into emotional pain. Pain is something we usually associate with physical origins. We are familiar with the pain of a toothache, the pain caused by bodily injury, or by an internal organic disorder. The pain we experience when we feel unloved or unwanted is just as real. When emotional needs go unfulfilled, there are real sensations of profound bodily discomfort, anxiety, depression, headaches, stomach aches, and unfocused fear. Need deprivation is a threat to the integrity of the system. It is transformed into pain because it is pain that alerts us to the threat this deprivation poses.

When the needs of a child for love and affection, touching, and safety are not met, pain signals the system to mobilize and take protective action. The child is driven to seek fulfilment of unmet needs in one way or another. If there is no way for the needs to be met, repressive forces will stifle the need.

Lack of fulfilment threatens survival. Pain is simply a notice of this threat, a notice of what is missing. It directs us to get what we need, and is ultimately itself repressed. The power of the pain is equivalent to the intensity of the need. If you don't get the love you need part of you is lost to yourself.

Later in life, we learn to substitute one need fulfilment for another, seeking symbolic or substitute gratification. A baby

17

who needs has no alternative but to either feel continuous agony, or shut off. He can't get to the store for cigarettes nor phone a pal to see a movie. He represses. Repression is an automatic response to the pain of emotional deprivation.

The threat from not being held and soothed early on, for example, sets in motion a complex series of chemical processes. The end result of these processes is a shutdown of that very threat. Awareness of need ceases. Instead, one begins to substitute gratifications representing substitute wants. Tranquilizers, cigarettes, or food do what touch should have done – relax us. Children need touch for proper development. If they don't get it, their development is slowed and growth is retarded.

As children, we need to express our real feelings to our parents. We hurt if our parents are indifferent. If they force back our resentment and our rage we hurt. We can no longer be ourselves and be natural. Our 'nature', therefore, is warped, and that causes pain. If you don't let an arm move naturally, if you bind it with tape, it is going to hurt. If you don't let emotions move naturally you get the same result. These emotions are part of our physiology just as an arm is part of our anatomy. If a child is hungry he needs to be fed. The need to express feelings is just as physiological as hunger.

A child needs to feel accepted for what he is. If he is not, he is forced to be something or someone else – the intellectual, the athlete, or whatever. He must rework himself, and that causes emotional pain. We all need to grow up in harmony with ourselves, to be comfortable inside our skins. If we are uncomfortable with our natural feelings we suffer.

Primal Pain

It seems simple to define pain. Whatever hurts must be pain, as circular as that reasoning sounds. But what about emotional pain that doesn't hurt in the same way as a toothache or a cut finger gives us pain? What can we call that? I use the term Primal Pain to designate emotional pain that goes largely unfelt at the time it occurs. Primal pain is a pain that doesn't hurt, at least not consciously.

Primal Pain is not like a pinch where we yell 'ouch', shake our fingers, and in a few minutes get over it. Primal Pain is like being pinched so hard you cannot feel it, so that the pain goes on forever.

Primal Pain is continually being processed below the level of conscious awareness, but that doesn't mean it is not there doing its damage. It just means that it is too much to feel.

The repressed pain of thwarted emotional needs is beyond description. When it approaches consciousness, it can drive people crazy or to suicide. Someone who is totally shut off cannot imagine the intensity involved. That is why when patients come close to Primal Pain they are sometimes obsessed with suicide. They are inclined to choose death over the direct experience of Primal Pain.

The most catastrophic pains are the early ones which are life-threatening. Pains such as coming close to death at birth, or the pain of the hopelessness of ever being loved as a small child are examples of such pain. The system isn't geared to tolerate pains of this magnitude. Quite the opposite: it is set up to produce a morphine-like product to block the awareness of the pain so that the baby will not die or, in the case of an adult, so that the person can get on with his life.

Primal Pain always brings repression into life. The amount of repression elicited depends on the level or valence of pain. The morphine-like substances we produce internally to repress emotional pain can be hundreds of times more powerful than commercially prepared morphine. When Freud wrote about repression he could only speculate. Now we have a much clearer picture of how it works and where in the brain it operates.

There is only so much we can take. Pain mobilizes the system like nothing else. It boosts the heart rate and raises the blood pressure. A newborn child, in the midst of birth, can stand a pulse and blood pressure of 200 for only so long before he is in danger of expiring. Repression shuts down that extreme mobilization. Later on we shall see how, when the repressive gates are lifted, the exact early memory is reproduced with the very same heart rate and blood pressure as occurred originally.

If we start to freeze, we hurt. When the pain is too much we go numb and feel nothing. When we start to thaw and feel again we hurt once more. That is the paradigm for emotional hurt. Emotional pain is repressed and forgotten. An emotional numbness ensues, an inability to feel. When the pain is later remembered, the hurt begins anew. Thus we hurt in the first instance when the emotional pain occurs, and we will hurt later if we allow ourselves to remember the original pain.

Pain, Need, and Natural Development

The reason we hurt is because an alien intrusion, blocking our natural tendencies, causes a dislocation of natural functions of the body. It hurts not to be natural. To be frustrated and deprived by one's parents, to react angrily and then to be threatened by them because of the anger, is to have one's system deformed. If we were meant to stand up at one year of age but anxious parents force us to stand at eight months, we shall hurt. The neurologic system will be affected. If we were meant to nurse for one year but were weaned after the third week, a basic need will have been frustrated. If we are resentful because our parents favour another sibling, and we are punished when we express that resentment, we hurt. We cannot be what we are and feel what we feel. 'Let me be!' is the frequent scream we hear in our therapy.

I don't know how to describe the pain I have seen in Primal Therapy. I practiced a psychoanalytically based psychotherapy for seventeen years and never saw anything like it. When one sees patients who feel one feeling, hour after hour, month after month, writhing and thrashing, sobbing and screaming, one just begins to understand what is compacted inside most of us. It is an ineffable experience. It is not comprehensible on an intellectual level. Once that pain is observed it is no longer a mystery why we later fall ill with heart attacks, strokes, or cancer.

The great wonder is how it is that such a gigantic amount of pain can reside compressed in our bodies without our being aware of it. It is repression we must thank. Repression diffuses its energy so that it is found in our high blood pressure, compulsive sexuality, asthma and colitis, in daydreams, posture and headaches. It is no wonder, then, that after a course of Primal Therapy, hypertensives average a drop of 24 points in blood pressure.

The needs and the pain are what drives us, using up tremendous energy. Repression detaches the energy of the pain from the experience of it. Someone with a lot of drive is generally someone in a good deal of pain. That is why the neurotic cannot relax. No matter how hard he tries to stop, his motor is constantly running and nothing can slow it down permanently. It is running on what I call 'Primal Fuel'.

The Mystery of Primal Pain

It is astonishing how electrical impulses and a chemical soup sloshing around the cranium can end up in a psychological state called hurting. What is that leap that transforms something happening to a jelly-like organ into something psychological? And how is it that by a psychologic manoeuvre, psychic self-deception, we can annul that pain and believe we do not hurt? This much we do know: pain signals are forms of information which, in sufficient quantity, manage to overload the system and produce the opposite – no pain.

Is emotional pain a feeling? No. It is what happens to feelings when they don't take their natural course. That is why feeling feelings ends the pain. Pain always involves unconsciousness. Until pain becomes conscious it is amorphous suffering. The suffering system travels along ancient nerve pathways closest to the midline of the nervous system.

The suffering system projects nerve fibres to great portions of the neocortex from lower brain structures such as the thalamus. That is why we know we are hurting but don't know why.

The pain system involves newer nerve pathways. This system is more precise, and tells us what is hurting, and often why we are hurting.

Consciousness of pain means consciousness. The discriminating pain pathways involve selective targets in the cortex that let us know what precisely is going on below. These connecting pathways transform suffering into pain, then pain into consciousness. Feeling a hollowness in the stomach and a constant ache or cramp is part of suffering. Feeling the emptiness of one's life is a connected feeling. Feeling depressed and despairing is part of suffering. Feeling the hopelessness of never being loved by one's mother is a connected feeling.

Connection dispels suffering and disconnection maintains it; this is a phenomenon we will explore in much greater detail later in this book. This means when you cannot feel a precise emotional pain, you are going to suffer. And when patients feel only a small aspect of an old feeling they will go on suffering from that portion which remains unfelt and unconnected. It is not that the patient isn't getting anywhere. Rather, there is just additional suffering that requires connection. It can't be done in one day.

We are discussing a quantity of energy in suffering, an energy that can be channelled in the body and the mind. A feeling of rage can be transformed into a severe headache. The rage is now contained in the symptom. When the rage is expressed – and it must be fully *expressed* not just *understood* – the symptom will disappear. When the rage becomes conscious through full expression (pounding, screaming), it is transformed into a feeling and is no longer an element of suffering. To be 'aware' of rage has nothing to do with being conscious of it. A person who must talk incessantly discovers that there is hurt inside his words. He feels, 'I must keep on talking to keep from finding out that no one listens.' It is a grab for attention. That kind of talking is symptomatic of a feeling.

The Primal Pool of Pain

In *The Primal Scream* I discussed the Primal Pool of pain. I believe this notion is as true today as it was then. What it means is that throughout one's childhood small pains accumulate and compound as the child encounters adverse events. It is a figurative description of what I have seen with patients, but somehow it reflects the fact that there is a build-up of pain to high levels. This pool must be drained somehow to take the burden off the system and to allow the person to relax. The tributaries to the Primal Pool can come from both physical hurts such as surgery, and psychological wounds such as being ignored. Both are processed in the same way. Enough surgery can accumulate into an overload just as enough rejection can. Therapy must drain that pool over time to lower the burden of pain and allow the system to right itself. This is done by reliving one bit of a feeling at a time, integrating and resolving it. It is the transformation of pain into feeling. That is how neurotics become feeling human beings.

There is a group of structures in the brain charged with processing and storing feelings. The limbic brain is a ring of structures under the neocortex. It organizes our emotions, acting as a capacitor, accepting a certain level of input and rerouting the excess of the feeling into other channels, organ systems, or the ideational mind. Thus it is a container for pain, but one with a limited capacity. When that capacity is exceeded, when there is an overspill of energy caused by emotional pain, we are in a state of acute anxiety.

There is an experiment with dogs who were given a slight zap of electrical energy to their limbic systems day after day. They found that it took a lot less stimulation to make them have seizures. The slightest event produced in them a massive global discharge of electrical energy ... a seizure.

This seems to be what happened when we were children. Insult after insult was processed by the limbic system. The pain accumulated until we were very susceptible to even the most neutral stimulus. Thus, the slightest frustration could lead to massive rage. In our brainwave studies a person entering a giant old feeling will have an almost epileptic equivalent in terms of brain activity. The limbic system is pouring out its stored energy.

Measuring Emotional Pain

We measure pain by its processing mechanisms, by brain-wave studies, vital signs such as blood pressure and pulse, and by hormones. The body does not distinguish between physical and psychological pain, (both stimulate the same repressive chemicals) nor does it distinguish between psychological or physical pain-killers. Someone can be given a suggestion that such and such a tablet will kill his pain and feel no pain, even when there is nothing in that tablet (a placebo), in the same way that someone feels no pain after getting a shot of a real pain killer. The mind is a strong pain-killing agent. It is as good, and probably better than any shot of morphine – for reasons we shall discover shortly.

Primal pain can be dampened, re-channelled, and diverted, but it cannot be erased. It cannot be cajoled or encouraged out of existence. An addict will never get over his addiction to pain-killers by these means. Even heavy electric shocks will not erase memory. This has been shown in animal research. Once something is learned, you cannot extinguish it. Thus a feeling, 'I am not loved', never leaves once it is set down in early childhood. It remains pristine pure and resembles Freud's immutable id-unconscious because it lasts forever and is unchanging. Life experience, being loved by hundreds, will never change that feeling one iota. Imagine! Part of our physiology, perhaps the only part, that is impervious to change. The reason is survival of the species. The painful feeling remains stored, waiting for its chance at consciousness and resolution. The organism is waiting for its chance to return to health and to its evolutionary destination. Freud, not knowing exactly about imprinted pain, gave this phenomenon a mystical aura – the id – but in fact it was only a duplicate of the early traumatic environment, now internalized. As we shall see in a moment the whole evolutionary thrust is to get rid of that 'inside' non-self and return to the real self – the healthy one.

The Nature of Emotional Memory

Every cell in our body 'remembers' its natural state. Take, for example, the one-celled amoeba. When it is put into a solution of water polluted with India ink granules, it will literally absorb those granules and store them in vacuoles. These noxious elements become part of its physiology. Then, when put in clean water (a healthy environment) the vacuoles will move to the edge of the cell membrane and discharge those granules. Thus, the amoeba restores itself to a healthy condition.

All organic life has certain basic processes in common. Every organism strives to achieve homeostasis, natural equilibrium. When there is early pain the memory and charge are stored intact inside the cells of the emotional brain centres waiting for their day to be released. These foreign elements are now part of the physiology.

When the environment is again propitious, when there is a warm, loving, therapeutic environment conducive to feeling, the old pain begins its discharge. The body is getting rid of stored harmful stimuli, just like the India ink granules. After pain is discharged, the body returns to its original healthy state.

I have implied that somehow emotional pain can accumulate and be stored. Clearly, this is a function of memory. We can respond to stress very early in life: even in the womb we code and store it. It endures as a memory. Implicit in the notion of reliving is that memory lasts. What used to be outside is now inside. All the smells, sights, and sounds of an early event are there every minute of our lives and can be called forth any second of our lives. What a miracle that a complete environment in every minute detail is in our brains and bodies as a duplicate copy. Moreover, we respond first to that environment and then to the outside one. The traumatic memory becomes a filter which determines how we later respond to events.

Why is there a duplicate copy of childhood events? It is one way to incorporate a dangerous environment internally and render it both encapsulated and innocuous. Internally, we can remove its explosive charge or at least be removed from its explosive charge by this encapsulation. We can keep it isolated internally until we are grown up and able to experience the pain. Then we can, so to speak, 'spit it out'. What is true for the amoeba is also true for all human life.

We even know that a foetus feels pain in the womb. Two investigators, Anand and Hickey, have pointed out that 'the nerve tracts carrying pain signals from the spinal cord to the lower centres of the brain are almost fully developed at 35–37 weeks of gestation ... EEG (brain wave) studies show well-developed electrical activity in both cerebral hemispheres at 26 weeks.' At that age the developing foetus is capable of the registration of emotional and physical pain.

In a report to the *New England Journal of Medicine*, Anand and Hickey further point out that after circumcision there is evidence of continued memory of the event. There are later behavioural changes which indicate the disruption of 'the adaptation of newborn infants to their post-natal environment.'

These researchers go on to say that the synaptic and cellular changes required for this kind of very early memory depend on the plasticity and malleability of the brain, which happens to be 'highest during the prenatal and neonatal periods'. The fact that early memory endures is crucial to the notion of being able to later relive emotional pain. Without coded memory such a thing would be unthinkable. Such emotional memory depends on the functioning of the limbic system, a part of the brain which both authors find 'well-developed and functioning during the newborn period'.

Capacity for Stress in the Newborn Child

It should not be surprising that Ananad and Hickey found that babies react to events much more strongly than adults. In a 1983 study of the stress response of babies undergoing surgery, Anand said, 'To my surprise I found that babies had five times the stress response of adults undergoing similar surgery. Hormone levels, blood pressure, heart rate and levels of metabolic by-products all skyrocketed.' The importance of this is that the response is obviously more than a baby can bear. Part of the response is blocked, gated, and held in storage for a lifetime, becoming the source of later tension. The emotional memory apparatus during all of this time remains operational.

Nor is the baby's stress response confined to surgery. It can be present in the case of emotional trauma as well. That is the function of the limbic system. This system contains pain receptors, the number of which are actually increased by · the presence of pain. But Anand is only proving experimentally what we have seen for decades: when a patient relives gagging and choking due to a lack of oxygen at birth, it is clear that it is not a fake experience. The patient cannot by any act of will catch his breath, and it will take seconds before he does. This is memory in its crystalline form. It is within the limbic system that one aspect of a memory becomes connected with another; a sight with a smell, a sound with a touch. When a patient is into his old feelings, all aspects of the memory ascend to consciousness and emotional memory flowers.

Richard Thompson of the University of Southern California investigated the memory trace in animals. He found that with repeated stimulation, certain nerve cells link with others to form a bond. As nerve pathways continue to become linked, movement across the synapse or nerve gap becomes facilitated, and that is what is responsible for the memory. It is like a switchman who has opened all the barriers so that the train slides through smoothly. It is, if you will, a 'groove' that makes later events channel themselves easily into it. That groove is responsible for habitual behaviour. If a baby comes near death, the thought of death in the face of adversity becomes a memory or a groove. Therefore, when this child becomes an adult, and he is faced with problems, his first thoughts may be of death and suicide.

Too often we consider the foetus and the newborn as some kind of blob where nothing registers because the foetus can't talk about it. We see from our observations, and from recent research, that the infant registers experiences with a great impact. Being able to describe or discuss the experience has nothing to do with that impact. Later on, the person will have all kinds of misperceptions and strange ideas when he tries to put words to wordless, early experience.

The infant, in fact, has a wide open sensory window, and is more sensitive than he will ever be again. He feels more because he doesn't have a developed cortex or thinking brain to dilute experience. None of this should be surprising when we consider that even plants remember. If you take a pea-tendril, which reacts to light, and put it in the dark, whatever happens to it will be 'remembered' until it is returned to the light. If you touch it in the dark, it will lean towards that touch only when it is light again. It has remembered and stored information.

Emotional Memory is not Conscious Recall

Emotional memory is not the same as conscious recall. We can easily remember our good times in childhood. It takes only a bit of recall. But no wilful conscious determination is going to recall painful, emotional memory. Those can only be remembered on an emotional level by the feeling system.

The idea of a hidden memory of pain is difficult to accept because pain cannot be recalled with ease, and because it is hidden. This is why we use the term 'Primal Pain'. It is like the force of gravity. It is a totally unconscious influence that is always there. If gravity had not been discovered, we would never have known about its effects. It is time to recognize the influence of pain. It is a force that moves societies while remaining our mutual, mass secret. When we consider that our internally manufactured morphine is found in the placenta and in the most primitive brain structures, we must realize that unconsciousness can begin in the womb. In a sense we are 'out of it' before we are in it, where life is concerned. Is it any wonder that we are not aware?

Primal Pain is the great hidden secret of our day, part of the mass unconsciousness; the unconscious conspiracy through which we all agree to deny the central realities of our time, our dubious legacy of repressed needs, feelings, and pain.

3

Repression: The Gates of the Brain and The Loss of Feeling

Gating: The Mechanism of Repression

The principal mechanism through which pain is repressed is called gating. Gating is a process which controls the *perception* of pain, not the pain itself, by blocking the mass of electrical impulses which constitute pain from reaching the higher levels of the brain.

Through gating, overwhelming pain, either physical or psychological, stimulates its own repression. This occurs through an electrochemical process whereby certain nerve cells and their connecting points inhibit the transmission of information. This gating system works throughout the brain, but is concentrated in certain key areas which organize the pain response.

The gating system separates thinking, feeling and sensing levels of consciousness and controls input all the way along the nervous system. Once gating and repression set in, neural circuits are functionally disconnected and seem to take on independent lives. Thoughts, disengaged from feelings, have a viability of their own. The energy of the feelings, meanwhile, reverberates in loops on the lower levels of the brain, cut off from thought processes.

Thus gating works in two directions: it keeps feeling and sensation from the thinking level, and it prevents ideas and concepts from affecting our emotional level. When we say that someone has 'lost touch with reality' we are unknowingly referring to the process of gating, which has effectively disengaged one level of consciousness from another. One loses touch with the outside world only after one has lost touch with the inner world. Losing touch with inside is a precondition for losing touch with the external world.

There are many graphic examples of gating at work. In football, players can often play an entire game with severely broken bones. They become aware of their pain after the game when the intensity of their attention has shifted away from the contest. Getting drunk is another example. After a night on the town a person may have no memory of what he did the night before. Yet he drove home while he was practically unconscious. He was operating, at the time, on a different level of consciousness.

The Gates of the Brain and Repression

By a happy circumstance of fate, but one which is not without ominous consequences, the feeling of great early pain turns into its opposite – no feeling. The phenomenon of gating enables us to understand how this takes place. As a first step, we need to consider how pain enters the mind.

Research into pain and its mechanisms has shed important light on emotional suffering and how it is processed. In fact, the line between so-called physical pain and emotional pain, which is undoubtedly a physiological reaction to psychological events, is difficult to draw. Thus the theory of pain which postulates a gating system in the mid-brain is equally relevant to physical and emotional pain.

The gate control theory of pain was developed by Ronald Melzack and Patrick Wall. By examining a phenomenon called TENS, transcutaneous electroneurostimulation, Melzack and Wall discovered that a gating system exists within the cerebrospinal system. By implanting an electronic device high up the spinal cord a patient was able to push a button on a transmitter and flood the area with electrical impulses. This in turn would shut off pain which had been transmitted from the spinal cord. When stimulated, this device would shut off great pain, such as that of cancer. There is no content to those electrical impulses. They are neutral, yet they send information to the gating system to inhibit pain.

Transcutaneous electroneurostimulation, TENS, suggests the mechanism through which we repress emotional pain. This is clear from the fact that pain is ultimately a mass of electrochemical impulses. When this mass becomes too great, impulses flood the brain and produce an overload. This overload stimulates the brain to gate pain and produce repression. The mechanism is automatic.

Gating of emotional pain works in two ways: when intensity levels tend to overwhelm the threshold, and when there is a cumulative effect that arrives at that same threshold.

Any pain which threatens the threshold of tolerance sets in motion a built-in anti-suffering mechanism which ensures that we do not suffer inordinately.

We see the principle of gating in shock therapy. The person is no longer in pain after a massive electrical jolt to the brain because he is no longer feeling. Massive shock to his brain has cancelled out part of his memory as well. The shock has helped in the task of repression when the system could not produce enough of its own chemicals to keep the pain under control.

Shock therapy, incidentally, is a massive input that stays in the system. I have seen patients reliving their shock therapy exactly as it happened. What goes in must come out eventually, whether impulses from a shock machine or impulses from being traumatized as a child.

Gated Pain Memory in Primal Therapy

What we have observed in Primal Therapy lends support to the gate control theory. Patients reliving a birth sequence will again show the forceps mark on the forehead. Where were those marks during all of those intervening years? Gated away, stored as a memory with a force, but never gone. What about those baby wails, those sounds of a one year old that forty-year-old patients make involuntarily during the course of reliving early traumas? Gated, but surging to be released. Gating a massive amount of primal energy is what produces an equal amount of bodily tension. When patients relive their pain the tension levels are radically reduced. Electromyographic studies indicate reduced electrical activity of the muscles.

Emotional shocks are no different than shock therapy. Having one's mother sent to a mental hospital, losing a brother in an accident, being sent to a foster home at a young age, or suffering from incest, all flood the brain system with a surfeit of electrical impulses that produce a shutdown. We are discussing an information overload. The gates are not too worried about content. It is the force of the trauma that counts. When the level of trauma, say incest, is great enough they swing shut.

Unfortunately, when the gates in the brain shut down against pain they also shut out our history with it. We no longer remember the trauma nor the needs and feelings that went with it. We are bereft of exactly the kind of memory we need to resolve the unfortunate and crippling effects of those old traumas. We never repress with impunity. There is always a price to pay.

Gating and the Repression of Pain: The Clinical Picture

The degree of gating or repression is commensurate with the amount of pain. Massive pain during one's birth can cause the kind of repression we have been talking about. It will take a great amount of energy forever after to keep that pain in its place. This output of energy is continuous because the imprint of the trauma never leaves. The amount of energy utilized is measurable. Patients reliving certain very early traumas can show jumps of several degrees of body temperature in a very few minutes. Such readings appear to be immediate demonstrations of the level of pain and the amount of repression which has occurred.

Gating and Severed Communication

Gating results in the blocking of communication from one level of consciousness to another. This is why so many memories remain unconscious. This is why one part of our brain – the thinking, conscious part – is often not in communication with other parts of the brain which contain important information.

Blocked communication, or repression, is well demonstrated in hypnosis, where psychological techniques can shut off the experience of pain and its memory. It is possible in hypnosis to achieve gating so profound that a person becomes rigid, can be stretched between two chairs (with the head on one chair and the ankles on another) and not feel a two hundred pound weight on his stomach.

The example of hypnosis is important because it demonstrates how psychological factors, simple ideas, can alter the brain chemistry and produce gating – a gating so deep as to leave only a primitive organism in its wake. Gating can not only separate ideas from feelings, but can suppress feelings so that the primitive survival brain remains. It operates, in short, on three levels of consciousness.

Unconscious memory can also guide a variety of co-ordinated actions. There is the sleepwalker who goes into the kitchen and cooks a meal while sound asleep, performing complex functions without the activation of top-level consciousness. There are those who have epileptic seizures and still manage to drive a car, select streets and make turn signals. Furthermore, they later have no memory of any of this. One level of consciousness was gated away while another was functioning perfectly.

Clinically, this blocking is apparent in many ways. A patient who was the victim of incest did not discover that fact until she was two years into Primal Therapy. She began talking to herself on the street and felt she was 'losing it'. She came into therapy not knowing what was wrong. Over many weeks she relived aspects of the incest until one day she faced it head on in the most horrific agony. Even the pieces of the memory were gated away so she could remember only the most innocuous aspects first. Her first Primals, the reliving of repressed pain, were about fear in the dark as a child; then the footsteps coming down the hall; later a shadow in the room; still later the sensation of something big and sharp between her legs; and finally, months later, Daddy! Thus, the strength of the gate has to do with the amount of pain. The system will automatically allow only a bit at a time into consciousness. It allows just enough to be integrated, and no more.

Physiologically, we know something about the way gating, or blocking, works. There are a number of studies on nerve cells which show that when there is a barrage of input, certain associated cells become 'silent'; they fail to respond further. This is another way of demonstrating how overload produces shutdown. If this happens in a nuclear plant, bells and alarms go off. If it happens to the human system, nothing happens. At least nothing overt. Below decks there is a constant flurry of activity as hormones spill into the system, body heat goes up, white cells scurry to and fro and brain cells recruit supporters in the service of repression.

Alas, the alarm is silent and no one is there to hear it. The alarm chimes and screams all of our lives behind the primal gate.

Anything done artificially to break down barriers of

communication within the brain resulting from gating is dangerous because it can churn up out-of-sequence pains. Drugs or bad therapy amount to the same thing – the possibility of flooding the cortex or conscious thinking brain with pain which cannot be integrated. Gating has an important reason for its existence: nothing less than survival.

Gating as the Base of Neurosis

The gating system allows us to feel one way and act another. It allows us to be in contradiction with ourselves. It allows us to remember the times tables we learned at age six in school, while having no memory of the emotions we had at the time. The reason is that we first gate the pain, then the associations that might bring it up, until we have blocked out all memories surrounding it – places, times, scenes, etc. When we suffer from shock, such as in a car accident, there is often amnesia. The same is true with early emotional shocks. The way most of us are born leaves us in a state of shock just after birth. It is no wonder that so few of us can remember our birth.

The gates are the agency of self-deception. A person is certain he is relaxed, while repressed rage elevates his blood pressure. He sees no connection between his blood pressure and feelings. If someone were to ask, 'What's making you tense?' he wouldn't know what the person was talking about. 'I'm not at all tense,' he would reply. Gating has sealed off awareness.

There are also some kinds of brain damage where the person can be in pain and take the attitude, 'I know I hurt but it doesn't bother me.' His appreciation of the pain and its connection to the suffering has been interfered with. In the old days, when surgeons performed frontal lobotomies (severing the frontal cortex from emotional centres) the same thing happened. The person was in pain but didn't seem to care.

The normal person maintains his coherence through a fluid interaction of all levels of consciousness. The neurotic maintains his coherence or incoherence through the opposite – a system of well-functioning gates that keep everything apart. Without those gates there would be no way to get through life. One would be in excruciating pain all the time. So the gates allow a patient to come to us complaining of migraine, and assure us she has had a happy childhood, only to discover one year and a hundred Primals (episodes of reliving early trauma) later that it wasn't at all like that.

The price of repression is always diminished consciousness. Neurosis is simply the extension of the natural process of shutting out overwhelming amounts of information (by which we are all bombarded) for the purpose of protecting the organism from overload. It would seem that pain is pandemic. The point of any therapy would be to reduce it to acceptable levels inside the system. In my opinion, to be one hundred per cent free of pain, given the society we live in, is possible only in theory.

The Evolution of Gating

The gating system develops commensurately with the overall evolution of the brain. An infant or foetus can repress. Foetuses in the womb have been measured as they 'tune out' loud sounds. But the repression is done with the primitive nervous system. It is only years later that he or she is going to have the wherewithal to gate on the highest cerebral level: to use ideas to block feelings, to rationalize to keep from hurting, to deny a reality that is right in front of him or her.

Brain development not only allows for emotions, it allows for emotional pain as well. With each and every pain there is the mechanism for its opposte – repression. A child, before he uses ideas to gate pain, can act against his feelings. He can act 'macho' and independent to deny his need to be a baby. It is an emotional cover-up. And speaking of cover up, those who cover up a good deal of their reality inside will be likely to do the same when confronted with reality outside later on. Their first impulse will be to deny and cover over; an extension of what is happening internally.

Gates preserve our internal reality in its pure form. They buffer and protect feelings; they are meant to be benevolent. The problem is that in becoming insensitive to ourselves we become insensitive to others. We don't see their pain; we can't empathize or feel for them. We don't perceive what we should perceive, and miss the obvious.

Later in life a person who is heavily gated or repressed may suffer from an auto-immune disease such as arthritis in which the real person, his cells and tissues, is attacked as if it were a stranger or alien to be attacked. We become allergic to ourselves.

Measuring the Strength of the Gates

Each aspect of the gating system seems to have a specific tolerance. By first-line gate we refer to repression of events which occur before, during or around birth. This includes events some months after birth. First line gates may have a capacity of ten, for example. Other gates higher in the brain may have a capacity of five or six. One trauma such as incest may overwhelm the gate with a valence of seven or eight or the accumulation of pains over time may ultimately debilitate a gating system. It is then that we need drugs to boost gating action. The way we see the collapse of the gates is in overt anxiety states, psychosis, infantile autism, or severe illness.

An LSD trip is the quickest way to break down the gates – diminishing cortical integrative activity while liberating pains set down early and low in the nervous system.

What we also see in some of our patients is a fragile gating system due to compounding of pain all through childhood – someone who has the worst kind of birth followed by rejection all through childhood. This is the kind of person who comes to us inundated and awash with feelings, and who later cannot separate out feelings. She will come into therapy and have a feeling about childhood mixed with all kinds of birth trauma. This confusing melange prevents the person from having one single integrated feeling. At this point, tranquillizers or painkillers are required to push down heavy valence pain and bolster the gates so that the person can integrate one feeling at a time into her consciousness.

By our brainwave examinations we are able to measure the repression or gating system. A repressed person has a typical brain-wave pattern. If he is not overtly anxious he has a resting EEG (electroencephalogram) of 20–40 microvolts at 11–15 cycles per second. This is low voltage, slightly fast. A less repressed person who shows overt anxiety (the breakthrough of pain) has a higher voltage of 50–150 microvolts at 10–13 cycles per second. When pain is relived the patient may drop to 20 microvolts (alpha wave) at 7–10 cycles per second.

Those who are actively suffering often have an EEG of 150–250 microvolts. And when patients relive early pains while hooked up to an EEG machine it can go higher. Here we see clear evidence of the pain and the gating system at work. We see what happens when it is overloaded. The high voltage represents a breakthrough of profound and early pain. The cortex is doing what it can to handle it but it has to work overtime. The amplitude of the brain wave increases significantly, as does the body temperature. Both indicate a great deal of work being done to push back the intruder. As pain approaches consciousness, the brain seems to go into a frenzy. The feeling is treated as an enemy. Why should that be? Why should something that is so much a part of ourselves be considered an enemy? That is something we shall explore as we go along. We shall see how we incorporate alien forces to render them harmless.

The minute the patient drops into the real feeling all biologic indices drop. The importance of this is that we have the means to observe gating in action. We can see it being overtaxed and we can see when it works well. It is working well in patients who feel nothing and complain that life doesn't give them much.

Contrary to the old canard about how we don't use much of our brain capacity, the neurotic is always using too much of his brain in the service of repression.

Pain and the Higher Brain

Pain may be one of the prime reasons for the development of the thinking brain. Adversity 'demanded' a higher brain to handle overwhelming input. In the same way that we flee to our cortex and its thoughts to handle upcoming pain, the lower brain cells seemed to have migrated upwards in evolution to form a cortex in the face of adversity.

It has been found that the simplest memories involve wide areas of the brain, comprising millions of nerve cells. When there is a large storehouse of painful memories one can only guess at the billions of nerve cells at work. There seems to be nothing that activates the brain, and then its gating system, like pain.

To recapitulate: there are a series of pains that dislocate the system and produce one neurosis. That is all there is – one neurosis operating on different levels of consciousness, manifested in thousands of ways.

There is one primary mode of defence – repression – with a multitude of symptoms that arise from that defence. Until now, the tendency in psychotherapy has been to concentrate on all those diversions from the defence, to focus on the many forms of neurosis rather than on its generating sources. This is as true in medicine as in psychology. We treat compulsions and phobias, migraine and ulcers as viable entities requiring different specialists, unaware that the source for all may be the same.

The reason that there is one defence is that the physiological processes of repression are set in motion to counter any pain regardless of its source. When the pains are massive and continuous, and repression is equal to the task, there is global repression with little chance for major act-outs. But more often there is some repression with leakages of the feeling upwards towards conscious-awareness. What the person does with that leakage is employ secondary defences. These are what the Freudians call primary defensive mechanisms: denial, projection, reaction formation, etc.

But the modes of defence are as diverse as there are people. Some defend by fleeing to their head, with ideas, philosophies and belief systems. Others defend by a flurry of activity which keeps the feeling away. Still others talk incessantly.

The function of the secondary defences is to take up the slack where repression leaves off. They have both a qualitative and quantitative aspect. The qualitative aspect means that the precise feeling impels a behaviour that usually embodies hope and the avoidance of pain. The quantitative factor involves the energy of the imprint. The strength of the trauma or quantity of deprivation determines the force of the defence. It is then that the person cannot stop talking and must constantly 'dump' his energy on others. The qualitative aspect could be the feeling that no one ever listened, no one was interested. Thus, the person forces the issue, making others listen all of the time. The force of the defence would also be found in how loudly they speak and the speed of their sentences. In therapy they will talk over feelings all of the time.

So we have one defence, repression, and then secondary defences which are the idiosyncratic ways each of us find to avoid pain and fulfil our unmet needs, while binding or releasing the energy of the feeling.

It is true that some use denial and others projection, but the truth is that repression *is* denial in every case of the real feeling. Every person in pain denies. The biology won't permit otherwise. There is no need to memorize all of the defence operations listed in the Freudian literature;

secondary defences are limitless. One patient I had used to clench her fists tightly just before a feeling. To insist that she unclench allowed her to get into old feelings immediately.

Neurosis is really about people trying to solve their pain and finding ways to get what looks like love. It is the most natural of human enterprises. Because we hide from our pain doesn't mean it doesn't exist. All we are doing is hiding from ourselves. Isn't that a paradox? To constantly elude the one thing that can liberate us. It is no wonder that we can be objective about anyone else but never about our 'selves'. That self is hidden away so that we don't know about it. The repressed feeling melds into one's behaviour. It is the past constantly found in the present. That is why the neurotic confuses past and present. The pain of being unloved stays behind in the unconscious while we go about trying to feel loved.

Pain is a blessing because when it is felt it sets in motion the forces of healing. We mustn't treat it as an anathema. Even though it looks like a threat, it is a benevolent force. It just waits until we are old enough and strong enough to feel it.

The Endorphines: Natural Pain Killers

How does repressed or gated pain stay repressed and linger on? The answer to this question lies in the existence of a natural substance produced by the body for the control and management of pain.

We now know that pain is gated both by the electrical system and a chemical counterpart which act together. When an electrode is placed down low in the brain of cats, for example, in a structure known as the periacqueductal grey, the electrical stimulation shuts down the sensation of pain. That gating can be reversed by injecting a chemical that over-turns the indigenous production of a morphine-like substance. The electrical stimulation causes the production of this morphine-like substance in the upper brainstem. And the amount of that substance produced seems to be commensurate with the amount of pain.

This morphine-like substance has now been isolated through the discovery of a naturally produced chemical identical in its molecular structure to morphine. It is called endomorphine or endorphine. Pain is both gated and managed by these endorphines and other inhibitory molecules. (I shall concentrate on the endorphines.) There is a large family of endorphines, each with a different function. Through the endorphines and their action, the repression of pain is sustained over time.

The discovery of the endorphines is only a decade old, and constitutes one of the most exciting developments in scientific research in this country. Actually, before the endophine molecules were themselves identified, their receptors were discovered. Hans Kosterlitz and John Hughes in Scotland made the initial discoveries about opiate receptors in the brain. In 1973, Solomon Snyder and his co-worker Candace Pert revealed the first incredible link in the chain: the body has a vast array of receptors to which morphine-based drugs could attach. These receptors are the reason that such drugs can affect us. Without the receptors, the drugs would wash through the system, unattached and basically harmless.

The implication of the discovery was that if the human body is endowed with receptors whose specific task is to receive and bind morphine type drugs, the body must produce its own internal (endogenous) morphine-like substances. Indeed, morphine and heroine have their effects only because their molecular structure mimics the molecular structure of these internally manufactured opiates.

Endorphines are manufactured all over the brain but particularly in those areas that deal with the processing and storage of pain. The importance of this fact is that pain not only calls into production its opposite, its 'antagonist', but does so in the same home, so to speak. When there is massive pain, the receptor sites for endorphines may proliferate to accommodate the accumulating burden. Long-term stress may use up our endorphine supplies, no matter how well we manufacture them.

Endorphines: Keys and Locks in the Gating of Pain

Between nerve cells is a gap called a synapse. In that synapse are secreted all kinds of chemicals or brain hormones known as neurotransmitters. They, too, either impede or enhance the pain signal. Such chemicals as the endorphines thus impede the pain signal and help to produce analgesia. Late information indicates that the inhibitory or repressive transmitters may work in global fashion, going where needed, and not just across specific synapses.

Their action makes us unaware of the pain. When we help patients down to lower levels of consciousness they feel that pain immediately. The body is always aware of pain, and shouts its message, but that message cannot get through the neural barrier. Instead it increases the level of stress hormone, elevates the body temperature, and causes a great increase in the amount of brain cells at work – all companions of gating.

The endorphines can only send messages of restraint and inhibition between the nerve cell pathways; they cannot make the pain itself disappear from the system.

After having seen shattering, early childhood pains in my patients, endorphine manufacture is understandable. Over a long evolutionary period, this kind of pain caused the creation of increasingly potent pain-quelling substances, indicating that nothing in the human system exists without a reason.

Endorphines and their receptors act as keys and locks. Endorphines are the keys which fit into the locks (the receptors) on the cell walls. Then the cell wall opens or 'unzips' to let in the endorphines. This entire process is the means by which information in one part of the body is transmitted to other parts. This is why endorphines and their receptors are known as informational substances.

In heroin addiction, the drug takes the place of endorphines at the sites and may also cause a build up of more receptors to accept increasing doses of the drug. In addiction there are now more receptors calling out for fulfilment, so that when an addict tries to come off the drug, the withdrawal syndrome is experienced. The pain becomes acute. When the imprinted memory of pain is so massive that our internal production of endorphine cannot put out enough supplies to quell it, the person needs something external to bolster the endorphine system. Tranquillizers and pain-killers are often summoned to fill the breach.

Based on my own observations, people who have had horrendous childhoods or traumatic births are ready candidates for addiction because the natural pain-killers, the endorphines, cannot do the job despite their power.

A person in the throes of the severe pain of a heart attack will be given a shot of morphine and suddenly feel comfortable. When the morphine wears off, he hurts again. Likewise, through endorphine production, we render ourselves comfortable and out of touch with what hurts. When that happens we stop feeling. Unlike the shot of morphine in the cardiac patient, we have what amounts to a constant shot of endorphine to match imprinted pain. Then as adults we wonder why we can't get any real joy out of life.

Endorphines hold the secrets to unlocking the causes of many diseases. They might even be said to act as a barometer of dis-ease in our system, for their levels indicate the amount of pain we are handling. Because of this intimate relationship, the onset of disease is often accompanied by high levels of endorphines. Once repression exists, we not only stop feeling but its existence keeps us from knowing that we are repressed. When repression reaches a critical level called depression, we are feeling the effects of repression.

What is interesting about repression is that it sets the limit of feeling. Almost everyone believes they feel. That is because they do feel – up to their repressive boundary. They only discover that they did not fully feel, experience all themselves, when major repression has been removed. Those who are more repressed have narrower boundaries of feeling than others. Still, since they have no other frame of reference, they may consider themselves feeling people, even though they can only feel at four on a scale of ten. It is only when one feels one's pain that the full breadth of the feeling scale is revealed.

We have seen that endorphines can be elicited by electrode stimulation in certain parts of the lower brain. They can also be stimulated by acupuncture needles and, importantly, by thoughts. Thoughts which evoke hope and/or belief can cause their production. It has been found, for example, that if a dental patient has been told he has been given a pain-killer when in fact he has been given a placebo, he will still feel less pain *and will produce increased endorphines*. Thinking that something is going to make us feel better will do so.

Why do Endorphines Exist?

Why are there receptors in the brain at all, particularly ones that are to receive a plant (poppy) derivative? Certainly, in evolution from plants to more highly evolved organisms, we never lost our origins. We utilize elements of our long evolutionary history that have helped us to survive. Endorphines are found in the lowest of animal forms, even in worms. More astonishingly, they are also manufactured by two-celled microscopic protozoa! They are the bedrock of evolution.

So it is no wonder that endorphines have a history which perhaps reaches all the way back to plants. Our systems seem to have some historical scanning device from our evolutionary past that might be helpful. Even human semen contains opiates. It seems that almost any body orifice is a means of discharging some of the stressors that exist in the human system. Almost any fluid in the body (including tears) contains evidence of pain-killing substances.

The Past is the Key to Survival

Why do we store the past? Because in it lies the keys to future survival. Memories are stored so that they can rise to the surface for resolution and integration. It is not as if traumas occur, do their damage, and then leave. Not at all. They remain in the system so that we can deal with them when we are older and stronger. Something like that must have occurred in the long process of human evolution. Nothing is ever lost in evolution; instead, it is suppressed and stored. We have the capacity for tails, but the genetic code has been altered. If we thought it might be useful, techniques of genetic engineering might one day develop to the point at which we might program tails again!

Endorphines are released regardless of the nature of the stress, be it physical or psychological. The system simply says, 'pain is pain'. This system allows us to be unconscious, and that unconsciousness is our genetic legacy. It means we can ignore, deny, and be unaware of a vast amount of trauma while living our daily lives. The endorphines are the agents and the origin of unconsciousness. They are also partly responsible for our current civilization. Without repression, most of us would suffer so much that it is doubtful whether civilization would have progressed at all. With the benefit of repression, however, we can keep on producing and working, even though racked by pain; in fact, it is often the pain that drives us to produce. We usually don't know we're in pain; we only experience its propulsion.

Neurosis is the gift of the endorphines. They are a blessing and a scourge. They make our own bodies a mystery, our behaviour a puzzle, and our symptoms an enigma. They save us and then demand that we pay back with our lives. That is their legacy.

Pain, Repression and the Endorphines in Disease

In 1984, at the National Congress on Endocrinology in Canada, K. Tsunashima indicated that the inhibition of endorphines was a useful cancer therapy for animals. After receiving cancer grafts, mice were injected with certain kinds of endorphines. The result was that the injections promoted cancer growth. Strange. Pain-killing chemicals promote disease; or, to put it even more succinctly, we could say that repression equals disease. When these same animals were then injected with naloxone, an endorphine antagonist, both their suffering and their survival rate were measurably increased. Many studies have come to this same conclusion. In essence, active suffering increases survival, while repression decreases it. Thus, pain plus repression equals disease, while anxiety with no repression can mean survival.

It is not just pain that makes us vulnerable to disease; it is pain plus repression. An experiment was done with rats in which their tails were pinched constantly. These rats become voracious eaters and, not surprisingly, their endorphine levels rose initially. However, when they were injected with naloxone, they first acted as if they were in pain, then went into withdrawal with 'wet-dog' shakes. Finally the symptom of overeating stopped. The symptom of overeating was reversed by naloxone, yet naloxone never interfered with the actual pain; it interfered only with the neurotransmitters that mediated the repression of that pain.

Current research indicates that anything that blunts pain – whether it be tranquillizers, anaesthetics or endogenous pain-killers, also blunts the immune system. Even a single shot of morphine compromises natural killer cell response. Natural killer cells are the cells in the immune system which kill invading antigens, the carriers of disease. When morphine is prevented from working by other chemicals, natural killer cell activity is enhanced. This important aspect of the immune system, therefore, varies in accordance with the degree of repression. Repression operates in the brain as well as in the minute cells circulating throughout the bloodstream.

Deep pain means deep repression, and that means an increased possibility of cancer. Analgesia, tranquillization, or chemically-induced calm, simultaneously lower pain and immune functioning. They are an ensemble. What affects one affects the other.

It has also been found that female fighting mice have smaller virus-induced tumours than do non-fighters. The more spontaneous and aggressive the mouse the less cancer-prone she is. The spontaneous and aggressive human may get a heart attack, but is less likely to contract cancer.

The way we live our lives is a reflection of our basic physiological tendencies. Research indicates that someone who is repressed and 'inward orientated' is much more likely to contract immune system breakdown diseases, whereas a high intensity type person is more prone to having heart disease or a stroke. Consequently, the formulas seem to be:

$$Pain + Repression = Disease$$
$$Pain + Suffering = Survival$$

The implication here is that active suffering is, if not curative, at least alleviating. Acute anxiety and pain, felt and directly experienced, therefore, would seem to be preventative of catastrophic disease.

Why should this be? Why would feeling anxious aid survival? Because, for one thing, the body is in harmony under such circumstances. One is hurt and one feels it. One is operating within a consistent reality. A peson who is hurt, but continues to function as though the hurt never existed, is obviously not in harmony with himself. There is an inner war taking place, with one part of the system fighting the other.

Contrary to our previous beliefs, feeling pain is adaptive in the long run, and not feeling pain is non-adaptive. Let me hasten to point out that not feeling pain is adaptive as a child, but becomes non-adaptive over the long run. Here is another one of those dialectics: what saves our life early on – repression – is eventually what kills us. So when one wonders if a person can die from lack of love, the answer is yes. A great deal of severity and lack of affection early in life create a deal of pain and its repression later on. Pain is repression's 'raison d'être'. It is brought into life by pain.

I have just cited the use of naloxone as a way of blocking repression. There is a chemical-free way of achieving the same result – have the person feel (i.e. re-experience) and integrate his pain. Primal Therapy will, in my opinion, diminish the required output of the endorphines and, therefore, repression. Unlike neurosis, which is like a continual shot of morphine, Primal Therapy is like a strong shot of naloxone. It aids survival because it eases repression naturally, by dealing with the element that brought repression into being in the first place ... pain.

4

The Levels of Consciousness and the Nature of Mind

We have seen that illness can result from a pattern of deprived need, pain, repression, and the development within the mind of a special category of memory called imprints. On numerous occasions in previous chapters I have referred to something called 'mind'. Mind is the structure or framework within which all this activity and drama takes place. In order to deepen our understanding of what illness is, and to lay the groundwork for seeing how Primal Therapy can lead to health, it is important to take a deeper look at what we mean by 'mind'.

For centuries the mind has been a mysterious place peopled with dark demons that haunt our daily lives, plague our sleep, produce strange dreams, and move us about beyond our control. For some, the mind is sacrosanct, not to be meddled with; they take a kind of 'let sleeping dogs lie' attitude. They are not convinced that their behaviour, symptoms, dreams, and ambitions are coloured by or determined by deep-lying forces. This is not only a layman's attitude, it is also the conviction of some schools of psychotherapy such as Behaviourism, who prefer not to consider 'mind', thus guarding their focus on behaviour to the exclusion of all else. Yet the very notion of the unconscious mind is in the zeitgeist, part of the collective consciousness of our time.

The problem of the mind has challenged philosophers and

51

scientists for centuries. Where it is, constitutes another vexing problem. Is it the same as the brain? Does it ride above the brain? If so, how can that be? How can a mind function without the brain? If it is something separate from the brain, then what causes it to work at all?

There are those who have spent a lifetime trying to answer these questions. For them the mind is something to explore and, like a mountain, something to eventually conquer. The very least they want is control over the mind. So there are mind schools by the dozens.

In general, the mind is considered something to fear; every religion sees the notion of man (and therefore his unconscious) as basically evil, seeing man as compelled to battle constantly against his impulses. The notion is that we have to keep the beast in us under control or we shall go crazy. Almost every current dynamic psychotherapy extends this religious idea into the realm of psychology, where mind is still considered basically evil, in the sense that we are haunted by demons that do not have to be exorcised so much as understood and controlled. It is time to set the record straight. We need to know what the mind is, what lies inside it, and how it works both in sickness and in health.

The Mind in the Body

Let me begin by offering a proposition: the mind is not just in the brain. The brain processes information from everywhere in the body. And every cell in our body is an information processor. Cells in the immune system store old information, recognize enemies, and stir the system into combat readiness. They remember when the same enemy was present in the past, and give orders to clone themselves to do battle. Is the mind, then, the immune system? The immune mind is. The immune system is a mind which has memory, recognition, and command capabilities. It has its own language – not words – but it certainly communicates. Just because it doesn't speak in verbal syntax does not mean it doesn't communicate. It may tell the natural killer cells about an attacker and urge it to readiness. Natural killer cells then multiply and enter the fray against cancer cells.

The immune system also tells the brain about its activities. It informs the hypothalamus, which stirs the other brain processes into action. One might say that the command centre for the working of the immune mind lies, not in the brain at all, but in the lymphocytes, the white blood cells which produce antibodies to fight disease. The immune system is but one system among many which process information. This information eventually reaches the brain, where it is co-ordinated. But there would be no mind without all of these tributaries.

As long as we equate thinking and verbal activity with the mind we shall go astray. Verbal activity is the product of a recent mind, the mind which was last to evolve in the human species, something that has come along after the most primitive mind. There was a long evolutionary leap between the mind that helps us survive and the mind that reasons and uses logic. The verbal mind allows us to say what is on our mind but not what is on our minds. The verbal mind may be cut off from the lower levels of organization and not have the foggiest notion of what is going on below.

The Survival Mind, the Feeling Mind, and the Thinking Mind

There are, in fact, three distinct principal minds. The survival mind is the mind which keeps us breathing and our blood pressure constant. There is also a feeling mind which generates and processes emotions or feelings. And finally, there is the verbal, logical, thinking mind – the mind which uses language and solves problems. Each of these, although interconnected in the brain, is a separate entity with different functions. Damage to the logical, verbal mind may not affect the feeling mind at all. Thus a person can express himself with emotion after sustaining certain kinds of brain damage, yet not know why. He can say, 'Shit, I hate this', but cannot tell what he hates or why. Humans can process emotions without using the section of the brain called the cortex, or thinking mind.

When both the thinking mind and the feeling mind are damaged, as in a car accident, the survival mind keeps giving orders to breathe and to maintain heart rate and blood pressure. We can be 'brain dead' and still live with a kind of rudimentary consciousness. Even during surgery, when we are anaesthetized, there is evidence that lower levels of consciousness are processing pain, and indeed responding to what the surgeons are saying.

Consciousness and the Three Principal Minds

The survival, feeling, and thinking minds function on three different levels of consciousness. There is clearly some sort of gating system that manages to keep these three levels distinct from one another. These three minds and three levels of consciousness evolved over the history of mankind. The survival mind came first, then the feeling mind, and finally the thinking mind. The development of a child recapitulates this evolution.

Initially, the events which occur from the time there is a well-organized nervous system (approximately at the third month of gestation) to about six months of life on earth are registered down low in the nervous system on what I call the first line. Events occurring after the sixth month are impressed on the second line, or emotional level. The third line begins in pre-adolescence and continues its formation even into our twenties; it is continuous with the development of the highest level of nervous tissue – the cerebral cortex.

Imprinted pain and its memory on the first line are the least accessible. They therefore tend to be the least believable later on because they are so difficult to retrieve and understand. No language is going to help in that understanding either, which further complicates the problem. It is a level that can be reached only on its own terms.

Second, as the infant develops, he or she begins to relate to a larger world than that of the mother's breast and the crib. At this point the limbic system predominates in the baby's responses to the environment. The infant can now develop emotional attachments to his parents and relatives. He can experience more than just physical discomfort and hurt. Now he can feel emotional suffering.

Finally, just as was the case in the evolution of the human species, the third level of mind, the level of thinking (cognition) comes to predominate around the age of twelve.

By adolescence, we all possess three full levels of consciousness which correspond to the three principal minds. These function as follows:

First Level: This is the visceral, sensory level which deals with sensation and mediates bodily impulses and states. This level incorporates the survival mind.

Second Level: This is the affective-expressive level that mediates the complex processes involved in the creation and expression of feeling and emotion. It is the level of the feeling mind.

Third Level: This is the familiar cognitive, or thinking, level. It also provides discrimination, comprehension, and meaning with regard to feeling states. This is the level of the thinking mind.

Each level contributes its part to the experience of pain. At the first level there is the raw sensation of pain. At the second level there is emotional elaboration of pain. At the third level there is the conscious recognition of pain.

Normally, a feeling or attitude that we have towards some person, object, or activity, is comprised of all three levels of consciousness: sensation, emotion and cognition. The three are interconnected and work in harmony. But when the feeling is overwhelming, such as in the statement, 'They don't like me', the fluid interconnection among the levels is disrupted. Now there is fragmentation and blocking.

Because each level has its own repressive system, it's possible to be cut off from the most primitive impulses and needs. For example, we forget to eat or are unable to sleep. It is possible to be disengaged from emotions so that one no longer knows what one needs or what one feels. In the same way, it is possible to be disengaged from thinking so that one has ideas and concepts that are completely unrelated to what is going on 'below'. The business executive who thinks he feels terrific is so disconnected from his own physical reality that it takes a stroke or a heart attack to get the true message through to his mind.

Pain: The Organizer of the Mind

Historically, over the centuries of human evolution, reactions to pain have given the mind its three level structural character. The brain has evolved according to challenge and adversity. Pain has dictated the structure of consciousness because pain was not just an ordinary experience. Pain occurred as a result of threats to the survival of the system. The ability to feel pain was the key to survival, biologically and psychologically. Those bereft of the ability to feel pain are in constant danger of being destroyed by something they cannot feel and therefore cannot avoid.

One of the root problems in psychology thus far is that either consciousness or pain was studied independently, but not one as the function of the other. From an evolutionary standpoint, pain would seem to be the central factor in which consciousness became organized into its present structure. I believe this to be true ontogenetically, as well, meaning that pain becomes the organizing principle in the development of our own consciousness, in each and every one of us, from the embryo to adulthood.

Gated and repressed pain is the basis for impeded

communication between the levels of consciousness. It is responsible for a kind of fragmentation and disconnectedness. Bringing pain to full consciousness will liberate a whole new system of consciousness rather than simply produce an awareness of one specific pain or another.

There is evidence indicating that the higher central nervous system – the third level of consciousness – exerts a powerful suppressive influence on the experience of pain. This suppressing tendency means that ideas or the third level can control sensory input and what can be experienced.

When the third level is lulled, as in sleep, coded memories in the unconscious return with alarming force in our nightmares. There the precise feeling from a birth trauma can ascend: feelings of being crushed, drowning, suffocation or strangling. It is not the unconscious we are discussing, although that is a convenient conventional term, but another level of consciousness, to which one has gained access. There is no biological unconsciousness; there are only levels of consciousness, which become unconscious when gated. There is nothing mysterious about this. The sensations of a nightmare that intrude into higher level consciousness in sleep is, unfortunately, there all of the time waiting for connection and release.

Mind and the Three Levels of Consciousness

The three levels of consciousness work all the time and make up the mind. Each level has its separate function and different biochemical system. The feeling level, or second level, is packed with endorphine receptors which act to gate pain. Down lower, at the first (visceral) level, where deep pains are imprinted in a structure known as the locus coeruleus, we find a heavy concentration of a stress hormone called noradrenaline. It helps mediate terror.

I call these levels of consciousness, from lowest to highest, first, second and third line. When a diagnosis is made of a patient and his status, our knowledge of the levels of consciousness allows us to make a simultaneous statement about the physiological brain and the conceptual structure we call the mind. Certain kinds of nightmares or preoccupations, for example, tell us what kind of material is on the ascent in our patients, how well defended they are, and what feeling to expect next. The absence of nightmares can also be an important diagnostic clue.

What we call mind develops in stages in the newborn infant as the brain itself develops in concentric spheres known as neuropils. The first line functions involve the anatomic midline, gastric, respiratory, bladder and bowel functions. They are controlled by the inner portion of the brain which is practically fully functional at and before birth – the visceral level of consciousness. The second level, or emotional component of the mind, centred on the limbic system, is also functioning soon after birth. It is only some years later, however, that the cortical, thinking, symbolic brain will be fully functional. In the meantime, traumas will be handled by the lower neuropils. Thus, the newborn will develop colic because he hasn't the capacity to become mystical. He needs a more developed brain for that. When he finally achieves it, colic may transmute into mysticism.

Illness and First Line Consciousness

The access to first line consciousness is one of the major contributions of Primal Therapy because it means that for the first time we can pinpoint the deep-lying sources of both mental and physical illnesses.

When a trauma occurs very early in life the visceral brain will deal with it, pumping out more acids, accelerating the heart rate, raising the blood pressure, and elevating body temperature. The visceral mind is the only mind equipped to deal with early trauma.

Pain and the Levels of Consciousness

A baby who is not placed next to its mother right after birth suffers on the first line. The reactions to this trauma will be in terms of the most advanced nervous system available. At the visceral level there may be colic, vomiting and breathing difficulties. A five-year-old who is constantly made to feel ashamed or guilty is suffering on an emotional level. Now the pain will be processed not only in the viscera, but in the more fully developed emotional centres of the brain as well. The child now has the wherewithal to act out this pain in school with his peers. He can now discharge the energy of the pain, something a newborn cannot do. The neonate suffers internally because there are no outlets.

The emotional level cries and sobs, and produces dream images which attempt to contain and circumscribe the pain. The cortex and its thinking mind becomes involved, trying to explain the inexplicable. Because there is a re-representation of the early trauma on this level, there is an attempt to make sense out of the hurt. Without full access to its source, the cortex does the best it can stretching logic to the irrational. Paranoid reactions are no more than the attempt to focus, without the proper historical information, a distant and inaccessible inner hurt (often compounded by harsh life circumstances). That is what makes the ideation seem so bizarre. The cortex, as the unwitting accomplice, projects those hurts outside: 'They are laughing at me behind my back.' 'They are out to hurt me.' If only he could know who 'they' are.

Memory is coded differently on each level of consciousness. That is why a patient reliving a birth event has no words, no baby cries and no free movement. What is amazing about these memories is that they remain absolutely pure and untouched by experience. They arrive at consciousness as though in freshly unwrapped gauze. The memory contains all of the details surrounding the trauma – no part of it is changed. The old environment is now an imprint which forces the system to re-create that environment in the present, first, to match the imprint and thus make rational what impels from the unconscious; and secondly, in order for the person to resolve the early trauma, albeit symbolically.

A woman who has the imprinted trauma of a weak and helpless father who could not protect her, may find other weak men in her life and struggle to make them strong – a symbolic attempt to produce a real, protective father.

We can see early imprints manifested in such things as migraine. The early trauma is often a oxygen starvation at birth in which the original reaction was vasoconstriction followed by massive dilation and the subsequent throbbing experience. An adult conflict can reawaken the migraine response. What may have gone unnoticed is the specific early memory concealed inside the symptom. The migraine attack, then, is a biological memory of survival and the attempt to conserve oxygen. One of the treatments for migraine is oxygen.

No level of consciousness can do the work of another. No cerebral understanding in the world is going to change an imprinted memory of a breech delivery at birth.

The feeling mind cannot solve a geometry problem, and the cortical mind cannot know by any act of will precisely the origins of a strange idea it may carry.

Because each level has its own memory system, one cannot try to remember a feeling. It has to be felt in its own way. The immune system remembers a viral attack for decades, while the cortex remembers with specific words and figures.

The appearance of birthmarks when patients relive their birth trauma is an example of specific level of memory. Forceps marks will reappear on the forehead or wherever else they originally left a mark. Pressure applied to certain spots, for example, where an adult was severely beaten as a child, can awaken the memory of the event with all of its painful meaning, and provoke the bruises to go with it. It is almost as if the spot on the back 'remembers' and 'recalls', when the stimulus is appropriate.

Thus, memory is retrieved in different ways, some of which have nothing to do with thoughts, scenes or verbal descriptions. We have memories of smells which are only reawakened by smells, memories of emotions felt, and memories of maths tables that have no emotional content.

The neurophysiologist Roger Sperry, of Cold Spring Harbor Laboratory, New York, has found that each nerve fibre has a unique chemical code that tells it where to go and where to grow. Every axon fibre of the nerve cell has an affinity (what he calls 'chemoaffinity') which is coded chemically to a matching cell. The crucial detail is that even after the nerves are sliced they will grow back in precisely the same pattern; a pattern that does not change as a result of experience. It would seem that something like this happens to circuits disconnected by pain and repression. They spend a lifetime waiting for the proper hookup, yet somehow instinctively sense that such a hookup may be dangerous if done prematurely.

Consciousness and the Functioning of the Brain

A well-balanced person has a balanced mind. There is fluid access to the lower levels, and an intelligence that serves the feelings and instincts. This allows him or her to react instinctively to situations and make immediate yet appropriate decisions. Football players have this capacity; they instinctively know where to run on the field. Their actions are not part of a deliberative, thought out process. The lower mind works and directs the body without too much interference from the logical, reflective mind. There are those who can neither move in this instinctive way, dance, or do the things that should be instinctive because they 'live in their head'. They have fled to their cortical mind and allowed it to take over. Thus, they fail to react on the basis of feelings, which are shut away, but react only with some elaborate, cortical process that weighs and balances alternatives. If you ask them how they feel, they are not sure. They begin to eliminate certain negative factors and decide if they feel good or bad. What they express is a decision, not a feeling.

Is consciousness the same as brain functioning? Are they identical? The overall gestalt of a brain in action is a different quality from the brain itself. We, as human beings, are more than the sum of our parts and so is consciousness. Mind is the overall brain in action. Mind is not identical with the brain, but an emerging quality. Mind is made up of brain cells but cannot be reduced to them. It then is capable of interacting with the brain to change its functioning and eventually its structure.

Consequently, the conditions of life make a difference. Rats raised in a stimulating environment early in their lives have a different cortex than non-stimulated rats. Their brains changed according to social conditions. Such social conditions alter the mind on all levels, and seem to make a difference in physical structure.

Similarly, repeated brain-wave studies showed that the brains of my patients changed in function and structure when they gained access to their lower-level functioning. The relationship of the two hemispheres changed, as did that of the various quadrants of the brain. How can we account for this? Consciousness changed brain function. Reliving shattering early events changed how the brain operates.

The Mind Versus the Body

The mind–body problem is an age-old one. Some think we are creatures of the physical brain with computer-like functions that offer only the illusion of freedom and choice. They believe this brain dictates our lives. For them, there is no 'mind'. This is an old philosophy that has been adapted by the Behaviourist school of psychotherapy. There is never a mention of mind in their approach. They stamp in and stamp out behaviours based on reward and punishment. According to behaviourists we are nothing more than a machine that responds mechanically to input like Pavlov's dogs.

On the other hand lie the mystics. They believe that mind is some special quality that does not rely on the physical brain. For them it is an ethereal entity that transcends physical matter and comes from other planes or realities. They believe the mind is inhabited by magical qualities and special consciousness that has almost God-like attributes. It does not flow out of the brain, but comes from somewhere else. Often it is thought to be 'God-given'.

The Nature of Mind

Does the mind start out as a *tabula rasa* – a blank slate upon which everything is impressed during our lives? Or does it already have special qualities? The debate has been confusing because until very recently it was not known that the events in the womb shaped the brain and its function and left a lasting impression upon it. It was assumed at birth that the brain was a blank slate ready to accept new stimuli. Whatever preceded birth was imputed to genetics.

We now know that the most crucial factor in psychological and physiological development is that of key events during the nine months of gestation. This is when trauma experienced by the mother can alter the brain system, the hormone balance, and the anatomy of the baby, not to mention its psychological state. I have cited a wealth of research in my book, *Imprints*, indicating how stress in mothers alters the neurophysiology of the offspring.

Genetic factors are at play as well. After all, we inherit hair colour and physical structure from our parents and grandparents. Why should we expect nature to stop with these characteristics? There is a whole history in the brain, as well. The abilities to be musical or artistic, for example, seem to have a genetic basis. So the brain is not a blank slate, but possesses certain tendencies which are either elicited or nurtured, or suppressed, depending upon one's life circumstances. An artistic family is going to cultivate the child's capacity for imagery. The fact that the child is surrounded by artistic works may shape his choice of profession. It is impossible to determine which was predominant, nature or nurture.

Watching my patients has led me to certain conclusions about the nature of mind. When the mind is fragile, naive and fresh, events are impressed upon it with an impact that will not be duplicated later on, except under incredible circumstances. That is why prenatal events translated from the mother to the foetus are so important. That is also why the birth trauma is so important. We have been able to measure the vital signs and brain-wave functions of patients reliving traumas of birth and know how shattering the valence of the trauma is. We also note the personality changes of patients who have spent months reliving these traumas. We can see how warping these imprints have been. If the reliving of them normalizes personality, it can be assumed that the original impact also warped personality development considerably. After all, we are dealing with the same imprint, only in reverse. Noting the hormone changes and renewed growth patterns afterwards, we can say that these traumas affected the whole physiology.

The lower the level upon which the traumas are imprinted, the more determinant they are of later behaviours and symptoms. When impressed on an infantile mind, they are generally of the highest valence and create the most widespread, disparate kinds of reactions. Patients who have worked their way down levels of consciousness over years of therapy finally come in contact with very early imprints made during birth or just after.

Hypnosis and the Levels of Consciousness

Another way to understand the levels of consciousness is through hypnosis. A person can have his critical consciousness lulled and descend to the time when he was four. He will talk like a little boy and remember every detail of his kindergarten classroom, something impossible to do when he is on the higher level of consciousness. The childhood memory is positively intact in all respects just below that level.

It is not surprising that one can feel no pain and can even undergo surgery while under hypnosis. When top level consciousness is set aside there is no longer an appreciation of pain. That is why you need full consciousness for the full experience of pain and for the return of feeling. Hypnosis, like neurosis, can make someone unaware of pain. It is an example of the split mind. I view hypnosis as a 'mini-neurosis' because it is based on making someone unaware. It takes more time in neurosis, but in both cases the authority figure is diverting the person from his natural feeling state. Both require a state of dependence on this authority figure. The problem is you cannot use a mini-neurosis to cure a real one. You can't get well unconsciously; that is a contradiction in terms. The sickness is due to unconsciousness.

This split in consciousness is evident in so many ways. Someone wants sex in his mind, but his body won't co-operate. Someone wants to stop eating so much, but the forces inside compel him to go on stuffing himself.

Hypnosis demonstrates that inner processes can be pre-potent over external reality. One responds to one's inner programme rather than what is in front of one's eyes. In hypnosis, the mind believes that a pinprick is the touch of a feather, even while the person is staring at the pin.

We can see how belief systems get their start. With thoughts no longer anchored into feelings, the upper level mind can be programmed to believe in unreality. The formula is, 'I'll believe in anything as long as it does not lead me back to myself.'

When a person is hypnotized, he can undergo an experience and then be told he will have no memory of it. And he doesn't. Imagine! A mental suggestion that can cancel a memory. That is how fragile memory is. Pain also tells memory to keep quiet, not to intrude or make a noise. In both cases it is the so-called conscious mind that forgets, not the lower one. As soon as one descends down lower, memory is right there in full flower. When our patients are less defended, they too meet up with stored and hidden memory.

Hallucinogenic Drugs and the Mind

Those who have taken strong hallucinogens may come into contact with the anciently evolved primitive mind, where high valence pains are engraved. The access is premature and the result is flooding. Thus, the person is driven to make the atavistic leap over proper conscious connections, and imagines himself into a 'higher consciousness', into past lives, or into some sort of cosmic unity – anything but the truth.

Such drugs are dangerous because they crack open the gates, sometimes for the rest of our lives. Paradoxically, what happens after that is that the person is in pursuit of some kind of mystical experience forevermore. He is in constant flight from reality, first the inner one and then the outer one. He is now in the position of someone who did not take the drug but had had such a terrible early life that his defence system is weakened. He now has 'faulty gates'.

The Mind and Faulty Gates

Faulty gates are nearly always implicated in what used to be called a nervous breakdown. We now know what a nervous breakdown is. Nerves don't break down. Defences do. When the gating system breaks down because of drugs, or more often because life has become too tough, the person may go crazy. He is using his now overwhelmed cortex to handle the onrush of early pain. He does the best he can, but it is not good enough. He no longer makes sense, is irrational, and imagines what isn't there. Actually, it is there, but it can't be seen; old shattering memories. The person doesn't know the source, but he senses danger, and focuses it externally. If the doctor doesn't know the source, he too focuses on behaviour and tries to dissuade the person from his ideation. Meanwhile, both the person and the doctor try to make sense out of something that already makes sense, once the hidden source is made evident. The human system is eminently rational. For every effect, no matter how bizarre, there is a specific cause.

During a nervous collapse, a person descends into a lower level of consciousness. If he could just know that, his anxiety would be relieved and he might be less crazy. If his obsession and anxieties are utterly mysterious, then he is even more frightened. Psychotics are often the most sensitive, insightful and perceptive people because they are undefended. That is why the put-together intellectual neurotic cannot sense what the crazy person can see. The neurotic wants proof for what he cannot feel. This explains why a leading scientific journal recently stated that there is no proof of the memory of early pain. Waiting for a numerical value to show that pain can be remembered is not necessary, as every suffering human being can demonstrate.

Sometimes what is going on below is so powerful that it constantly intrudes upon the top level. We daydream much of the time; sometimes we drive all the way across town and wonder how we got there. We were immersed in another world while the thinking, directive mind took a figurative back seat. The psychotic is simply living in his daydream without sufficient objectivity to differentiate reality from fantasy. So we have the phenomena of mental (third line) breakdown and a breakthrough of lower level imprints.

We have learned that the process of integration cannot be hurried; one must be ready to accept painful truths. These truths are not the kind that can be 'confessed'. There are stronger truths – confessions by the body, if you will, that have a pain valence far beyond what can be dredged up voluntarily.

It is these stronger truths that force the higher cortical mind to seek out magical and mystical ideas. Unreality is the religion of the gated person. Or is it the other way around?

Consciousness Versus Awareness

There are two basic ways to become unconscious. The first is to undergo powerful events before there is a developed cortex; these generally remain undelineated because there were no words or concepts to help out. The second is to have events occur later on that are too strong to feel and so therefore must be repressed out of consciousness.

One way in which we can become unconscious concerns the experience early in life of receiving a series of psychological blows that cannot be integrated by the brain. Suppose one's parents are divorcing and one of them is leaving the household. For the child, the memory of such an event remains well hidden, as does its meaning, which is that the child will never be with both parents again. All of the pain and its attendant memories becomes unconscious. The person then walks around in a semi-coma for the rest of his life and isn't even aware of it. He is as unconscious as if someone hit him on the head. Great parts of himself are inaccessible. He cannot learn from his past history because it is buried in his mental archives. He will repeat patterns over and over again because he is unconscious.

It is always possible to help someone later on to become aware of these events, as is done in conventional psychotherapy. But you cannot make someone conscious. Aware, yes. Only the experience of pain can produce consciousness in neurotics. It is a state arrived at from inside, never from the outside.

Consciousness is a state arrived at alone, never in company. Awareness can be given to someone. Consciousness cannot. Awareness can be played with, manipulated, and altered by force. Consciousness cannot. One can be aware of others in a most perceptive way (seemingly conscious) as a means of self-protection, but it is a weapon rooted in a defence of self, and is not the case with consciousness. Consciousness is enduring and rock solid. It cannot be forced, coerced and exhorted. It is an organic reality. Awareness is disengaged consciousness.

No amount of awareness can produce what we see in therapy – a person reliving events around birth in the grips of a primordial brain causing salamander-like movements that may go on for over an hour. What arises after this kind of experience is a new quality of consciousness.

Penetrating the Unconscious Mind

There are criteria to determine how deep unconsciousness is. The ability to respond to stimuli is a key one. The less the strength of the stimuli needed the more conscious the person. If the person can feel a pin prick, he is pretty aware. If he cannot respond to deep pain he is more unconscious. In the realm of the psychological, the same is true. A person who can no longer respond to pain either in himself or in others is somewhat unconscious. It would take a lot to make this person respond to anything. The strength of the stimuli needed to rouse him out of his unconscious torper would have to be enormous. He cannot see the suffering in his children, or his spouse, because of this unconsciousness. It is because of this that someone can seemingly be very aware, yet totally unconscious.

I remember seeing one patient who used to leave her young child alone so she could attend awareness seminars. She saw nothing of what was happening to her child.

With an unconscious emotional life, one neither perceives nor understands and is a victim, unable to use past experience to comprehend the present. Someone who never had a mother keeps on projecting his past onto women in the present, and cannot see their faults. His needs predominate and suffuse reality and judgement. Without access to feeling, a person makes stupid choices and decisions.

One has to ask, 'Where is the real person in all of this?'

She is the one suffering. She feels the pain. So nature has done a wonderful thing. It pretends that the earlier brain belongs to someone else. They are two worlds apart. That lower brain might as well belong to someone else, since the upper brain cannot ever recognize the pain the body is undergoing.

The New Age thinkers talk a lot about consciousness and the higher mind. They believe that you can transcend to higher levels of mind unknown to ordinary mortals. They concoct rituals to rise to these levels. Yet, the only way to rise to a higher consciousness is by descending to lower levels. That is the true dialectic of mind.

It is paradoxical. Those who claim to have achieved a state of bliss and cosmic calm come to our research laboratory, where we find a mind that is racing a mile a minute and a body in a panic state. Billions of neurons are busy in the job of repression. It works and the person believes he is calm or has achieved nirvana. Repression's job is to deceive. There is nothing quite as infinite as self-deception – the great gift of our advanced civilization.

Those into magical thinking want to believe in some special mind that is cosmic, God-like. It is nothing like that. What some seem to want is to ascend to a state of peace or bliss. It is when one descends, however, and makes the unconscious conscious, that one finds peace and calm. There is no greater inner harmony. It means the end to inexplicable tension. The minds are finally unified. If you are without pain, you are already at the highest level of consciousness possible. There is nothing more than that.

The Dream Sleep Process and the Levels of the Mind

The whole dream sleep process is eloquent testimony to the three levels of consciousness. The story we make up for ourselves in the dream is another way we keep our self-deception going. After all, there is no audience for this story.

We are the actors and the audience. It is a biological necessity to keep us asleep and sane. The dream allows us to have our needed rest. The sleep-dream process reflects the structure and function of the brain, a brain that does not change during sleep. The same processes are at work day and night. During the night it becomes clearer. Here the three minds are evident and measurable. They have different brain-wave signatures. Deep sleep uses up enormous supplies of the inhibitory chemical serotonin. The long, deep brain waves reflect deep repression at work, and finally when suppressive chemicals are exhausted we move into higher levels of consciousness and higher levels of sleep. Less repression equals more consciousness.

Our daily sleep cycles reflect the three minds. We go to sleep and descend slightly to the next lower level of consciousness below thinking (the level of feeling) then to deep consciousness (the level of visceral function) then back to the dream or feeling level, then to fully awake (the thinking level). This cycle seems to reflect the origin of each level of the brain as it evolved over time, recapitulating our phylogenetic or evolutionary history each day.

This cycle also reflects the origin of the brain's development in our own personal time. We wake up out of the unconscious into full consciousness each day, just as we first developed a primitive brain which finally flowered some years after birth into a fully developed neocortex. There is no great mystery about each of the survival, emotional and thinking minds. When individuals have access down deep we see first hand what is there, and what there is seems to be nothing more than imprinted memories from a long hidden past. No id, no unchained lust and aggression, no need to for meaning, no mystical entities – just a material brain with imprinted memories from the past. The so-called unconscious is laid bare for all to see. Most of all it is no longer a mystery to the person involved. All is understood – the deep motivations, the dreams and nightmares, the symptoms, the relationships – everything that matters. As long as repression

exists, one can impute all sorts of qualities to the unconscious.

Sleep, Dreams and Nightmares: How to be Neurotic in Your Sleep

The brain doesn't change structure when night falls, and the
levels of consciousness don't melt away during sleep. We
descend down the levels of consciousness during sleep just as
we make that same descent during a Primal session. The
patterns of sleep, dreams and nightmares are the equivalent
of certain behaviours done during the day. The only difference is that they are done in a relative state of unconsciousness. Since the neurotic is largely unconscious, there is, in the
end, very little difference.

There have been literally hundreds of books on sleep and
dreams and a great deal of research. For our purposes it is
enough to know that there is something called dream sleep or
REM sleep that has a peculiar brain-wave signature; and
another deep level of sleep that has yet another signature,
large slow waves indicating deep levels of repression. Those
are the two basic sleep levels that alternate during a night's
sleep. Those levels clearly correspond to the first and second
level of consciousness I have just discussed. The second-line
emotional level where dream sleep takes place is also where
non-verbal images are manufactured. Those with access can
be frequent dreamers, artists, in pain, or all of the three.
Access means to experience images and pain at the same
time. The 'suffering artist' is redundant; unless of course the
artist is real and herself.

Dreams have many functions in the psychic economy.
They are usually the result of current input which often triggers off past imprints. If buried feelings are strong enough,
then no daytime trigger event is needed; they will arise all on
their own, a process of inner prompting. It is the same as
during waking; if inner feelings are strong enough they can

produce anxiety and neurotic behaviour without any special stimulus. Otherwise, a relatively minor current event can set them off. Dreams, by and large, deal with buried needs and feelings. As top level consciousness is lulled or put to sleep we have access to the lower levels. The trick is how to have access and still not feel the direct impact of early traumas so we may sleep and get our needed rest. Enter the dream. The dream is designed to wrap a symbol, image and story around a feeling so as to make the feeling unrecognizable for what it is; otherwise, the pain would shoot up unmasked and we would be awake and confronted with our internal reality. Dreams are only symbolic because of repression of that reality. Their function is to keep us unreal. So they have a dual function to protect sleep and our neurosis.

The dream is responsible for diluting the energy of the feeling in the story and its images. It is a form of camouflage. We say 'Boy, did that dream make me nervous or depressed.' Wrong. 'Boy, did that feeling of nervousness and depression make me dream a depressing story,' is more like it. If we were aware during the day we might say, 'Boy, did my feeling of loneliness and alienation make me believe in aliens inside UFOs.'

Secondly, the dream is an attempt to make rational and coherent the feelings we necessarily have access to when we descend the levels of consciousness during sleep. The dream has a further function; it does what we do during the day – that is, what we are forced to do each day, and that is recreate the imprint in the present in order to try to resolve it and heal. So the story in the dream is the symbolic analogue of the real feeling. The story represents the early situation that rises towards consciousness for connection, integration and healing. Sadly but fortunately, it is turned away by the gating system. This gating keeps us from knowing the feeling and its context, allowing us to form symbols around it. The symbols rush in before we have to recognize the feeling. It is also the case in the 'true believer', who has adopted belief systems, mantra, special rituals, so as not to feel his deprivations and their agony. It is the 'true believer' who loves dream analysis. It is essentially the same in all neurosis – blocking and rerouting. Neurotic act-outs are derived from rerouted needs and feelings.

When feelings are too strong, when deeper lying feelings mix with second line feelings the image factory isn't strong enough to make a coherent structure in a dream and we wake up out of a bad dream; feeling all the same rotten feelings that exist in the early situation. The fear, disgust, anger, confusion, etc. In the dream state there is a rise in body temperature, exactly what happens to our patients who are put in touch with the dream level (second line) of consciousness during a session. It is a sign of the work of the body handling pain and doing its job of repression.

Nightmares are the nighttime anxiety attack; and indeed, the physiological concomitants of a nightmare are exactly those of anxiety; sweats, pumping heart, feelings of dread and terror, shakiness, etc. We usually don't wake up screaming because most often the trauma has occurred before the capacity to scream. So in the nightmare we open our mouths to scream but nothing comes out. If we do actually scream the terror is more likely to have occurred after six months of age.

Nightmares occur when we are ending deep sleep with its deep repression. When the first line pain is enormous and gating cannot do its job there is a sudden breakthrough of the imprint with all of its sensations – choking, smothering, feeling crushed, strangled and asphyxiated. What this means is that the pain has used up the serotonin (and other repressive chemicals – for what is sleep but the effective *repression* of aspects of consciousness) supplies that ordinarily go into keeping us asleep and rested. The result is that the deepest lying pains shoot to the surface abruptly, an end-around the second line.

Here is an example of a birth-provoked nightmare: I'm standing in line at customs trying to escape from some vague danger. Suddenly, a customs officer comes over and arrests me and puts me in prison for trying to escape. I am sentenced to death. My cell is so small I feel squeezed and crushed. I find a hole to escape but when I try to get out I get stuck. It's too narrow and I can't move. Now I know they're going to catch me and I'm going to die. I wake up in absolute terror.

It is crucial to understand that nightmares are forms of defence. Against what? DEATH. Quite literally. For the person in a nightmare is the same as the person on the verge of reliving his birth or other early life and death trauma, his vital signs are lethal in an attempt at fleeing and repressing the pain. His heart beat and blood pressure are inordinately high. If those were allowed to continue for an extended period of time the body is at great risk. So the person wakes up to calm down and slow down those functions that could kill him. Therefore, dreams are defences against nightmares, and nightmares are defences against death.

Paradoxically, we wake up out of a nightmare so as to remain unconscious – *showing the distinct difference between awareness and consciousness.* We become awake and 'aware' (of our current surroundings) in order to remain unconscious (of ourselves). Being awake and seeing the 'reality' of the room, the lights reassure us, so we do not have to face our pain directly. Other times, when awake, we become unconscious, i.e. faint, so as not to be conscious of the unconscious. The system does whatever it must, awake or asleep, to ensure that we remain neurotic and unconscious (of our imprints). Dreams are the way the system ensures neurosis. Otherwise we would be conscious and whole. Without dreams (which means being without neurotic outlets) we would never rest and would be awash in pain all of the time.

One of the ways we check on this theory is to observe the progress of our patients vis à vis their dreams. As they feel deep feelings they no longer have nightmares. As first line feelings are on the march nightmares increase. They are the harbingers, portending serious pain en route to consciousness.

The story and images of the dream are the logical symbolic extension of the imprint. If one were afraid of one's father one may dream of menacing Nazis all of the time. One may be as powerless against the Nazis as one was against the father. And the dream portrays this. One can't escape. One is being punished for no reason. One's weapons break, etc. One patient constantly dreamt of losing things. He couldn't find his wallet, his car, his house and his clothes. He felt the feeling: the great loss of his mother early in his life which he never fully faced. In therapy it proceeds from 'I've lost something'. What is the feeling? 'I feel so lost.' 'I'm a lost little boy. I lost my mommy. Mommy! Come back Mommy!' And now the dream symbol has been transformed into the feeling it is. This, of course, takes place over a two hour period and not within a few minutes. So in therapy the symbol has been transformed into the feeling, while at the start of neurosis the feeling was transformed into the symbol. That is why I say that Primal Therapy is neurosis in reverse. The higher the valence of the imprinted feeling the more likely we are to see the same recurrent theme in a dream or nightmare.

When the hurt is too much and the containment difficult the brain goes into overdrive in an effort to hold back the force. That is why it must concoct the most bizarre stories in the dream to hold back the most excruciating suffering. Thus, alligators come out of the water and follow the person around even into restaurants. The great terror of one's childhood, the inability to have escaped a family that was in disarray, all are wound into the story. The brain does during sleep exactly what it does during the day against the very same force – it develops bizarre or psychotic ideation.

The dream story is no different from a sexual perversion or a phobia. It is a way to circumscribe and contain a feeling. The dream and ritual are condensations of thousands of early experiences but relatively few needs and feelings. They are the symptom, the representation of one's whole past. When a flasher does his thing he often reports that he seemed in some kind of 'coma' during the episode. He is really in the dream state acting out without any conscious control. He is deficient in top level inhibitory consciousness exactly as if he were asleep; thus, he is operating on a lower level of consciousness.

In one case (cited later) the feeling of the exhibitionist was, 'What do I have to do to get you to show some feeling?!' His ritual was a succinct symbol of a lifetime of living with a mother who showed no emotion whatsoever. The child needed some reality, needed to know the impact of what he was saying, feeling and doing. Having never been aware of the feeling, much less relived it, he continued to act it out. The dream is the nighttime act-out.

Because the symbol is the offshoot of the feeling (losing things to the patient just discussed meant the loss of his mother) it stands to reason that there can be no universal symbols applicable to all. The symbol is only specific to the feeling of the individual. Therefore all dream analysis is useless. There are no symbols that have any grand meaning that an analyst can divine. The only way to make sense out of a dream is to feel the feelings inside it. That is why we have our patients relive the dream as if it were happening now and fall into the feeling, which inevitably takes them back to the original situation and makes sense of the whole thing.

Understanding your dreams will never change your life, all the books making such claims to the contrary notwithstanding. Understanding symbols of feelings is almost useless; not quite as useless as *understanding* your feelings and thinking that will change you. Feeling them is what it's about.

There is nothing magic about dreams. They are, by and large, the stories we spin to make sense out of our unconscious; to make the unconscious make sense. The imprint and unconscious feelings *always make sense* when in context, so we have the patient relive the dream, feel the feeling in its original context and arrive at resolution. This should be a great relief to analysts, Freudian, Jungian and others, who no longer have to reach into their unconscious to calculate what is in the unconscious of their patients. And it should be relieving for the patients who need not talk about their dreams *ad nauseum*. Instead they must talk about their real life and its problems that require help.

Freud called dreams 'The royal road to the unconscious',

and a whole school of dream analysts arose as deep divers into the unconscious, trying to fathom what lay there in their patients. What they overlooked was that despite the fact that sleep and dreams do occur on an unconscious level (a level of consciousness not normally accessed during the day) the gating system never slept and it saw to it that the real feelings came up in masked form, no different then how feelings were masked during the day.

It follows from what I am saying that there can be no such thing in therapy as 'dream work', the endless analysis of dreams. It would be the same as the endless analysis of one's neurotic behaviour in the hope that the understanding will make the feelings go away, a patent impossibility. It's just manipulating symbols. Dream work is going through the motions of getting well without having to do it really. It's another symbolic act-out preferred by heavily symbolizing individuals. Neurotics too often choose neurotic ways of trying to get well.

It is true that not each and every dream has this primal content or has deep meaning. But significant dreams are always primal in content, and nightmares are but the break-through of very old, remote and deep lying sensations. I say 'sensations' rather than feelings because feelings are more to do with dreams. First line material – traumas before, during and soon after birth – occurs before the feeling brain is fully developed. An interesting sidelight to this is that when a patient relives a life and death event around birth there is no look of terror during it; yet when they come up to a higher level feeling terrifying things that happened at five, one sees great fear on the face as the feelings approach. We see terror in the face of our women patients in every case during the reliving of incest, but when they descend to birth the psychological aspect of the terror is not there even though the body seems to be in a frenzy.

There are times in our therapy when there is a sudden breakthrough of deep material. The patients makes very succinct statements, and those statements are identical with what a person feels during a nightmare; i.e., 'I'm smothering in here. I feel trapped. There's no room to breathe. Your behaviour is crushing me. I'm numb. I can't move. I'm going crazy. I feel terrible anxiety. Doom is lurking. I'm all confused!', etc. Sometimes it takes a paranoid turn: 'They are trying to trap me. They are out to make me go crazy', etc. We explain immediately that there is a rupture in the defence structure, certain feelings are on the rise and we help the patient to feel them. If it is too much, medication is sometimes indicated. If we know what the feelings are we tell them to the patient, anything to make it specific and reassuring.

The reason that the statements made by someone on the verge of a breakdown (into the unconscious) are succinct is that the second line hasn't the force to mitigate or vitiate the feelings or sensations and alter them into something else. So they erupt full blown. If the feelings happen to a non-patient, a psychotic break is in the offing because the person has no idea about what is happening to him, what feelings are coming up, or even that feelings exist and are rising. His defence structure might be crumbling due to current harsh circumstances (a divorce, loss of a job, a death in the family) and he is suddenly in touch with a deep level of consciousness that has lain dormant for a long time.

The more therapy a patient has the less he dreams in symbols because the unconscious has now been made conscious. There is now a fusion of the two and the dreams show it. The person is usually himself, saying real things to real people and still managing to stay asleep. That is because the heavy charge value of the feelings have been removed. So one can be real on the unconscious level, or, if you will, conscious on the unconscious level. Being conscious of the unconscious effectively erases the unconscious as a significant driving and motivating force.

5

Alietta

The following case history exhibits all of the aspects of Primal Therapy we have discussed thus far. In this journal, kept by a patient during the initial three weeks of treatment, the process of reliving is carefully documented in vivid terms. The journal is followed by reflections at several later points in time which document the long term benefits of therapy.

Sunday, 10 October

I am now in the motel room, in which I have to stay for three weeks without talking to anyone, watching TV, smoking cigarettes or grass, masturbating or having any kind of sex at all. In brief, where I am supposed to concentrate on myself.

Every morning, starting tomorrow, I will see my therapist. I am very excited. Primal Therapy. My last hope in this life. I am expecting everything from it, from the ability to love, to the possibility of being loved if I become someone else – the real me? – to happiness. . . .

I just spent five insane months, the culmination of the increasing madness that my life has become. I was protected by a perfectly well functioning outside. 'Your only craziness is to do any kind of therapy.' That's my family and friends' impression. Yes, the outside is quite well trained to make believe. Only I, inside, know how totally unhappy, how totally on the edge of the deepest chasm, how close to the last fall I am.

I realize that I am always cold, my teeth are clenched tight when I am lying down, probably when I stand too. My body is, in fact, stiff. I never wanted to pay any attention to all that, and I suddenly notice and feel it, having nothing else to think about. I like this moment of forced solitude, so longed for in the last months, this retreat within.

What is it going to be like to be a 'feeling person?' I force myself into trying to 'feel' right now, whatever there is to feel inside me. It is strange, it burns, it physically hurts ... I have the feeling that it is going to be horrible to go down into all this past (totally black now), because just thinking about it sets my throat on fire ... and I feel uncomfortable ... I expect the whole voyage to be fascinating.

Mary is my therapist. I don't like it. A woman. 'How do you feel?'

'Great, if you want me tense, send me to a party, not alone in a hotel room. I'm used to that. I like it.'

Some tears through random memories, but when she tells me to tell 'them', I can't talk. Did they ever *really* talk to me? After that, nothing, blackness. I feel totally blocked. I leave rather disappointed. Is that it?

Here I am, trying to wander around my youth. Well, I get nothing, I try ... a few irrelevant images. Are you going to be able to help me through? You claim you have the cure. I am afraid. What if it doesn't work?

Tuesday, 12 October

A lot of tears today. When I arrived, Art tells me that if I am not following the rules of the therapy I can't go on with it. Yesterday, at the end of the session, I told Mary how much I'd love a good cigarette. Horror on her face ... but I didn't touch any, and today I am surprised and puzzled at Art's aggressiveness. A trick? Probably, because Mary goes back on Art's bust a few times during the session, asking me what I felt when he spoke to me. 'Nothing,' I answered.

Today, I was in Porto di ... in our summer house, going

down the steps, hitting that ball. It pounds so clearly in my head now. It leads me to my total loneliness as a child, always by myself, and that makes me cry. I was sad inside. It is the first time I realize I was feeling something as a child!

Afterwards, I cool down for a while; lying on the floor, a memory is about to come to my mind, which I am blocking. 'Trust yourself,' Mary says, her voice extremely soft, 'what is it?'

'I am not too sure … long, long ago, papa hit me hard. Somebody had to say: "Stop it, you're going to kill her," but it is so foggy, I am not sure. I can't believe it … that scene doesn't bring any emotion, and I am a bit ashamed for having it come to mind.'

'What did you want from your father, Alietta?' Mary asked.

I am reluctant to answer the question. The answer is so obvious.

'Well, I wanted him to …' It is not so easy, my body becomes tense, I am silent, blank; then a vivid image comes suddenly: Papa writing at his desk almost every night, very late; I see him so clearly. It is amazing. I am next to him, and my head does not reach the platform of his desk. I see his hand sliding on the paper, writing in blue with his big pen. It is sort of magic, and I watch him, totally immobile, absorbed in the fascination of his hand.

Mary asks me what I feel while watching.

'Nothing.'

'What did you want him to do?'

Silence … I feel like I am on the edge of a very high cliff, and don't want to jump.

Mary waits a while, my body sweats, I am cold, then I hear her say softly, 'What did you want him to do, Alietta?'

This time I jump, or something jumps in me: the feeling. I explode into tears.

'I wanted him to touch me, to take me in his arms; I feel a huge tenderness for him, and a powerful desire for him to cuddle me in his arms and touch me.'

Mary tells me to ask him to touch me, and I go with the flow of my want. I ask him to touch my hair and my neck with his hands. It brings lots of tears, because while I am feeling my need for his tenderness I see his hand moving, sliding on a paper, writing in blue with a pen, indifferent to my need. I am very tired after the session. I didn't know I had so many tears in my tears' tank.

Back to the motel. I sleep a little bit ... a little bit? until 10:30PM. The whole day, in fact. My body sure has a good defence there. I never slept so well, so soundly, so quietly. I also feel really tired.

Wednesday, 13 October

I really don't know how long I can stand this. I hate the idea of going someplace every day to cry and suffer and hurt. Today I went back to the death of my sister, Flora. I also cried about Papa talking to me endlessly, for years after lunch, after dinner, spinning his wheel, following his lost dreams, rambling on and on, giving in to his insatiable need to talk. And I listened to him, all those hours, all those years.

Mama had to tell him to stop and let me go to bed. He hardly heard her and went on, and I was listening as if under the spell of a snake, not saying a word. It was the only attention he ever really gave me, and it was not even anything he was giving me, because he wasn't talking to me. I could have been a stone, or anyone. (That hurts and sends me deeper in the feeling.) He just needed an ear. I was an object, an object to fulfil his need. He was planting in me, 'faithful disciple', the basis for my future acting out, all those phoney values I had for so many years.

'I hate it, stop it, stop it ... stop talking, you drive me crazy, stop it!'

When I first start telling him that under Mary's recommendation it is difficult, I feel very self-conscious. It is extremely hard. How could I talk to him now? I never did in my youth. Seeing how difficult it is makes me realize that I have to do it, to open the block. When I finally do, it takes me to a surprisingly strong anger. I lose control for a few seconds in a huge rage, and I release some of that exasperation that built in me for so many years. After I have gone wild, which I like (it feels good to be kind of taken over by my feelings), all kinds of obvious things that I didn't understand before come to my mind.

I have always listened intensely to the men I have been with, and they have all been people with problems who needed to be listened to for hours. I have never really dared say a word about myself, and I always found them 'fascinating', and loved them for their problems. Fascinating. Now I understand ... trying to get love by giving them what they needed. Also, I bought into all the phoney values my father had, that I knew later were false. My instinct, something in me, was telling me they were false. When I was home later, older, I was fighting him on them, trying to show him how false they were. But somehow they always caught up with me; some of them always stayed in me and kept me from totally following my own convictions. He lived in a false dream, denying those parts of reality he didn't like or that hurt him. Some of that dream sank and nested in me. I feel some of my distortion and my anger at it.

I am exhausted after the session, but kind of happy. I consider that I had my first primal today because it took me over, and I understood a lot of things very clearly; in primal language, they call that 'connections' or insights. A little piece of the curtain has been lifted, a microscopic piece, but a piece all the same.

Mary told me to see *Five Easy Pieces*, because of a scene I mentioned to her that I couldn't talk about when I saw it in New York last year. I had to leave the theatre when the 'hero' comes back home after years of absence. He finds his father very aged, in a wheelchair, unable to speak any more. The hero starts talking to him, telling him how much he wishes they had communicated more and were closer, and how much he loves them. I had to leave the theatre very fast, bursting into tears, not knowing what was happening.

I was starting a primal. Today I am glad it is not playing; I am afraid to see it again. And I don't feel like hassling to get out; I am tired.

Thursday, 14 October

A guy at the pool gives me a joint. I don't even have a big temptation for it and it is against all the rules of therapy to smoke it and go out to dinner with him, which I do. I get very high, feel very guilty about it, and then decide it is too late to regret it. It is really nice, and I see a few weeks later how stupid and self-destructive that was, and how much tension it released. In my session, I cannot get into anything seriously. My mind is literally all over the place. I feel all dry inside; my thoughts are racing by; I can't concentrate. What a waste. I only have myself to blame.

While leaving my session, frustrated and mad at myself, I see other primal patients for the first time, suffering like me in their isolation. I see a blonde, very angry looking, tough, 'better stay away from her' lady who seems very big to me. And two guys – one looks rather dumb and kind of nice, like dumb guys often do, and the other is a rather good-looking blond.

Sometimes I wonder what the hell I am doing here. Is it me – in the therapy of the last hope? Difficult to believe. When I think of myself at twenty, the world was mine. I felt I was on top of it, I was very successful at anything I did. Men liked me, life was easy interesting and fun. Nothing was difficult for me. I had lots of friends. That was before the fall, before something in me started to disintegrate, before the drinking, before the drugs, before the suicide attempts and the days in a coma. I still had the strength to put myself back together, start functioning again, put on a smiling face. 'Everything is fine, mamma. I am just dying inside and I don't know why.'

Friday, 15 October

Finally, something happened today. I spent a great night again. When I wake up, I recognize this kind of half crying still in my chest. It is the way I cried as a child. A few tears on the way to the Institute. I don't really feel bad, but I know somehow that I am on the edge of something. While lying on the red carpet, waiting for Mary, I am deadly cold. It is extremely unpleasant and frightening; to avoid it I move and look around to see if something is blowing cold on me. It is so strong, but the room is not set up to trick me. Then Mary comes in. We go over my reading of *The Velveteen Rabbit.*

'Did you like it?'

'Yes, and I cried twice.'

'Oh yes? When?'

'When the rabbit is so happy that he cannot sleep after the boy says to him that he is real because he loves him.'

Talking about it and something Mary says makes me cry again, heavily. An image comes to my mind: my aunt playing the piano for me. In this memory, what strikes me is her warmth and niceness to me. I hear the touch of her nails on the keyboard of the piano. I feel her tall presence behind me and I am small. I cannot remember what Mary says each time to take me back to my feelings, but I find myself suddenly in tears, talking about my cousin's death, and I am freezing again, terribly cold. Mary tells me to feel that coldness. I feel it and I get extremely scared!

'Let it happen, Alietta, don't run away from it.'

'Easy to say, I am so scared ...'

I finally get into Flora's death. I didn't know I loved her so much. I remember this moment, the day she was buried, when they carried the coffin outside the church. When it passed by me, I 'saw' her lying inside, dead. Everything sunk inside me; I turned and staggered.

Today I see her again, and it is intolerable. The feeling that made me stumble comes up with a frightening strength. It is, 'Don't leave me. Don't leave me, please.' Again the storm: I cry, my body folded on itself, as if to protect itself from the too intense pain. I hurt, I cry. 'Don't leave me.' The feeling takes over.

While I am crying I realize that all my life I have left people, men mainly, because I was afraid they would leave me. While I am resting, images of the desert start invading my mind. The Sahara, my love for it, how deeply it always attracted me. I describe the way I feel about it to Mary, and tell her what the desert means to me and how strongly I identify with it. It reminds me of the first time I took acid. I started describing the desert to a friend of mine. He told me later how powerful my description was, and that he felt the strange fascination the Sahara had for me. It became a total death trip, a horrible nightmare. It seems that each time I focus on death, the desert is linked to it.

I don't know how, but then I switched to Flora telling me her dreams in the morning in Roma, when we lived together. Suddenly, I am back in our room in my childhood house which I see for the first time since I left it fifteen years ago. I feel a need for the kind of half-crying which drove my mother so crazy. I start doing it, and it develops into screaming mixed with anger. I hear Mama saying, 'Shut up or I'll give you something to cry about.' My anger swells and my screams start going out of control.

I am deep in myself. I scream 'Mama', and cry. I feel some desire in my legs; they feel heavy and yet I want to move them, to kick them. I start doing it, although a bit self-consciously. I am there in my childhood room, in my bed crying, and nobody is coming. Anger, anger, that's all that I feel now. 'Why does nobody come? I am small, and I want somebody to come.'

In five months of psychotherapy in New York I didn't remember one thing about my youth or early youth, and here, in five days so many things come back. When they come up they are usually announced by a boom of my heart which then pounds faster. I hold my breath and concentrate on every image bubbling upwards. Only one thing remains foggy, something behind the window that I couldn't see, yet I am sure is there. Later in the day, announced by the boom of my heart, it dawned on me ... a crib, a pink crib.

Now I am telling Mary, and the crib is not just a crib any more. There is a baby in it ... my brother?

I remember that crib; the baby in it ... is me, the clips my mother is putting on to hold the sheets tight so that I don't move. My legs feel tied up. They can't move; I hate it. I see her coming towards me. I am all sweating. She takes me in her arms and puts me on her bed to change me. She is huge. Her face is above me. She looks so young; I never remembered her before like this. God, I love her.

Tears come to my eyes, mamma. I feel strongly an immense and powerful desire for her to hold me. My tears are drying up, I can't talk any more. I see her with a very small infant in her arms and she is very big. Suddenly that baby in her arms ... I want to be that child close against her. My heart is pounding. I am that child. I feel a strong and immensely powerful desire for her to hold me. I want to feel her cheek and neck next to me. All resistance in me breaks down. 'Please, Mama, take me in your arms or I will die.' Tears are gushing out. I am folded onto myself, lost in my need, unconscious of the time it lasts. Then my tears slowly dry up. When I want to talk I find that I can't.

I see myself in a nappy, small, held against her chest, holding onto her like a clam. I feel what that infant feels. It is weird. I need to feel her so much, or feel my need of her so much. It is such a new sensation for me. I obviously lived it once, except I never let myself feel it with all its power at the time. Now the feeling I have is 'it feels like it is not a new feeling, but I feel it for the first time.' I am in a childlike position, a little bit convulsive, and I kick and hit my hand on the floor. I am the only one to be surprised at those movements which my body wants to make and does. When I have calmed down I am lying on my back again; my legs are no longer encased in lead. Mary: 'How are your legs?'

'All right now.'

She is smiling, so am I, and my smile suddenly makes me incredibly high. I feel light and happy and burst out in joy and laughter.

'I made it. We broke this terrible resistance I thought we would never break. I went far back, I can make it.'

I feel great. I have never felt like this before in my life, never, and it is fantastic. I FEEL. It is only a beginning, but now I have no doubts about the therapy any more, or about the possibility that I'll make it. I know it is right. My legs, so dead and heavy before, suddenly want to move, to dance. My whole body wants to be let out to celebrate a new lightness, something in me that is coming alive, and is irresistibly taking me over and making me laugh in exhilaration.

Goodbye, gloomy unhappiness. I feel so great.

Outside of the Institute I utter a huge Indian-like yell which surprises some Americans in the street. Many people talk to me today. My happiness shines; I feel it, it is a great day, I have wings, I have hope … 8:30PM. I am in bed.

So many things happen constantly. I just remember these cramps I have in my legs. They are the 'growing cramps' I had when I was a child. I also remember Mama rubbing them at night with camphor to ease the pain and how she left the room without kissing me, her chore finished.

Tonight, group session for the first time. It is really weird, this huge room with almost no light, people just getting down on the floor and starting to get into their feelings.

One of them, Mike R., gets down on the floor with a baby bottle, and I see him sucking on it. I can't help wishing that this kind of thing will not happen to me in the course of therapy, finding it slightly ridiculous, which I know means I am scared. I have a lot of fun watching this for a while, but later, when many people are moaning, screaming, talking to their parents and all, I find it beautiful and moving.

All these people are suffering and being reborn and cured through their pain, and there is nothing ridiculous about it. It is just very weird. In a way, it makes me feel how sick I am, and how much more free those people are. I hope it will help me feel less self-conscious about my own feelings, and that one day I'll be able to do all kinds of extravagant things, if my feelings call for it. Yes, I am trying to reassure myself, because, in fact, I am scared.

I have primaled and that is the 'blood-chilling scream' mentioned on the cover of the book – the one I dreamt so much about uttering when trying to do the therapy by myself.

Tonight I am calling 'Mama'. I want her to be with me, and wanting her hurts a lot. An impulse makes me leave the room like a prisoner leaving jail, with a huge sense of relief and the feeling I will never be able to go back into it again. I am sitting outside in the corridor when Lenny, who I like, comes over and tells me I should go back.

'Of course, the first time it is difficult, but you must go back. It is a feeling for you if you can't take it. Try to feel why you can't stay; feel that. It will keep you busy for a while, and who knows, maybe you will get into something.' He smiles a child-like smile.

So I go back into hell, and I feel a feeling, an old one. I want to get out, I hate everybody, I can't stay in the room any more than I wanted to stay at home as a child. I kept running away since I was five years old. I remember now how unhappy I was, what despair I was in. How sad it was for a little girl to feel that way. I was running away from home all the time, just as I have been running away all my life around the world, like a comet, never staying anywhere really, so I wouldn't have to feel that nobody loved me at home, or anywhere else in this world. After two hours of the group scene I don't feel like running out any more. The light comes back on. They wait for a guy to be finished with what he is into, which seems to be something deep, then Marc and Joshua sit in two chairs.

People are lying or sitting on the floor, or crying, or whatever they are into. They start saying what they have to say to finish their feelings, or get into a feeling. It is very interesting to watch the whole thing.

While someone is talking, everybody is silent, most watch

except those in their own primals. Sometimes the person talking can't be heard because of someone crying, or a huge scream suddenly goes off in the air, and a body swirls in violent agony, or someone crosses the room screaming, 'I hate you, I want to kill you', and throws himself to the punching bag, saying, 'I don't know who I am, and what I want.' (When the feeling is rising, the patients might take the time to put on the gloves, then they can really let their rage burst out and express it.)

I have never been in any therapy or any group of this sort, and watching this is totally phenomenal for me. How can these people be so free and have the courage to say all this? I am amazed, more even than during the time when the group was in the dark. One guy tells the group about being tied up by his father and made to watch him for hours while he made a whip. He has a lot of difficulty talking. It is obvious that the memory of the whole scene is coming up as he talks, and he is totally wrapped up in the emotion of it. 'He is carving the whip handle and showing it to us.' I notice that most of the therapists have tears in their eyes. So do I.

Evening

While I am getting ready for bed I see images of our summer place. I see the faces of my brothers and sister and other children, and Christina, my friend at the time. I haven't thought about her in thirty years. Our parents were very close; she was much more open about life than me. Her sexuality developed very early, and she made me discover this secret part of myself that she felt was worth more attention than I had given to it until then. So on the beach we put shells in our 'shell', and thought it was very pretty. It is funny to remember. We were so young and cute, and thinking of these kids' games, I fall asleep smiling, laughing. For how long?

Tuesday, 21 October

'The session was great today,' says Mary. I was running through scenes on the beach where I vaguely saw myself crawling on my ass in the sand, feeling miserable about this miserable condition.

Then, I started really hurting at the memory of Papa beating up my brother Joe badly. I lived it strongly again, with the sense of my helplessness, the desire to tell Papa to stop, and also my fear of him. I saw him as a giant, out of control, something like Jupiter, unleashing his gigantic power on a mosquito. I was there totally and I was re-experiencing the fear that he'd kill my little brother. All that tumult of feeling is boiling in me, and I realize through the pain of the primal, all the bad, deep bad, Papa has done to us by not loving us. (That's pretty obvious to me now, for the first time really.)

When the storm is over, I see myself holding my brother in my arms, both of us alone on the beach, and how protective of him I felt. Them against us. I also realize that all my life I have tried to make my father happy and to be what he wanted Joe to be – in other words, to be his son. I was so afraid of his gigantic and violent anger, and I thought that maybe that way, he would finally accept me.

Papa made me feel that as a woman I was automatically limited. I had to prove to him that I wasn't and defeat him on his own ground. Maybe then I would mean something, be like a man, live a man's life. That was my goal, to prove to myself that I could do something for myself. That's what I believed at the time. In fact, I was only pathetically acting out, still trying to get Papa to love me.

Mary explains to me that the primal process is like a wave that unwinds little by little, lets the person feel and relive the past, following the body's rhythm, revealing everything progressively.

Friday, 24 October

Last night I wanted to get on my knees and talk to Papa, ask forgiveness for all the horrible things I said and am going to say again, while in primal. I knew the kneeling would do something. As soon as I get down I burst into heavy tears and feel the hurt of Papa's death and start talking to him.

Mary has me tell her the story of Papa's death, four or five years ago. It is difficult. My whole body is shivering and shaking heavily.

I see Papa's coffin being taken away. I see myself watching ... the wave, the despair that I held in so well at the time ... a huge scream. 'Papa don't go ... don't go ... please don't leave me ... don't leave me ... I love you.' I am hurting a lot and it increases. I can't take it. It hurts too much. I scream because the hurt is too big; it is horrible.

I stop trying to get hold of myself, but it is 'open'. Something has broken open the cement of my defence system, and through the crack, the fire and then the reality burns. The demons which I kept tied up and pushed down and ignored for so long can finally break the lid, unleash themselves, and leave me. Then my body wants its part, and I decide to let it do whatever it wants to do. It never had any autonomy before with me. I am conscious about what my body seems to want to do. Nothing extraordinary in fact, but sucking my thumb at my age, in front of somebody I met only a few days ago is still difficult. My legs seem to be tied up together. I can't really move them. Weird. I realize that they have never been apart from each other through all the sessions. My body is holding onto itself. I try to uncross by legs and I can't. It scares me. I cry very childishly. I am still not used to the strange sounds that come out of me, and I am too conscious of them to really let them come. The thumb sucking is good, but I am too tired. I calm down progressively. I feel spaced out and worn out, after the big tornado.

I am stunned by the agony my whole self goes through and the inevitability of it once it has started. My face is ravaged and my skin is chaos. It is an earthquake that has shaken me.

Last night, I remembered showing Papa my first drawing, with all its colours and my pride in it. I did not know what to do with it. He gave me a vague smile, indifferent and polite, a 'very good, little one', and went right back to his daydreams. I never drew anything again, I never showed him anything again. I never showed anybody anything.

Neither did I ask him to take any interest in me. I didn't want to be faced with his indifference. Everybody was good enough but me. That's why when somebody I love gives what I need to someone else, I resent it so much. It makes all the old feelings come up. I called it insecurity. So did the psycho-analyst. It is obviously more complicated than that. It is my own experience specifically, and not a typical insecurity that anyone would have; only I can discover what my past is and understand it; nobody else.

And I understand so much every day. My parents always said, 'If you want to cry, cry in your room. You are not inter-esting when you cry; you bore us.' That's right, so I put on a brave smile for life, and went through it like this, only my smile was becoming sadder and sadder. I was not allowed to have feelings because they bored my parents. I had to hide them, to progressively kill them to be accepted. I had to kill the living part of myself, the feeling part, in exchange for them to accept me there. I feel a devastating pain at this real-ization. Another piece of the same puzzle or, should I say, of the same feeling?

Then, my body starts being restless; something I am not going to like is coming up. I get angry, really angry ... foetal position and childlike cry. I still can't get over hearing myself cry like this; I am not sure what it is. I feel very strange.

The tension I have felt a few times in the last weeks is stretching my shoulders and settling itself in my nape. My head is pushing, pushing, I don't know what. My legs are full of feelings. They help me push too. I am in the black, in a strange atmosphere. I don't know what's going on. I keep pushing. The lighting is strange. I am in the womb. I want to get out of it. As soon as the idea comes, I reject it. Can't be. It is too freaky an idea. I am banging my head against the wall and pushing like mad. Mary doesn't seem to find it freaky at all; she is not even surprised – as if it was the most normal stuff in the world. Well, it blows my mind.

Tonight, it is as if slow death is descending upon me. Death. I have always been obsessed by it. The fear of being alone in the dark is still there. I am alone, I have always been alone, I am never going to make it alone, I need help. I am so scared. It is as if I am going to die if nobody helps me, if nobody comes. I am totally still, I don't dare move, and slowly I feel myself fall irresistibly into a powerful drowsiness. A part of me becomes totally panicked. I have to get up and get help. Someone has got to come or I'll die. But I don't move. My body refuses the smallest movement. I feel drugged and I am going to die. I try taking a big breath of air and find that I can't breathe. The panic grows and, with it, my need to breathe. As I try to open my mouth, I feel it distorted in a silent scream. I am choking and I choke until I feel myself falling in a black hole. 'Where are you, Mama? I need you to help me. I am dying.' I have no idea how long I stayed in this narcoleptic state. It seemed like an eternity.

Suddenly, from somewhere far away in me, I feel an overwhelming need to move, a fear of it, too, the need to scream, to shake myself out of this death. Something in me refuses to die. A part of me, still alive, is growing. I have to summon up all my will power. It is a physical need. I have to move, I have to get out of it. I have to get out.

While I am forcing myself to move, to shake that incredibly powerful lethargy, I am screaming an inhuman scream, and my body starts moving in erratic movements. I start kicking, my back arches violently, every part of my body aches, it tenses up to make me push, to crawl in weird motions that I do not understand and that are totally out of my control. I just need to do it with all my strength. It is extremely hard, but I have to do it. I keep pushing, arching, gagging. I can't breathe. I am dying again. Again, I fall into the coma-like state, and again that little flame gets me out of it. As I was pushing and trying to breathe, I suddenly felt I was making it. I could breathe; I could open my eyes. From very deep in me, an explosion of amazing intensity rushed over me and grew into an unexpected bliss. I made it. I Made It. I am alive. And suddenly a flash. I am Born!

The joy was powerful. I was laughing. I was feeling the blood flow quickly through my body. Every part of me wanted to move, to stretch, to jump, to express the incredible joy I was now feeling. It became pure ecstasy, the ecstasy of simply being alive. I was laughing alone in my dark room and I recognized having never felt like this before. Was that what being alive could be like? How phenomenal. A few tears at the realization that it had never been like that for me. I had only felt pain, never joy, but now it was there and I wanted more of it. A new addiction to life was starting. It was fantastic. I was exhausted and yet I wanted to jump up and down, to feel my body move and dance. I was finally born. The insights started pouring out. Yes, birth, unmistakably so.

The agony of death, the struggle to be born, and finally coming out into this world all by myself with no help, only because of my determination not to die. That same determination has kept me alive through the worst, and has kept me searching for something to save me. It led me to therapy, and here again it is only I who can do it and save myself. I know now I will make it. I had to leave my mother's womb in which I was held prisoner, slowly suffocating for too long. I had to get out of the control of her body. I had to leave my home because I couldn't stand the permanent control I was subjected to, the rigidity of a Catholic bourgeois education. I had to be able to do what I wanted because otherwise I would die. And the child I was did die slowly through all these years of repression and lack of love. But now I will get her back, and Alietta is going to live again. I asked my mother later what had happened at my birth. At first she didn't remember, then she acknowledged the fact that she had to be given drugs to allow her to relax because I couldn't get out.

Group

The man with the whip, Raoul, is explaining his constant humiliation by his father. He is always excusing himself. He keeps talking and seems to have some difficulty getting into his feeling. He says he made the whip and brought it with him. He shows it to us. Bernard reaches over to him and takes the whip in a very threatening way. I am watching, fascinated. This place is full of the unexpected. Raoul is looking at Bernard with fear, like a small terrorized child. Suddenly, Bernard, who is very big, acts as if he is going to hit Raoul, and instead of touching him, hits the wall very hard. Things move very quickly. At the very second it happened, Raoul is on the floor primaling deeply, and almost everybody in the room has their nose in the carpet. 'Please, Daddy, please, don't hit me.'

The memory of my very serious suicide attempt, and the pain my ex-husband was putting me through at the time comes back. I had left him without a second's hesitation. When I did, it wasn't really a rational decision. A powerful force inside me was actually in control, making me put distance between him and me. I had rented myself a separate apartment. I just had to do it. But why? I never really understood where that power to leave him came from, but it was irresistible – as if my life depended on it. I had to put a definitive distance between the source of my pain (him), and me, if I was to survive. As these words go through my mind, I suddenly understand them. His totally controlling attitude was reawakening the feeling I know now: the impossibility of letting myself be controlled, birth, intolerable pain, helplessness, death.

All I could do was run away from the apparent source of rejection and pain. When I was hurting over the separation I put distance between me and myself, me and my pain. I took an overdose of pills. There was nothing dramatic about it. I didn't leave a note to anybody, I just wanted to sleep forever. Life wasn't worth living if that's the way I had to feel. I remember those sad days. I was being transported by ambulance full speed through Rome's crowded streets on my third day of the coma. I have no recollection of it, but since then I can never hear an ambulance siren without breaking into tears. Today I am sobbing softly, 'I tried to kill myself because you didn't love me.'

The Halloween Party

Somebody told me that every year Janov has a Halloween party for which all of us are supposed to dress up to express how we really feel about ourselves or what we hope to be. It is certainly the heaviest part of my life. It is like Fellini. I feel as though I am hallucinating. When I walk into the room I'm greeted at the door by something I hate – a skeleton. It's made of paper, but it's like the ones I saw as a child, and it was enough to scare me to death. There's another one hanging from the ceiling.

John is in the corner, but he doesn't know how to costume himself. He's wrapping himself in miles of silver paper and he gets up and says, 'I was a machine to make money. It's a good image of me,' he says, and then has a feeling of being nothing but a money machine instead of being loved for what he was.

I don't have the slightest desire to feel tonight. I'm fascinated by seeing humanity as it really is. I don't want to miss a second of it. There's somebody hanging from a giant cross in the corner. I hear he is an ex-priest. There is another minister tearing pages out of the Bible and throwing them all over the room. Meanwhile, he's in his usual dress. It's a touching and powerful sight, some kind of grotesque realism. There are patients in nappies sucking on bottles. Another giant fellow has a safety pin to keep his nappies up. There's a beautiful girl dressed in white like an angel with wings and feathers.

She pulls Kleenex from her box, but with non-angelic rage, and has an idea that she's always been made to be an angel, although that's not how she really felt. There's a ballerina who was forced to take lessons in her early life, who dances with a great deal of anger and resentment.

One man came completely in chains. He's naked, and he is really Prometheus, and I keep wondering how he managed to tie his hands and feet together. There is a tennis player, complete with racket and visor, recounting how he has been a transvestite all his adult life and the feelings he had about wanting his mother to show some feeling. There's a guy in a sailor suit next to a naked girl who's always been afraid to show her body. But she's showing it now. Meanwhile, another naked man with an erection is screaming, 'It's not dirty, Momma! It's not dirty! It's just me!'

Another man is dressed in a prisoner's outfit, dragging a heavy plastic ball, and a woman is sitting with a little red doll in her arms, talking baby talk to it. Meanwhile, group is going on as usual, people are standing up and talking about their costumes and what it means, falling on the floor and screaming. It seems like absolute bedlam.

I can't wait for the post-group, when Art takes his chair and the action really begins.

The feelings behind some costumes are pretty obvious, and lead the person into their feeling right away. There's a lady in a nurse's uniform who took care of her hypochondriac father all of her life, and was feeling so angry about all of his demands and how she had sacrificed her life for him, never marrying. Her rage was unbelievable. Another girl in a very sexy costume has said how she has always been sexually seductive, although underneath, with her nappies still on, she was just a baby, wanting love and to be held.

'This girl was an orphan,' Janov says with a very soft voice (the kind that makes you want to jump straight into his arms and cuddle there all winter). 'She's okay. You all recognize yourself in her because you are all orphans with parents.'

I cry so hard now, but I want to stop because I don't want

to miss any of the 'show'. Art asks George why he's wearing chains, and George says, 'Because I could never show my pain. I could never express myself. I felt so tied up by their misunderstanding of me and my needs.' He's crying and wailing. After George gets through screaming and crying, Art kneels down and unties his chains. It is a nice symbol of discovery.

Afterwards, there's a girl, Rebecca, who is wearing an angel costume. Art asks her why she's wearing it. She looks at the floor and doesn't answer, like a stubborn child. Then she starts talking. We all listen in perfect silence, tense. What she says is so indirect. I can feel how all her words pass through her screen of pain. She's detouring all over the place. She sounds like a machine that's out of order. It's frightening. My heart shrinks, listening to her. She finally reaches the wound, at the end of her interminable monologue. 'I always had to be an angel. I had to be so well-policed, so well-behaved that I could never be angry or resentful, or say anything that was slightly displaced.' And then she falls to the floor in a rage, pounding and screaming. 'I hate what you did to me! I hate you! I hate what you did to me! I hate everybody!' Her wings are flapping and she's writhing all over the floor in her burning hatred. While she is screaming, another man stands up. I can only guess that he's a man because he is dressed in a very green dress. He has a wig and looks strange. I don't recognize who he is. His confession is a painful one. He is a homosexual, and for him to come in a dress was difficult. He said that he masturbated twice in the Institute toilets before coming to group. He was so scared because he knew he had to say all this. When he gets scared he masturbates. He proceeds to undress slowly in front of all of us. I watch in fascination. What he was trying to do was transform himself from woman to man, while he was calling in a baby voice for his mommy.

There is a lady in the corner who remained a helpless child all of her life, and she's wearing a little baby dress. It was the only way she could get anybody to take care of her – first her mother, then her husband. Some guy is naked now because he lost the pin to his nappy. Another is wearing a computer and says that all of his life he's been a machine, functioning very well mechanically, but never feeling. The ballerina is dancing with a freedom she has never known before, because she was always so uptight and terrified. She really is graceful. And then she screams at her parents, 'Look at my ugly body! Look at my ugly body! I have always tried to hide it, I hated myself so much. But look at me now, because that's all there is to me. If you don't like me, that's too bad. I am what I am.' And she is smiling and smiling.

The whole thing reminded me of *Marat-Sade.* It seems beyond imagination this night. I will keep it in my memory forever.

Saturday, 1 November: Last Day of the Three Weeks

My new primal life is nicely organized, now that the motel time is over. I am going to share a house with Arlene, my friend. It looks like we will have to stay in LA longer than I thought. I thought the therapy would last three weeks! My primals are very strong. I am very angry or I feel like I am going crazy, like last night. They are heavy and fully of feelings, weighted with sobbing. I get overwhelmed for a while and then, 'poof', it is gone. I like it when it unfurls like that. I am opening up more and more. The mud is pouring out of me and I feel cleaner inside. In group last night, I had this terrible feeling of having been fucked up, thinking, 'Don't kill me. Please, you are killing me. Not me. Stop it.' I am hurting deeply and feel the impossibility of changing anything about it. I am crushed by the feeling of what has been done to me. I feel that all my life, every minute of it, has been a nightmare. I feel it, for the first time as I never did. How ironic that my life looked so nice from the outside.

Last night, feeling the misery of my life, I felt again that Papa always made me feel small, like nothing, in fact. I didn't exist and that's why I always denied myself everything. I am nothing, because that's how they treated me. It explains why I was becoming more and more insecure lately. I can't believe that anybody could love me because deep down inside I really feel very small, rejected, bad and uninteresting. Unlovable.

Monday, 3 November

I see Papa's eyes. They scare me deeply. I feel my fear very well now. I am really afraid of him. Could that have influenced my attitude towards men? I always played it cool, but was actually, literally, afraid of them. I am now reflecting on the disaster of my life. Every insight shows my sickness and how deep it is. Do I even have any freedom left in me to be myself, or am I entirely programmed by the pain? What a devastating thought! One thing is sure: thirty years of my life have been lost.

After feeling the terrifying reality of it, I rest and reflect on these three weeks. They have changed my life already for many reasons. The most obvious one is that I am now confident of the primal process. It happened for me and it is a great relief. However, the fear that it is all going to stop now that I am on my own is tenacious. I will discover later through birth primals that it is a 'big' feeling for me which belongs more to the past than to the present. Right now I am in awe of everything that has happened. I am elated and crucified by the reality I have discovered in me – elated because my ability to feel pain means hope. I have seen how it works; I have recognized it. It is me finally emerging, and that feels good. It is as if those little pieces of my past, of my feelings of my memory, needed to be conscious in me for me to be – or to become – complete. I like tearing away bit by bit all those pieces of myself from this total darkness where they laid for so long. What is extravagant is how it is all there, in the agony of Pain, waiting for me to rediscover it.

How powerful, how excruciating the pain is. I couldn't have any idea of this and I don't think anybody who hasn't felt it can have any idea. Such power has to exert a force when repressed. It seems to me that every bit of who I am hinges on these memories, these powerful needs, and the immensity of the Pain. It is worse than I thought ... and better. I measure now the immensity of the disaster, but I also have hope. One day, I will have a life again. It is entirely up to me this time. These three weeks have been the most fascinating of my life. So now I have to go on with the rest of the voyage. How deep, how long, how far do I have to go?

Five Years Later

It has now been five years of unexpected agony and great joy. Time to look back. I suppose the main event of my therapy and of my life is my birth. And that, of course, is quite a surprise. What is absolutely amazing is that this remote event is at the root of everything I do, everything I am. It is the pivot of the very basic tendencies of my personality.

The scenario I know by heart unfolded on a very grim November day, during the war. My mother was giving birth. She wasn't ready to open up, and I was ready to be born. What I learned later is that the signal of birth is given by the baby when it is ready to be born. So I must have done just that, but my mother wasn't ready to open up. Something in her body was fighting the natural process. Did she not want that baby? Whatever the reason was, it affected my whole life. When the signal of birth was given, and all my motions were keyed to that goal, I started going down the canal and all was fine. I should have gone out but I couldn't, and started suffocating. Very long. It might have actually lasted only a short time, but in my primals it feels like an eternity. So I suffocated, and slowly started to die, all the way to the very edge of death. In a last surge of survival, my body tried desperately to get out, to get some air, and make this intolerable feeling of suffocation and near death disappear. My survival instinct took the shape of a gigantic rage, making me push with all my energy in a desperate effort to be born.

Again, I was defeated and fell into nearly fatal asphyxiation. Again the rage to make it, to get out, and again the defeat.

Eventually, I was born, already modified by the experience. I was born with a huge bar across my forehead, purple with rage and obviously furious. The midwife warned my mother of all the 'good' times in store for us. She had never seen such an angry baby. She proved to be right. I couldn't be told anything. My total distrust for my environment made me refuse all orders, all constraint. My need for freedom was the main force behind my actions at all times. It created trouble with my parents, teachers, and generally anybody trying to curb me. I couldn't stand any interference with my will because it meant death. It was immensely powerful.

When I left my husband, the superpowerful force pushing me to put distance between him and me was the power of birth. He was enclosing me in his set of laws and I couldn't take it. I had to leave. I had no idea then what that force was which was pushing me to leave him, but I had to do it.

The other facet of it was the fact that nothing could stop me. Any serious obstacle had to be surmounted. I had to make it. I could never feel stuck or helpless. If I did, I literally felt like I was going crazy; the memory of near-death would start ascending – unbeknownst to me – and I would have to make it through. To avoid those feelings I enlisted all my powers in everything I did and was therefore successful.

I bred the solitude I lived in, the impossibility of commitment. I avoided any hint of dependence because, just as at my birth, dependence (on my mother) meant the danger of death. The necessity for freedom was the other aspect of it. I was never again going to be in anybody's power. Never again was I going to be at someone's mercy. So I was always my own boss, fully responsible for myself. If I wasn't, the near-death feeling was immediately ascending and transmitting itself in the form of incredibly powerful migraines. Every time an obstacle would raise its ugly head, a migraine would surge. I suffered from them for twenty years, and I had no idea where they came from. Now I can get rid of them by feeling the birth feeling of being stuck, being totally without oxygen and dying. After each of those feelings, very hard to relive, I can feel my migraine recede and disappear. Now I know where it comes from and what to do about it.

The feeling of utter loneliness was the other powerful drive behind my behaviour. My mother wasn't helping me to be born, and I learned from this that nobody would be there when I needed them, that I had to count only on myself, that I shouldn't expect any help from anybody. That too reinforced the solitude of my life. I could never share my troubles with anyone, act vulnerable, or ask for anything.

My mother didn't really want me being born and it made me feel deeply unwanted. That feeling was reinforced later by all these seconds in my youth where she and my father made me feel like they didn't want me to be around. They didn't enjoy my presence, my company, or merely the fact that I was alive. They made me feel that my existence itself was all a mistake and that everybody would have been much better off had I not been born.

So, feeling unloved, I thought it was all my fault. Why didn't they love me? What was wrong with me? Unconsciously, I hated myself for not being loved. I was a monster. Otherwise, why so much hatred and violence towards me? Why such inhuman treatment? I was less than a dog. I could not love myself since I was so bad. It made me distrust anybody who wanted me or loved me. Not being loved by my parents ensured that I would never be loved by anyone. I just could not accept it. It also made me incapable of giving love. And yet all I wanted in my life was to be loved and to love. What a sad irony.

The other powerful force in my life over which I had no control was the need to 'get out' all of the time, especially when anything went wrong. These basic tendencies weren't conscious, of course. They constituted my 'personality'. I was a difficult child, independent, strong, and a loner. I couldn't be moulded into what they wanted me to be.

The rest of my childhood only reinforced those basic

tendencies: my parents' lack of real interest, their total lack of real love. They didn't talk to me. Although my father was talking to me for hours he was really talking to himself. They never paid attention to any of my pains or needs. And I kept them at a distance. So I ran away. I had to get out. Whenever things went wrong I got out. I didn't communicate with them. I kept to myself. I never asked for anything.

All I was hoping for was to get out of my family as fast as I could. That I accomplished. They were only too happy to get rid of me when I was fifteen. I had to get out and take my life into my own hands. No power over me. My freedom was in sight. I was going to make sure never to lose it again. I kept packing my bags whenever a lover or friend asserted their power over me. In the end, even my tolerance of that became thinner and thinner. I was packing my bags all the time and spinning round the planet. The last time I packed my bags was to come to therapy.

The other totally 'far out' consequence of my birth has been my suicide attempts. When getting out of a situation was no longer enough to lower the pain, when putting distance between the source of the pain and myself was no longer enough, I put distance between myself and my pain. I tried to kill myself. The birth memory had taught me that after agony, suffocation, and near-death, death itself represented an end to the agony I was in. The equation stayed in my system. Whenever the situation seemed to hopeless, whenever I was no longer in command and the hurt was unbearable, the obvious way out was suicide. Really, it was the reawakened pain which was pushing me in this direction, and the ultimate solution I sought was the one attached to the birth experience. My whole life was directed by it, and not only did I have no idea of it, but I was totally powerless to do anything about it.

Fifteen Years Later

The insights have become deeper and more complete. After

so much time I am still astonished at the power of the primal. I still have one once in a while, but the pain has finally subsided. I do not have to feel this experience so often. Only when life brings up some old unfinished pain do I have to feel this. It is very rare now. Feeling always brings clarity and simplification, and I can now deal with reality and the present, and no more with the past.

My life is now very much in order. I am no longer my father's son. I am no longer a hard-driving business woman. I am no longer after success, but only after fulfilment of my real self. My real self is now in command; my life is much simpler. I have found love at last, and I am able to love and be loved. I am now an artist. This is what I should have been from the beginning for it gives me great satisfaction and peace. It is the real me. I sleep well (I was always an insomniac), I eat better, I don't drink, nor am I a dope addict any more. I am generally much healthier. I used to have infections, haemorrhages, and there was often something wrong with me. My eyesight was deteriorating rapidly. After two weeks of therapy, having lost my glasses, I lived without them for two weeks before I realized I didn't have them.

Now years have passed and age has caught up with me. I am a lot softer, easy to be with, and a lot more open and warmer. I even go to parties, although I still don't like doing that much. But it is not the crucifying experience it used to be and very often I enjoy it thoroughly. It is easier to be with people. I don't run away or pack my bags. Instead I stay and feel the feelings. I like to listen to music and grow flowers. I enjoy more stability, and don't spend my life in airplanes.

My sex life is normal. For years I had to have birth primals before I could experience an orgasm because my body had been so shut off by the pain of birth that the pain always preceded the pleasure.

I look more relaxed because so much tension has left me for good. My dreams are no longer symbolic. If they are painful, all I have to do is get back to the feeling contained in them and get to it.

I feel I got what I expected from Primal and more. I know who I am and what I am. I am no longer a mystery to myself. In fact, I am not sure I still have an unconscious. So much has surfaced and become and remain conscious. It is a great relief. My life is in order. All these years of pain have paid off. I am finally happy.

6

How Early Experience is Imprinted

There is a special category of memory which I call imprints. Although the term imprint has been used with a different meaning and in a somewhat different context by students of animal behaviour, it is uniquely descriptive of how pain is impressed in the nervous system.

What are Imprints?

Imprints, as I use the term, are repressed memories which find their way into the biological system and produce distorted functions. These distortions can be both organic and psychological. The formation of imprints takes place during early childhood development, and falls off critically after about the age of ten. That is, it would take a much greater force after that to engrave an imprint than at the age of two, for example.

There are two ways in which imprints are set in place. One is through the experience of a single, excruciating drama. The other is through a series of events during which certain needs remain chronically unfulfilled over a period of several years. The feeling, 'No one wants me,' may have its origins in a specific traumatic event, (being sent very early to boarding school – the favourite sport of the English) or it may arise from a series of minor events which produce an incremental impact over time. After enough rejection it starts to dawn on the child that no one wants him. I say, 'starts to', because before the full light of realization it is repressed and begins its underground life. The above ground life is trying to get everyone to want him (even the waitress serving him coffee). For every underground feeling there is an above ground counterpart act-out. The connections have been severed and rerouted so that the act-out seems natural and evident.

A parent who really feels that the child is in his way will continuously treat that child as if he were not wanted. And sooner or later, the imprint sets in: 'I am not wanted.' Now the physiology has been changed and the personality reflects that change. It is not produced by one shattering event, but by one shattering feeling spread over hundreds of events.

The illnesses we suffer from later in life – the psychological ones and some of the organic ones – are the result of these bits of frozen history. Feelings of loneliness, worthlessness (if no one wants me it must be because I'm worthless), despair and hopelessness are all translated into disease. These early memories and feelings will continue to warp the system as long as they remain repressed, blocked and unconscious. Changes in the biochemistry and neurology of an individual contain the memory. It is one way the memory is imprinted. The imprint then becomes a danger, a 'foreign element' to be reckoned with. And the system thereafter cannot be itself but spends its life trying to get back to normal (discussed in detail later on). The alien intrusion (a father's rages, for example; being sent to a foster home) makes the child feel fearful and unsafe. The child cannot be herself and the system goes into the defensive mode. There are changes in brain wave patterns, hormone output, muscle potential, and changes in the brain to accommodate the pain; namely, added receptor sites for pain to deal with the inundation. The system can compensate for the intrusion only so long before a vulnerable organ gives out and disease follows. Any later therapy for whatever illness that occurs will eventually have to 'right' the system back to normal. An example will help make this clear.

Impact of an Imprint Upon the Immune System

Some years ago a patient of mine was preparing for a trip to India. In order to strengthen her immune reactions she was required to have inoculations for tetanus, cholera, and typhoid. A polio shot was thrown in for good measure. She received all the shots at once and within an hour she had a high fever and agonizing constrictions throughout her body. She vomited continuously. Two days later there was a serious itch in her vagina which was diagnosed as herpes, one of the worst cases the doctor had ever seen. Some years before she had noticed a slight vaginal irritation which had been diagnosed as mild herpes, but at the time of these vaccinations she had not been sexually active for nine months.

Two weeks later she developed a fever that went on for over a month. After six weeks of this fever, she began to relive a traumatic, near-death situation from very early in her life. The fever brought on by the inoculations triggered off an imprinted memory of a similar traumatic past event. The combined force of the inoculations and the imprinted memory was overwhelming. When she finished reliving the earlier trauma and the trauma of the inoculations, the fever ended and she was on the road to recovery.

Within my patient's encapsulated experience lies a great deal of information about the imprint and the nature of disease. In this particular situation, too much was asked of the woman's immune system. It was asked to react and integrate the inoculations for all three diseases. In addition, the shots mobilized the imprint of the old near-death memory which, when intermingled with the present shock, became overwhelming. The herpes virus, which had been held in check, was now 'liberated' to manifest itself overtly.

Although this is an example of physical illness, the realm of mental illness is the same. Too much negative input, the loss of a job, a partner, a marriage, etc. can combine with the imprinted early loss of a parent to overwhelm the system and result in neurosis or psychosis. The current stressful input literally jiggles the antennae of the nerve cells to reawaken specific feelings and memories. That is why the neurotic reacts in the present as though he or she were in the past.

Inoculations are but one way the immune system can be overwhelmed. A woman who loses her spouse also has a weakened immune system and is five times more likely to develop cancer. A chimp whose mother has been killed by hunters suddenly falls ill and dies for inexplicable reasons.

Imprints as the Memory of Trauma

Trauma is an input into the system which is more than can be accepted and integrated. When something is too painful for the system to absorb, it is a trauma. One experience may not be traumatic but when combined with other experiences, it produces a feeling which is traumatic. Traumas remain as pain memories of a special kind which can be recalled and relived. When we are old enough to withstand the full onslaught of an early childhood drama we can feel the total impact and begin its integration.

Traumas are impressed into the system with the force of the original event. As soon as traumatic stimuli are recorded in the body they are split into two parts, one which can be immediately felt as pain and discomfort, and another part which goes unfelt, is gated away and kept in storage as suffering. Trauma creates a splitting of the self. A wedge is driven between the real self and the unreal or unfeeling self. The part of the recorded traumatic event which is unfelt and held in the memory bank becomes a continuous and reverberating source of energy in the brain and body. Imprints based on trauma contain both the memory of the event, and the encoded record of the feelings associated with it.

The manner in which imprinted trauma functions can be inferred from the research conducted by Wilder Penfield during surgery on epileptics. With the patient awake, Penfield stimulated certain cells of the temporal lobe with an electrode and found that the patients would relive certain events from the past even while they were aware of doing so in the operating theatre. Two levels of consciousness were functioning at the same time. There was a simultaneous focus on the past and the present. When Penfield removed the electrode, the memory stopped. When the electrode was replaced, the memory began again. The patient could smell the smells, see the images, and hear the sounds exactly as though he were 'back there'. Clearly, the memories had remained and could be recalled as a living experience by putting an electrode on the scanning mechanism in the brain that retrieves long-term memory. At that moment the patient was in the experience. It wasn't a matter of just talking about a memory. It was a reliving.

This important experiment demonstrates that our mind can hold detailed memories and associations without being able to access them in a conscious state. Imprints are such memories. An imprinted trauma leaves a 'trace'. This means that certain nerve networks become 'grooved' so that they interact more readily with one another. Thereafter, messages will travel along those nerve pathways with greater facility. The child who learns to be afraid of her father and then of men in general reacts to present situations on a trace memory. The imprinted fear of men has become grooved, and ensures that the next time she is with an adult male she will be just as afraid as she was the last time.

Imprints and the Emotional Centres of the Mind

The limbic system is located along the borders of the lower part of the neocortex. It is a functional unit of the brain which is made up of portions of the thalamus, hypothalamus, hippocampal formation, amygdala, caudate nucleus and mes-encephalon. Linked in a unique way by fibre pathways, these structures control various behaviours including emotional expression, seizure activity, and memory storage and recall.

One of the key structures in the limbic system is the hippocampus, which is often considered the gateway to memory, and thus the gateway to the unconscious. The hippocampus plays a role in the organization of memory after an event has occurred. The thalamus, which lies just above the hippocampus, is responsible for the 'print' order that results in permanent, long-term memory. When a person suffers from amnesia, for example, it is sometimes the case that the print order was never given; something has interfered with thalamic functioning.

This print process may work in the following manner. We see or sense something, stimuli are perceived, and the hippocampus is informed. The hippocampus then tells the thalamus to print, or imprint, the scene. Once this process has taken place, with a few hours' delay while the biochemistry changes to convert the memory into a long-term event, nothing can erase that memory. It will remain for the rest of our lives.

When an event is traumatic, the message of that emotion is shunted to another place in the limbic system, including the thalamus and the amygdala. They handle part of the suffering component of the imprint. When either structure is lesioned suffering stops. The thalamus can relay painful information outside the limbic system to the neocortex, or thinking brain. But the neocortex doesn't suffer. It remembers and recalls in great detail, but a trigger or stimulus is needed to activate and release the suffering component of memory from the limbic system into cortical consciousness. Otherwise the memory will remain without emotional substance and be literally disembodied.

The importance of the relationship between the limbic system and the cortex in the thinking brain is that it is possible to understand oneself and one's behaviour solely on the cortical level, even to remember one's childhood in great detail, while being cut off from the feelings which constitute the guts of that memory. Cortical memory can be detailed and complex, and at the same time remain detached from the suffering factor. The suffering I am discussing is almost beyond description and has nothing to do with a few sobs or tears. That is why it is disconnected.

Without a reconnection of thinking to emotional memory, the suffering component or pain associated with the memory remains as gated circulating energy. We have found a therapeutic method for retrieving that suffering component, in small doses, which can be successfully integrated into the personality until there is relatively little unconscious left; for that is largely what the unconscious is made of – unintegrated pain.

The limbic system and its storehouse of emotions is what eventually shapes our perceptions and our projections – how we see reality. The amygdala is loaded with endorphines and functions not only as a storehouse of pain but also aids the gating function. Thus, the place where emotions are organized is also the place where they are suppressed. When too painful emotions move out of the limbic system towards the cortex and consciousness the morphine-like opiates block their route. Cortical consciousness means pain. It also means resolution of pain if it can be integrated.

As one moves down from the cortical processing area towards the limbic system one encounters heavier concentrations of the opiates. Thus, in the face of shattering feelings first organized in the hypothalmus, structures such as the amygdala are capable of spewing out endorphines to block the way of these feelings to consciousness.

The amygdala receives fibres from the cortex, but also sends projecting fibres up to the surface in the cortex. The ascending feelings, blocked by the internal opiates, continue to send their energy upwards and outwards. They are constantly trying to escape from the emotional warehouse and connect with their proper home in consciousness. So the feelings surge towards consciousness for resolution, while the gates prevent it. Thereafter, how we see ourselves and the world will change. Once there is a load of unconscious pain, no conscious act of will can make one real or straight. Gates do not yield to pleas. They are merciful and merciless.

The fact of a two-way fibre network between the limbic system and the cortex means that information arrives from outside and is immediately controlled by other prepotent information sent up from inside. That is why if you don't perceive yourself properly you will not see the external world as it is.

The imprint of memory isn't a 'thing'. It can't be localized in one specific place in the brain. Rather, the imprint is spread throughout the system. Memory is held by changes in the chemistry of neurons, by waveform patterns of electricity, by changes in the blood cells, and even in the content of our saliva. Indeed, memory might be said to be held by every cell in our body.

Imprints, Pain and Feeling

The fact that needs and feelings are gated on the way to consciousness allows us to act out our feelings symbolically, to think thoughts derivative of our feelings but without direct connection. We are no longer guided directly by needs and feelings so we behave indirectly. We work hard and act smart in order to feel loved, instead of feeling the hopelessness of ever being loved.

The feeling of stored hopelessness usually arrives at the cortex in the form of hope, its dialectic counterpart. Along the way, hopelessness has been transformed into its opposite. Somewhere along the voyage to the outer reaches reality has been changed into unreality. Repression has its sworn duty to keep part of us unreal. Neurosis arrives when more of us is unreal than real; when we are more unconscious than conscious. Clearly, there are levels of neurosis depending on how unconscious we are. Neurosis is the enduring change in the psychophysiology brought about by early experience.

Once unreal, a person may become a true believer, finding hope in the flimsiest of places because his hope must find a home. He will find special diets, vitamins, anything that he can put his faith into because having trust and faith in someone is basic. It is only when all avenues for hope disappear that one is again brought in touch with the inner imprint of hopelessness.

To be unreal, for the neurotic, means survival. He must have hope, however unreal it might be. So long as hopelessness lies deep down, hope will spring forth continuously. That hopelessness shapes how one sees the world. One may seem to be a perpetual optimist because the alternative means to be plunged into the depths of pessimism and despair. Optimism, thought to be a healthy trait, may only be a good defence. This person cannot see the futility in a certain programme, project or effort. He is driven to circumvent reality – the original one.

Illustration of the Imprint

Apropos of the imprint as a force of memory that endures, the following is a report of a patient who had a constant pain in her back. She told me that it was enough to make her cry during the three weeks of Primal Therapy. There were two places that hurt her all the time. One was a small spot on her left shoulder blade, the other was a line of pain stretching from the top of the right shoulder down the whole length of her back. Here is her account in her own words:

Alice

In one particular session I had begun to cry about hurting so much physically. As I sat up afterwards, I felt a hand grabbing me in the exact spot on my left shoulder where I hurt. I had the distinct feeling that someone had grabbed me there. I fell into feelings and relived a scene in which my father and mother were fighting. It turned out to be the last day my father was in my life. I was very frightened and was clinging to my mother's knees. Suddenly I felt a hand grab me by the back of my shirt and literally whip me backwards away from there. I was stopped by crashing backside into the bedpost. Afterwards, I heard my father leave the room and go downstairs. Then he drove away. Before I started feeling, I had no idea what happened when my parents got a divorce. It was so traumatic because of the meaning of that day. I would never see my father again. It is still painful to remember that scene. The two pains in my back were recurring in exactly the two locations where my father's hand had grabbed me, and in the line down my back where the bedpost engraved its knobs on my back. After some time, the pains have finally disappeared, and they have never come back except in connection with those same feelings of my parents fighting and my father leaving me forever.

How the Imprint Resonates with the Present

Dr E. Roy John of New York University conducted research with cats and found that when they were conditioned to the pairing of one neutral stimulus with a painful stimulus, then later presented with only the neutral stimulus, their brain wave patterns duplicated the earlier event in its entirety. The cats responded to the past imprinted painful memory rather than to the current reality of a neutral stimulus. The imprint, in this case, was measured via certain waveform patterns in the brain.

This is what happens to humans. We act in the present while responding to our past. We are seemingly in neutral situations, say with a male authority figure, and our brains are conjuring up ancient fears of authorities from our first days at school. That is why in neurosis it is so important to focus on the past and one's childhood, because the precise brain wave patterns of that past are ever present in the brain.

It is not only the brain wave patterns that remain. When someone relives an event every relevant cell involved originally is gathered into the memory. A patient reliving a lack of oxygen at birth is actually oxygen-starved in the therapy room. I recently conducted an experiment with someone who had relived a birth sequence the day before, where he did rapid deep breathing for over twenty minutes without one sign of a hyperventilation syndrome. The following day I had him breathe deeply for three minutes while sitting up and not in a memory. Here he showed every sign of serious hyperventilation[1], light-headedness with a tendency to pass out, facial twitch, and hands contracted into what he described as 'claws'; unable to straighten or unclamp his hands. The question is why in a feeling can he breathe deeply for a long period of time with no adverse signs, and yet when out of a memory can do the same exercise with serious effects?

The answer seems to be that when in the grip of a memory all the cells are responding as originally. The blood cells were oxygen-starved and are again deficient during the reliving. Therefore when there is deep breathing there is no hyperventilation because the body actually needs the oxygen, whereas when not in a memory the body does not have the same need, and goes into hyperventilation syndrome.

Breathing is controlled in the brainstem, an area saturated with opiate receptors whose functions are partly to control pain. This means that pain and breathing have some common elements. Deep breathing alters the opiate flow and therefore is able to change the defence against pain. Shallow breathing can be an important defence against feeling; and to force deep breathing is to break up the defence structure. This often results in flooding and a massive input of heavy feeling. The cortex, unable to integrate such an onrush, goes into

---

1. Where the breathing rate is deeper and faster than necessary for the exchange of carbon dioxide and oxygen, causing an excess intake of oxygen and lower levels of carbon dioxide.

overdrive and begins to conjure up all kinds of fanciful, mystical and unreal notions.

There is a school of deep breathing therapy with rather fancy techniques and names for what is essentially hyperventilation. When these therapists deprive the top level cortex of oxygen, and therefore of its coherence and defence capacity, the brain struggles to deal with upcoming pain. The person then fabricates living past lives and other notions beyond reality. That is because has been driven beyond his own reality. The reason that the person is not aware of the upcoming pain is that it is immediately absorbed by the ideational system. Due to this kind of hyperventilation a person can believe he has been 'born again' simply because he has been put in touch with a birth trauma. Deep breathing exercises can make a person believe that he has travelled back to another life in biblical times. These are what I call the 'benign psychoses'. To be real at that moment would be to suffer the agony of the devil. Benign psychotics join cults and live in the realm of the mystical, to try as best they can to keep *unreality* going. They are using ideas to defend against feeling.

The lack of hyperventilation syndrome in my patient who was immersed in a past feeling raises some important questions. Where was that lack of oxygen stored all of this time? And why and how is it re-created by memory? That lack was stored not only as a brain memory but as a gestalt over the entire system, and ultimately finds itself in the blood cells. To be locked into the memory, then, is to reawaken blood cell reactions, as well. That is why neurosis is found everywhere in the system, because so is memory. Poor circulation (or high blood pressure) in the extremities, therefore, can well be a memory, or part of a response to a memory. It will continue its effects as the physiological component of the memory until the actual traumatic event is full connected to consciousness.

Early memory with its exact physiological concomitants is always trying to assert itself in exact form. Thus, there are those who have frequent inexplicable hyperventilation bouts, because the early memory of suffocation is ever-present and rising towards consciousness. Because the memory is not fully accessible, what reaches the top is simply the physiological state; i.e., the loss of oxygen, and/or the rapid heartbeat. This is the early memory, disconnected, transported into the present.

There is still more. What my little experiment means is that old memory is continuously prepotent (takes precedence) over current reality. So here we have a patient in a ventilated room with plenty of oxygen while his body is crying out for oxygen. He acts as though he is oxygen-starved because he is. It is no different from a person who is love-starved early in life, whose system cries out for love even while it is plentiful in adult life. He cannot feel or accept it. The misery of oxygen deprivation, as with emotional deprivation, is found in the blood cells and can only be re-found in those same cells during a reliving. *Imprinted memory seals off the possibility of external fulfilment.* This is because *adult* filfilment is not what the body needs.

Because the system needs yet rejects fulfilment, the act-out towards fulfilment is set in motion. We keep trying to feel love in the present, yet feeling unloved is registered deep in the system. Repression sees to it that present love does not penetrate the levels of consciousness to where the real feeling lies. That is why the neurotic needs more and more current fulfilment in an unceasing parade. The best he can ever achieve is a sop for his feeling. There are many traumas associated with birth, any one of which sets repression in motion. Mere physical separation for hours at a time just after birth can be traumatic; and certainly being put in an incubator away from human contact for a long period of time is likewise damaging. What repression does is prevent continued full consciousness at the time of the event because connected consciousness means that the system continues to react fully; and that reaction can itself be life endangering. Unconsciousness through repression aids in suppressing the vital functions which might otherwise leap into life-endangering zones.

Integration of these early pains is impossible because integration means consciousness, and that again means danger. Being disintegrated is a survival mechanism. It is, in a sense, a defence against integration. Better for the neurotic to be fragmented than to be fully conscious of his agony.

Repression prevents the knowledge in the adult life that is safe to fully know what happened. Thus, the experience is encapsulated by repression. We can see how this might work practically. A newborn strangling on the cord must no longer fight and react in a combative way. Repression allows the newborn *not* to react and therefore to conserve oxygen for survival. This lack of reaction allows for a drop in the vital signs that ordinarily could be lethal, and thereby prevents the destruction that could take place with consciousness.

What neurotic behaviour involves is the act-out of an experience or of the feeling underlying many experiences. The act-out is a repetition compulsion where the system re-creates the early environment in order to master and integrate it. One patient was bound into an attitude, 'I can't try any more'. Everything was too much, as it was at birth. Even in tennis when the going got rough he gave up – the unconsciousness attitude – 'It's too much. I can't win. I'll stop trying.' If he couldn't gain a lead in the first game he would invariably manage to lose the set.

The central reason for the act-out is to create the conditions, albeit symbolically, where healing can take place. The body knows that only in the original context can healing occur. So it constantly attempts to reproduce that context in order to heal. Clearly, one can only heal where one is wounded. If the early assaults occurred on a lower level of consciousness, healing can only take place on that level.

One patient who spent three weeks in an incubator right after birth developed an overwhelming feeling of isolation and alienation. She isolated herself later in life and had few social contacts. There was something 'removed' about her (having been removed from social contact at birth). What she had done, and what neurotics must do, is create a matching environment to the internal feeling, thereby lessening ambivalence and creating the possible conditions for healing. Matching the inside to the outside provides coherence for the person. This helps make sense out of what is going on and provides a rationale for one's internal feelings. That is because doubt is even more painful than certainty. A psychotic idea is better than the feeling of desperate futility.

The act-outs, discussed in detail later, can be as simple as being nice constantly in adult life in order to mollify an irritable mother (originally). The hope is to make her gentle and kind through others. The hopelessness of it all gives rise unconsciously to the *behaviour of hope*, also known as neurosis, which is then applied indiscriminately. Or someone is a continual 'helper' always ready to take charge and lend a hand, in the unconscious hope of helping enough to help himself, something the parents never managed to do.

If the field of psychology understood and accepted the notion that healing can only occur in its original context it would immediately change the face of the profession. No more magical notions about hypnosis, confrontation groups, acupuncture, psychoanalysis, existential analysis and other current manipulations, which at best can only chance the face of neurosis. So long as overwhelming hurt is blocked from reaching its proper neurological destiny, so long as connection to consciousness cannot occur, there will be no healing. As we shall see later, the fever that every patient runs as she approaches catastrophic early pain is the first sign of the healing process in progress.

What we think of as neurotic behaviour, i.e., the symbolic act-out, is not really neurotic; it is the first step on the path to normality. It is re-creating the healing conditions as best as repression will allow. So *neurosis is the symbolic means we use in order to heal.*

I should add that not every neurotic re-creates his early environment. There are the counterphobic types who studiously avoid any situation that brings up an early feeling. These people are further from their needs than the others.

It's the difference between those who still try for fulfilment in one way or another, and those who give up trying. For example, if the counterphobic feels helpless, he avoids any situation that might put him in a helpless situation. To be in the hands completely, say of a bureaucrat, leads immediately to anxiety. The original helplessness, perhaps at birth and later when one was helpless in the hands of tyrannical parents, evokes the old fear again. But, by and large, the inner environment and its original reactions are reproduced again and again by the neurotic.

The reason that the neurotic feels unfulfilled, such as our woman who began life in an incubator, is that *fulfilment was not part of the original memory she carries around.* No amount of being with people is ever going to change a basic feeling of loneliness occasioned by being removed from one's mother for long periods very early in life. One might use drugs later on to cap that kind of pain, even while one is unaware of it. Even if one recognizes the existence of pain, it is almost impossible to know its source because repression won't permit it. Remember, the job of repression is to keep part of us unconscious and prevent healing. There is no way to alter a basic feeling of alienation and isolation from above; neither encouragement, social contact, nor advice will change the feeling and its pressure, it will only change the obvious behaviour for a time. There will usually be a regression back to the original feeling.

The system literally, and in every way possible, is living in the past. That is why past memory supersedes current reality, and why we respond internally first to the memory and only later to external reality. When a person is no longer operating on an early level where memory resides they can in no way duplicate the experience later. The baby cries of a two-year-old cannot be done again no matter how hard one tries when one is out of the feeling. Likewise, the lack of oxygen cannot be replicated again, no matter how strong the will. There are concomitants to memory that lie only on that early level and on no other.

There are implications here for serious mental illness. I recall seeing a woman some years ago who was diagnosed as pre-psychotic because she was having hallucinations of a scraping sound in her ears. No matter how much psychotherapy she had, she still heard the sounds. After six months in my therapy she relived a birth sequence of the side of her head and ear being scraped against the pubic arch. The hallucination stopped. Previously she was simply subject to a disconnected memory that seemed like hallucinations. As in almost every case of symptoms it is simply a sign of history intruding itself abruptly into consciousness, particularly when the defence system is weak.

Psychiatrist William Gray believes that all thought is embedded in feeling tones which help to code memory and integrate thoughts as they are formed. His work has been advanced by Paul La Violette, a systems theorist, who thinks that experience is coded and stored in the brain as neuroelectric waveforms which are elicited by early events which have similar waveforms. Gray is proposing that the emotional content of an experience then serves as a kind of code label for what is stored in the memory bank. (I use that term figuratively.) This code label responds to memory traces with which it is in tune, which in turn provoke the retransmission of the experience in its originally encoded form. In other words, something in the present resonates with something from the past that has been stored in the memory bank, setting off the original memory once again with all of its force.

The use of the term resonance to describe this process is not merely figurative. There seems to be a precise frequency that will resonate with the membrane receptor in the amygdala. This then activates neuronal discharge, i.e., emotional reactions. These resonating messages are triggered by vibrations in the protein molecule sticking down through the cell membrane. Such molecules act virtually like cellular antennae which trap a certain frequency of information and translate it into a feeling-memory. The signal coming in seems to have a code similar to those signals already lodged in the emotional warehouse. When old experience is added to new and the combined feeling is too much, the hypothalamus cannot integrate the input and shunts part of the experience to other structures.

As long as this shunting continues, complete healing, both physical and psychological, cannot take place. This is why the shunted experience must have as its final destination the hypothalmus where healing is initiated. That is the meaning of integration.

The following case illustrates the kind of resonance of which I have been speaking.

Harry

One day, entering a reliving episode, I started coughing up clear fluid. I could hardly continue as the feeling of drowning was so strong. I began to have a painful irritation in my sinuses, and I had the distinct impression that they were full of soap. It felt almost like a couple of spikes thrust up my nostrils. My screams became muffled, then turned into these hideous, muted whoops. At the same time, I was flat on my back and reaching my fingers and toes as high to the ceiling as I possibly could.

I wanted desperately to get off my back to breathe, but found I couldn't without leaving the feeling. Then the scene focused: my mother was holding me under water! I was an infant, and she had evidently been giving me a bath in the kitchen sink in a most sloppy, hurried manner, and was actually drowning me. Whatever she was thinking, she held me pinioned under soapy water in the sink, ran the tap directly over my face, and swished me around in the water where I lay limp. I suppose it's when I seized up in her hand that she flopped me up on the kitchen table where I came to in a puddle of water.

The amusing thing about this horror story is that later she

always refused to believe that I was allergic to Ivory soap. Whenever she'd buy it I'd sneeze and cough, my sinuses would run, and I'd complain. The reason for her disbelief?

'But you can't possibly be allergic to Ivory. That's what I used to wash you in when you were a baby.'

Imprints and Chronic Need Deprivation

Imagine that you go to a park and see a father playing with his son. They embrace and you suddenly feel something in your stomach, a kind of cramp. It is painful because it brings up an unfulfilled need to be held and touched by your father.

You see a violent argument on the street and you develop a panic attack. The violence has set off a memory of your mother's violence that you tried desperately to avoid. You are so shaken that you can hardly function for the next two days. The current situation has resonated with a feeling and scenes from the past.

Notice that it is feelings which allow perhaps thousands of disparate bits and pieces of early scenes to be coded in similar ways. For example, there can be hundreds of scenes of Mother looking sad and being depressed, creating a feeling in a young child who doesn't know any better that 'I am responsible for her unhappiness,' or 'Mama seems unhappy to be around me.' The child is never able to understand that it is Mother's problem, and so he acts out trying to make Mother and others happy so that he will not feel responsible for their sadness.

Feeling binds the information from separate but related experiences together. E. Roy John's cats conjured up the brain waveform patterns of a time gone by. They acted 'as if' the old environment with all of its details (in this case, the painful stimulus) still existed. If the cats could talk, they would say, 'I feel as if I'm going to be punished again, just like I was the last time.'

To a person who was unmercifully criticized as a child,

one present-day criticism can be devastating, even when there is a host of praise at the same time. The criticism has set off an old feeling of being worthless. Praise is ignored. The one criticism has resonated with the past.

As soon as something in the present resembles an old imprint the body reacts as it did originally. Neurotics avoid the kind of situations or the kind of relationships that might set off an old pain. The system, in that sense, becomes a radar device directing us away from anything that might upset us and bring up the past. The more painful the past is, the easier it is to be upset. It is what I call having many 'buttons', or a high level of resonance. A person loaded with anger, for example, can be irritable all the time and almost any obstacle can set off that old irritability. The same is true of fear. Someone with a load of terror will find that almost anything will make then afraid, whether it is a relationship, crowds, high places, elevators, or any other neutral stimulus.

The following case history is a classic example of the kind of resonance I am talking about, and is typical of the way in which many neurotics act. Eating, in the case of this person, and feeling full, evoked an old feeling of complete emptiness. In a paradoxical twist, the more empty she was, the less she had to feel the emptiness of her life. The more full she was, the more empty she felt.

Karen

I'm anorexic. What that means is I've systematically starved myself for the past seven years. My rationalization for almost never eating was that I wanted to be thin. I wanted to look consumptive, with jutting hipbones and hollow cheeks. I envied people who were so ill they had to be fed intravenously. Boy, you could lose weight that way! I was never fat, but I was never thin enough. More than that, I always wanted to be empty. I got crazy when I felt full.

Most people I talk to get crazy if they don't have some

*food in them. All I know was that my feeling full was
certainly more than anxiety about getting fat. It was something profoundly systematic. If I ate too much I became
light-headed, dizzy, and irritable, with pains in the back of
my neck. This translated itself into an urgent need to vomit.
Vomiting brought a sense of relief from some enormous
pressure.*

*I hated this obsession with food because it meant that I
was always thinking about what I was not eating. I never
understood the reason for this bizarre reversal of body
responses. Why was I always so driven to stay empty? I'm
beginning to understand it now.*

*Most people who are deprived early in life of food or
love somehow remain in touch with that deprivation. They
seek out some kind of fulfilment. They try to get love
somehow, somewhere. But others are deprived beyond
their capacity to integrate. They and their bodies simply
shut down. They disconnect from their own needs very
early because the pain is just too much to face. These
people, myself included, avoid warmth later because it
reminds them of what they didn't get. They don't want
anything to upset the apple cart. They are fine the way they
are.*

*The same is true of eating. I avoided it because feeling
full reminded me of how empty I felt. If I stayed empty I
didn't have to feel it. I began to eat a bit of food in therapy.
How odd, and how obvious – food as a cure for someone
who is starving himself. I began to feel a great pain with
this food. I woke up at night with a terrible back pain as
though the small of my back had a crank in it which was
tightening my legs and spine. It became difficult to breathe.
I couldn't bend any more. I didn't know what was wrong.
Trying to describe it with words like 'helplessness', 'worthlessness' and 'loneliness' was inadequate. I just had to feel
it.*

*All I knew was 'I feel empty'. I also felt, 'I don't know
what is going on.' I suddenly had an image of myself as a*

baby lying in the crib with my eyes wide open, all stiff and tense, and then 'WHAM' ... the connection! I knew I wasn't supposed to cry and bother my mother. I wasn't supposed to cry or hurt or need. Rather than risk the sight of her angry eyes, a far cry from the warmth I needed, I clenched my whole body and bore it in silence. Time seemed to go on forever in my feeling, minute by minute of pure pain, of waiting for her to check up on me.

All of my life I waited quietly for her to glance at me, to see that I was suffering. I remember standing at her bedroom door after a horrendous nightmare, looking at her sleeping and trying to mouth the word, 'mama'. I would tiptoe back down the hall to my room and spend the night paralyzed with fear. Still, I thought, 'Maybe she will come.'

I was never able to ask directly for what I wanted. I was yelled at and called a nuisance and a bore if I cried. It became easier to withstand it internally. Although my body was registering stress, my mind simply quit paying attention to the need messages. After enough denial of its needs, my body no longer bothered to communicate them. It was like an endless shock. Stiffness became my mode of survival.

Feeling full was like a huge lie and it drove me crazy. I didn't know it, but my body did. Starving was my way of keeping pain at bay. If you don't get any warmth in your life, you don't have to feel what you've missed. You just stay in your igloo. If I stayed thin, there was always the slim chance that my mother would notice I was dying and take care of me.

A person under a heavy load of pain will take a completely neutral situation – a woman on a street corner, for example, and concoct a whole scenario about what she is thinking or going to do. Here the old pain resonance is enormous and the energy is flooding the cortex causing it to fabulate. This is psychosis.

Resonating energy can also be released internally, resulting in extensive physical symptoms. In that sense, cancer could be the 'psychosis' of the body. When cancer is generalized, it functions in the same way that the cortex does, acting randomly and overspilling boundaries.

Increased pain actually takes up an increasing amount of space in the brain. As painful experience accumulates, an increasingly larger area of the brain is devoted to pain, until the major part of the brain becomes, literally, a pain processing machine. It is then that current experience is constantly filtered through most imprints; neutral events become translated into painful ones. 'Can I do this for you?' becomes perceived as, 'Why?! Do you think I'm helpless or dumb?' 'You were marvellous today,' becomes, 'So you think I wasn't marvellous before?' The current situation is 'fighting' against the imprint. 'I feel helpless and dumb' becomes the primary meaning by which all present day events are interrupted.

Tranquillizers may dampen the imprint enough so that the pain does not intrude. The more pain, the greater the dose required. I have seen patients who attempted suicide by ingesting doses that would have been lethal for almost any human being, but who were only put to sleep for twelve hours. They had such massive amounts of pain activating the brain that the medication could not induce death.

The imprint of pain thus fixes a permanent imbalance in brain function and in body biochemistry. A trauma at birth in which the baby had no alternative but to give in to the experience passively (as, for example, when the cord wraps around the baby's neck) will imprint a tendency towards passivity. It produces a biochemistry that accommodates and expresses that passivity.

Imprints and Our Genetic Destiny

The imprint of pain even seems able to alter our ability to fulfil our own genetic destiny. It may be that the DNA molecule that transmits the genetic code is changed by pain so that cells respond to a different or slightly altered code. Whatever the mechanisms, the repression of the imprint seems to have a global effect. We see empirical evidence of this in children reared in an orphanage who do not grow to their genetic potential while institutionalized, but begin growing again when placed in a loving environment.

The reality of an altered genetic programme is important in disease because there is good evidence that such alterations produce catastrophic illnesses. In some kinds of cancer, normal genes become oncogenes, cancer-producing genes. Researchers still do not understand why this is so, but I would submit that imprinted pain is one key reason. The massive imprint of pain puts pressure on normal gene cells and finally alters their structure, rendering them lethal.

A most interesting experiment by G. Miller Jonakait *et al.* at Cornell College of Medicine lends support to the above. In this research mice were stressed with an apparent alteration of the genetic code as a result. Embryonic nerve cells expressed the genetic potential differently in those mice which were subject to stress. The developmental period was extended, and changes seemed to occur at a very fundamental level.

We have seen further evidence of changed genetic expression in our male patients who, after many months of therapy, will begin to grow facial hair and chest hair, even at the age of forty. Others at that age may develop wisdom teeth for the first time. Women have experienced breast development in their twenties and thirties. In others, foot size and height increases. What should have taken place during adolescence was somehow delayed for decades.

Let me be clear about this point. Due to global repression a good deal of our genetic code is dormant. When the imprinted load of stress has been addressed and experienced there is less repression, hence less inhibition of genetic expression.

The genetic unfolding, in such cases, has evidently been

retarded. I doubt that such critical blocking could take place with impunity; a price is paid at some point. Something strong enough to impede genetic development in an individual must have a severe impact on the physical system.

Repression is not just a psychotherapeutic term, but an actual physical process that works everywhere in the body. Repression is found in chest hairs, for example, or at least in the genetic code for their growth. Some male patients develop these hairs suddenly after a year or two of therapy. What has happened to those hairs when they do not develop? They were waiting to be let out. Their normal code of growth was aborted and a different code substituted. There must be pressure there, even for something as seemingly insignificant as hairs. The original code is always trying to unfold.

There is always an infant and child in us trying to get out. When we manage to let down our adult defence systems the child in us surges forth. New chest hairs and new breast development are part of the adolescent breaking through.

When the imprint of pain is felt, the system will begin to 'right' itself. As we have found in our research, the brain's hemispheric relationships and physical processes will normalize. This is as it should be, since each one of the original alterations in our body's physiology was part of the imprint. The reality of cellular imprinting is vital to an adequate understanding of how to treat neurosis.

Here is an example of an imprint in which the memory of helplessness felt towards the person's father replayed itself with devastating effects in the present. These are the words of the patient I will call Linda.

Linda

An experience I would like to pretend never happened occurred four years ago when I was living in Paris. I occasionally went to a bookstore for poetry readings where I met a man who was, by reputation, a poet. I remember thinking that he was a dirty, violent-looking man who couldn't be trusted, but I thought, 'Oh that's unkind. How do you know? He might be a fine person. Don't judge too fast.' We spoke and he asked me for coffee the next evening. At the time I was trying to be more 'worldly'. I agreed.

The following evening he wanted me to go with him to his room to get some of his work. I didn't want to but I thought, 'Give him the benefit of the doubt.' I went to his dirty, tiny room, full of morbid surrealist prints and a few books. He proceeded to rape me, threatening to break a glass and cut my face if I didn't co-operate. I found out how much he hated 'stupid American cunts'. He let me get dressed and at the first opportunity I ran.

I felt so stupid, ashamed and foolish. How could I let such a thing happen to me? Years later I realized that my judgement was clouded by my 'I'm a good girl' Christian ethics, which were just another way of trying to be so good that somebody would have to love me. My ability to say 'NO' disappeared, and I became helpless again, just as I had been with my father.

Imprinting in a Critical Period

The impact of an imprint depends upon how life threatening the original situation was, when it occurred, and whether it occurred during what I call a 'critical period', the time when the need MUST be fulfilled to avoid trauma.

Events during gestation and in and around birth are generally the most life-threatening; their impact is often the greatest. Not being held at the age of nine is not nearly so serious as not being held during a critical period, just after birth, when touch is absolutely necessary for development. When needs are not fulfilled during the critical period, there is the greatest injury to the system, and no amount of later fulfilment will change the imprint and its force. If the mother was sick and could not be with her child just after birth, could not give her the warmth and cuddling necessary, that child is going to suffer. Later touch may attenuate the pain, but it cannot and does not weaken the imprint of the original deprivation.

A monumental aloneness just after birth can produce in a person a lifelong terror of being alone and a need to be surrounded by an entourage all of the time. Having friends around all the time is a way of avoiding that early pain; it is an act-out against the feelings.

The critical periods are genetically determined. If, at the age of one or two, we were fed on some rigid schedule instead of when we were hungry, there will be a lifelong impact that no amount of ease about feeding later on will erase. The baby is starving and is not being fed; that is its immediate reality. Later on, the adult may develop neurotic eating habits. The minute an adult is hungry, the old memory of starvation is unconsciously reawakened and he must eat immediately or he will get a headache. Or he will stuff the food down without thinking, until he is bloated or sick, all to keep away that starving feeling, a memory of which he has no conscious awareness.

No one would dream that colitis at the age of eighteen is related to a series of traumas that occurred at the beginning of a person's life. Who could guess that ulcers at thirty are related to traumas in the crib where systematic starvation was taking place? When that starvation took place, at the age of six months or one year, the stomach secreted powerful acids such as hydrocholoric acid. That secretion later became an automatic response to hunger or any other kind of stress. When secreted often enough, these corrosive acids literally burn holes in the stomach. The focal point for later stress reactions thus becomes the original organ involved in the trauma. This trauma does not happen because one doesn't eat on time at the age of fourteen. The critical period has long passed.

Closets of Our Minds

The means by which the force of the imprint is cleared out of the system is simply by addressing it one-to-one on the level of consciousness where it was laid down. When the feeling in the imprint is felt consciously, its bioelectric energy is finally released and connected to consciousness. Then the imprint becomes a simple memory; one cannot, nor does one need to, erase a memory. That stays. What we can do is eliminate the force. We are told that disease strikes us randomly and for no particular reasons. Nothing could be further from the truth; nature's force is never random, nor without due cause. The imprint is the central reality behind many afflictions. It must not be ignored.

7

Acting Neurotic: Symbolic Acting Out

Neurotics are comprised of two selves. The real self is the pained one, the one we have to feel in order to become real. The other self – the unreal self – is the accomplice of regression and the oppressor of the real self. It is oblivious to what is real, embraces magic, the mystical, and what is beyond worldly knowledge. The neurotic is forever a victim of what is beyond her knowledge. And she acts-out those forces all of the time. She acts in the present as if it were the past. It is a constant attempt at the resolution of past needs and traumas done symbolically. Symbolic acting out means acting in the present with the force of the original unconscious need. The unreal self must remain in a haze, busying itself with trivial pursuits and abstractions so as not to feel any pain.

I have discussed the needs of a child and what he expects from his parents. He expects to be loved, totally accepted and approved of, protected, wanted and respected. He expects this because it is normal, and because inherent in the human condition is the fulfilment of those needs. The system instinctively knows what it needs, and an adult parent in touch with his or her feelings instinctively knows these needs as well, and will fulfil them. An adult removed from his own needs, however, is not going to be able to fulfil the needs of his child.

The child has no reason to expect lack of fulfilment. He cannot imagine that he is on this earth unwanted, an accident of impulse-laden lust. He cannot imagine that he is in the way or that babies are born by accident. Yet, sadly, he may learn this soon enough through the attitudes of his parents. They are the whole world to him. If they do not love and adore him, if they do not approve of him and accept him as he his, he will seek substitute fulfilment later on, trying to make up for what he never had. That is the essence of what I call 'symbolic acting-out'.

The World as a Stand-in for Parents

In the case of an adult whose needs were not fulfilled as a child, the world becomes a stand-in for what the parents should have done. Needs must be fulfilled somehow or other because they are essential to normal growth and survival. Institutionalized children, for example, who grow up without love, do not grow physically at the proper rate. They fall ill more often than normal children, they learn more slowly, and their physical co-ordination is poorer. All this happens because they were not held, caressed, and given affection during their earliest days on earth.

The problem is that parents are not replaceable. Needs have to be fulfilled when the child is young. He must be held and kept close just after birth and in the first few days of his life. It is critical to survival. All the loving years later by a boyfriend or girlfriend can never make up for that early lack of touch. Because the system is always trying to make up for what it lacks, the child, and then the adult, seeks out substitute fulfilments – symbolic sources of gratification. Need drives, and a driven person is one who needs.

A child who is ignored by harassed parents will try to be the centre of attention later on. He might be diagnosed as narcissistic in adult life, but the fact is, he was ignored. That is a simple example. A child who was ignored may also feel worthless, not worth anyone's attention. Depending on later life circumstances, he may act out his feeling of worthlessness by displaying a certain timidity in social situations, a diffidence and apprehension towards others.

A good example of acting-out was explained by one of my patients: 'I never went for love straight. Girls who sought me out and made the first move as though they were interested in me set off anxiety. Finally, at forty-two, I was with a girl whom I was dating for a long while. She was aloof most of the time and slightly affectionate part of the time. Perfect. She finally said to me that she thought we should break it off because I was not, and was never going to be, the man of her life. Just right. I struggled like crazy to make her want me. I immediately proposed marriage and she resisted. I wrote and called and never gave up ... until I had the feeling ... the most obvious of all feelings. My mother never loved me and never showed any affection. I finally found a perfect substitute with whom I could struggle. I needed someone who didn't love me. Basically, my mother made me feel unlovable. To be with someone who loved me would be going against my type.'

Neurotic behaviour is a self-fulfilling prophecy. Someone may feel unworthy, and goes about proving that she is. When she is with others, she acts like she doesn't exist. She is then treated as if she doesn't exist, which reinforces the problem. What she secretly hopes for is that others will see her fear and apprehension and draw her out. It rarely happens.

It is not normal, nor in the order of things, to be timid and shy. A person may keep everything inside because he sensed early on that he couldn't talk to his parents about himself – they were too busy with their own needs. He marries and has marital problems because his wife complains that he keeps everything inside and never confides in her. But this is only secondarily a marital problem. The real problem, as is so often the case, revolves around patterns from the past. It is easy to counsel the wife in this case and say, 'Why not accept him the way he is. Maybe you should draw him out. That is just the way he is.' But it isn't the way he is. It is the way he has been made. It is what happened because he wasn't loved.

Such a person can change, but not by being drawn out. He

can change by feeling his original need to be drawn out by his parents, a need which says: 'Listen to me. Hear me. Be interested in me. I'm your son. Love me.' To feel all that is to know hopelessness.

Hopelessness is the key to change. When he allows himself to feel the need to be valued, he will discover all over again how little his parents care. Keeping everything in is the way to keep the pain away.

The Birth of the Act-Out

Act-outs are not necessarily the result of one single trauma. They can often result from a series of very small traumas that go on for years and summate into a meaning, such as 'They want me out of the way. No one wants me. I don't belong.' These are common feelings which later produce an act-out. One patient compulsively had to join organizations. Unconsciously, she was trying to hide the pain by feeling she belonged, something she never felt as a child. Many dinners and conversations at a table where she was excluded by her parents, many outings where she was left out, left her with this feeling.

Such a person might go to a therapist who remarks, 'You seem to need to join a lot of groups.' The patient reflects, 'Yes, that's true. I guess I need to belong.' That is not quite reliving the agony of being set aside at dinner night after night, feeling like a leper because parents come first for each other, with the children never counting.

Hopelessness is at the bottom of so much acting out. I recall seeing one radical activist who was constantly engaged in one cause or another trying to make a better world. The feeling he had in therapy was, 'I have to make a better home life or I'm going to die.' The world he was making outside was but a substitute for the better world he needed at home. The struggle in the social world was a way of keeping his hopelessness at bay. Thus, despite all the betrayals, the corruption and degradation that he saw in the outside world, he never gave up his struggle as an activist.

The Struggle: Re-Creating the Imprint

Symbols are representations of real needs. Thus, we later get involved with those who can re-create our early lives. One marries a critical person like one's father, and then struggles thereafter to try to earn his approval symbolically.

A woman who needs to be dependent and infantile will act out that dependence on other people. She will expect her mate to take care of everything and to baby her. He won't want to because he has needs of his own, so there are problems.

When a neurotic feels the past in its full agony, she might say, 'You know, I'm okay the way I am. It was they who were not okay.' In seeking relationships, she never went directly to someone who could love and approve of her immediately. Her history made her feel disapproved of. In choosing a partner she could struggle with, she created a symbol of her past. For this woman to find a partner who loved her without reservation would leave her still feeling tense and dissatisfied. If she were to choose such a loving partner, she would then feel really hopeless, because she would still feel unloved. If you feel unloved, you feel unloved. It cannot be painted over. The woman had to *struggle* for love, for in the struggle lies hope. Feeling totally unloved by one's parents will stop the symbolic acting-out.

To be disliked and criticized when you are five or six leaves you believing that there is something radically wrong with you. Being in the struggle for approval in the present is at least being on the right track. The symbol is just one step removed from reality. For example, a person acts very sweetly and tries to please everyone, because in that nice behaviour lies hope of feeling loved and approved of. That behaviour continues in the present because one cannot stand another drop of disapproval added to that past. It helps avoid any reaction that might trigger the terrible hurt from childhood. No matter how many times the person is stepped on and betrayed, the sweetness inside them lives on. That is what provides the continuity of neurotic personality.

Parents put children in the struggle when they don't let them be themselves. For example, constantly being put down makes the child struggle to feel good about himself, and so he struggles to be appreciated or approved. He is trying to normalize. The young child doesn't know that it is abnormal to be denigrated. He grows up with a deficit of which he is unaware, and therefore automatically struggles for fulfilment. If, however, early on he learns that there is absolutely nothing to be had (and children sense that without any conceptualization whatsoever), there is no love but *there is no struggle.*

Thus, if parents simply ignore the child and do not give him a way to struggle, a way to be neurotic in order to feel a semblance of love, the child will suffer, will be chronically anxious, will grow up without effective defences, will forever be closer to his pain, but he will not have a deeply systematized and compacted neurosis. In short, he will have access to himself later on.

When a parent dislikes a child (too often, the parent is a child herself who resents having to act like a parent when she wants to act like a child) and is constantly critical or irritable it creates a new need in the child; a need to act in a way to mollify the parent. The child is so busy acting-out this new need that he loses touch with his real needs – to be loved just because he is alive. The child can no longer be himself or know who he is because he is now in a desperate struggle to ward off anger.

In therapy he must first feel the manufactured need and then perhaps months later will get to the feeling and real need – love me. It is in that feeling – love me – that allows the person to become himself again. That is, the bottom line need which was lost long ago and that finally allows the system to right itself. So first, the person will feel 'Don't be mad at me, please!' And then, 'Love me!' The sequence or reliving must follow that order in reverse; one cannot skip steps in therapy.

The child's behaviour is like a radar system; the slightest hope of love in the parent will direct the child to try to be what the parent needs for him (parent) to feel whole. It's the way, almost genetically, that neurosis is passed down from one generation to the other. Unfulfilled need in the parent deprives the child and produces that same unfulfilled need in a child. A father who feels inferior can only feel half-way decent by putting down the child in order to feel superior at least to someone; the child feels inferior and then, decades later, does it to his child. His act-out is unconscious because his need is.

Another simple act-out is the inability to say 'no'. If parents always demanded complete obedience and the child was never allowed to express his own will, he will later carry on that behaviour by not being able to refuse any request or demand. He's going to feel like he must say 'yes' immediately. The pain involved is very simple. To have expressed one's own will meant punishment, disapproval, and lack of love. Acquiescence becomes the rule.

One patient had a governess who took care of her throughout her early childhood. Her mother was always travelling, and was very much a jet setter. The mother and father were always away. The child got a feeling very early that she was 'second best'. And whenever she asked her nanny for her mother she was shamed for being 'such a baby'. She spent her life never asking for what she wanted, and always chose second best because she felt second best. If she went to a dress shop, she chose the one she didn't quite want and, in this way, re-created her childhood over and over again. Getting second best was a struggle to keep the hope alive, and in turn the struggle was kept alive by the hope.

One anorexic had the following insight: 'I needed love, not food. They stuffed me with food instead of affection.

Now when I eat, I feel something is wrong. I'm not getting what I really need, so my body rejects it, and I throw up. I starved to keep my hope alive.' Unconsciously she felt that if she ate she would lose the chance for the real thing. She stopped eating and became emaciated.

Anorexia, incidentally, is a large subject which I shall not discuss here except to note that I have treated numerous patients suffering from it. It comes from diverse sources, and usually originates very early in life.

One patient I treated was abandoned by her parents and sent to live with her grandparents. It always felt wrong to her, as if she never had a real home. She needed a real home like all her friends at school. Later on, in any loving relationship, she felt this kind of 'wrong' feeling, and had to break it off. She just would not accept any substitute for the home she did not have as a child. She was compelled to act out this need in the present. This act-out was the cause of much of her adult pain because she could not sustain a relationship, no matter how good. She was compelled to end it on the basis of one excuse or another. She had no idea what she was acting-out or even that she *was* acting-out. Ironically, what she was trying to do through her neurotic behaviour – to feel loved and at home – is what prevented her from getting what she really wanted – love and a home in the here and now.

Another of my patients was a man who had suddenly been sent to an orphanage when he was eight years old. He was then shifted around to many foster homes. When he grew up, he never settled in one place, because it was never the right one – the one he had lost early in life. His wanderlust was based on the unconscious hope of finding a real home. But he never did. He never felt at home anywhere (because he wasn't). The minute he felt he had stayed too long in one place, he had to get out and get going.

Hidden Meaning of Behaviour

Symbolic acting-out is probably as diverse as people. The person who has to accumulate money finally gets rich, yet needs more to keep himself from finding out that there was nothing to get. Money becomes a substitute for lack of love. Money, in fact, is a frequent substitute for love. Those who were deprived early in life often have an inordinate need for money. Some simply steal it. They want something for nothing; they want to feel loved without having to do anything for it. Stealing is a symbol of that need.

There are others who are sexually promiscuous in order to make up for the lack of affection and touch early in life. That, too, is a symbolic acting-out. What starts out as a simple uncomplicated need can end up ramified in a thousand different ways.

A young man, for example, who had lost his mother at a young age, was always slightly ill at ease. He had what he called a 'malaise', and spent his adult life in a kind of 'vague waiting'. If he was on vacation, he had to rush home and check his mail. What was he waiting for? As it turned out, he was waiting for a letter from his mother. Until he felt how deeply he loved her he never knew how much he missed her, and how unable he was to accept her death. So he arranged his life to wait for almost everything. He deferred all of his pleasures; he was always waiting for the right news. He compulsively played lotto on television, once again waiting for the big news.

This poor soul could never relax; he was always expecting his mother. Waiting, and its slight tension, were essential. Whenever he got something he was waiting for he was disappointed. Even his new car meant nothing to him. It wasn't what he really wanted. Is being disappointed over your new car neurotic? In his case, yes. He found reasons, of course; the paint wasn't right, the rear view mirror was too small, etc. But those weren't the real reasons. This man was wrapped in infantile desire. The eventual feeling and recognition of his needs was liberating. He was liberated from hope because hope lay nestled in the waiting.

I remember treating a psychotherapist who had honed his skills as an interviewer. All of his life he had been asking people questions, because there was one critical question he dared not ask, 'Where is my mommy?' She died abruptly when he was five. No one told him anything, and he sensed that he dare not ask too much. It all seemed like such a mystery. Thus, although it didn't seem neurotic at all, he developed a skill that made him productive as an adult, while he acted out symbolically. I never could have drawn that conclusion if he hadn't had a feeling that clarified the meaning of his actions. So it is clear that neurosis as symbolic behaviour can be quite subtle, and the attempts to measure and reveal it must be subtle as well.

A child who grows up with deceitful parents may have a need to trust so he can finally feel that he can depend on someone. In adult life, he misplaces his trust because he needs to trust so badly. The need dominates his reality and forces him to become involved with untrustworthy people. So the struggle begins. Being deceived is perceived as 'their' fault, and it is. But it is also the person's own need that sets up the deception. Until it is felt for what it is, it will go on and on. One needs to be totally vulnerable in order to experience the feeling that one's parents couldn't be trusted and that early life was shaky and unstable. Only then will the present cease to be dominated by the old need.

Acting-Out One's Birth

Symbolic acting-out can take place when one stands in line and suddenly develops a feeling of tremendous impatience, almost a panic state. This may be a birth analogue of waiting to get out. It may also have a compounded quality because one's home life was terrible, and once again the person 'could not wait to get out'. A history of failure, due to this impatience, can derive from such a trauma, even though it may have lasted only minutes at birth. The ability to see things through, to work patiently towards a goal, to study towards a long-term target, to develop relationships over time, are all impeded by the inability to wait.

It is not, of course, always immediately evident that a form of behaviour represents neurotic symbolic acting-out. There are no psychological tests for this sort of thing. But anything anyone does can be neurotic or not, depending on the history behind it. It is not something someone else can decide. 'Is that neurotic? Am I neurotic?', one can ask, and no one can really answer. The individual is the sole archivist of his history, and in that history lies the answer.

Another of my patients, whose therapy was going slowly, didn't seem to understand the feelings she went through. She just seemed dumb. She was exasperating. Then, she had the feeling, 'I don't want to know anything. Knowing was too painful. I've tried so hard not to know the painful truth – they didn't like me.' Her lack of curiosity and apparent stupidity were symbolic act-outs. She eventually became unable to even watch the news on TV or read the paper. It was all too painful. To know meant to hurt; that was the equation that ruled her life.

Even behaviour that seems quite normal can be deceptive. The person acting young and seeming to be in full vigour, as was the case with one patient, was acting-out a refusal to 'act his age'. He had to stay young because to act his age meant to give up hope for the love he had not received as a young child. 'I won't grow up until you love me, Momma,' seemed to be what he was unconsciously saying.

Freudian 'transference' is just another symbolic act-out in which old feelings from the parents are transferred onto the therapist. It doesn't do any good to analyze that transference and understand the act-out with the therapist; it is much better to feel its source. Then the symbol will evaporate by itself. There are events by the thousands with many feelings that play into an act-out. Readers can supply their own examples. Typically, in an act-out, the intensity of the behaviour is based upon the strength of the need (the amount of deprivation), or the valence of the trauma.

Resolution of the Act-Out

Many different kinds of therapy have addressed neurosis and its act-outs. There is a therapy, for example, called 'Directive Daydreaming-Guided Imagery', where the therapist actually creates stories for the person and directs him towards resolution. It is believed that this symbolism resolves neurotic behaviour, and it does – symbolically. Unfortunately, it won't change the underlying need and feelings. A scenario might run like this: 'The wife is critical. The boss won't let up. Let's imagine now how you go to them and tell them off. Assert yourself! Ah, you see, you can do it.' A nice dream.

Act-outs that work are effective neuroses. Those that don't are ineffective neuroses. When the act-outs work, we are relatively at ease. When they don't, we are again face-to-face with our pain. It is then that someone goes to a therapist to get his neurosis fixed. He is usually given drugs to feel better. Repression works again, this time induced by drugs, and ensures continuance of the act-out.

It is not as if there is a personality that acts out. Acting-out is part of the personality, and almost everything a neurotic does is an act-out. This is because all of one's behaviour is directed by unrecognized feelings. The way one holds one's jaw, one's posture, the squint of the eyes, the way one speaks, acts and walks, are all included in this spectrum. Nothing escapes. Nothing can.

What most conventional therapies do is offer insights into the symbolic act-outs of the patient. The therapist usually has to guess what exact motivation is behind it. Until the patient feels, they both have to guess. Because the knowing brain came along millions of years after the feeling brain, we cannot expect it to know secrets held in trust by the lower one. Indeed, we developed a cortex so that we wouldn't know; otherwise we'd be awash in feelings all of the time. To understand an act-out, even to understand that it is neurotic, won't change a thing. It would be the same faulty logic to imagine that understanding a virus would cure an infection. Too often, however, sophisticated understanding of an act-out becomes another act-out, a defence against feeling. In this way, one can go through the motions of getting well without the pain involved.

What the neurotic chooses for his therapy is something that will usually bolster his neurosis; a psychotherapy without roots for a patient bereft of his history. The unreal self is at work choosing its act-out. In the name of progress, most current dynamic psychotherapies deal with the unreal self, focus on the here and now and imagine that they have offered something new to the patient. The problem was that for years they focused on the past, but because they were talking about it rather than reliving it, all was in vain. The problem was not the focus on the past, but the way in which this focus was approached. To be free means to liberate the real self.

Prayer can be another symbolic act-out. We pray for protection, love, and caring. With just a slight turn of phrase, we could apply these supplications to depriving parents as well. Yet despite that, it sometimes takes many months to enable patients to even begin to ask their parents – much less beg them – for what they pray to God for every day. The reason is simple: a deep despair and hopelessness lies within these needs – a hopelessness which is very difficult to confront.

The patient will say, 'What's the use? They can't love me, so why ask? It's safer to ask God.' Whether the parents can love or not hardly matters. The need remains, and when the person asks his parents for what he needs, the pain is there. In therapy, when such patients beg their parents for love, they encounter their hopelessness. As one patient puts it, 'The original primal supplication (the begging) turned to prayers. In therapy, they turned back into my agony.'

Once real need is repressed and rerouted, we forcibly become less direct and more symbolic. It cannot be otherwise. That is why, advanced primal patients have direct, nonsymbolic dreams. That is why those who have felt their need and its pain have a direct quality about them. They're more perceptive, having perceived the most important reality of their lives.

Neurosis is a lifetime sentence, a prison with invisible bars that circumscribes our choices, interests and alternatives. We are forever its helpless victim until we feel.

8

The Birth Trauma:
The Life-Long Consequences of Birth

'I had just gone through my birth Primal, and later it hit me that the pain inflicted upon me by the steel forceps and the terror of convulsing tissues and muscles, which had for hours laboured and throbbed and pushed and kneaded me, desperately trying to expel me, cast me into life ... that all this is so amazingly analogous to what happened to the embryo of the human species. We are still in the "labour pain" phase of the overgrown embryo struggling for its right to live. And in that incredible, barren, overheated therapy room BIRTH is taking place; not just of this or that patient, but of a new species; the first bodily evidence is beginning to appear. It is so very slowly sliding millimetre by millimetre; the infant screams and screams and he begins to live. Whosoever is born there is the original parent of the true and complete human product. Every one of them is Adam and Eve ... the beginning of humanity' (a patient).

Neurosis Begins in the Womb

One of the most striking aspects of imprinting is that it can begin before conception. The foetal environment is a neighbourhood which can be filled with contaminants, pollutants and noxious chemicals. There the suffering is silent, the harm secret, and the damage invisible. Mother may be anxious, irritable and depressed, all of which is translated chemically and infuses the system of the foetus. Mother may smoke like a smokestack and contaminate her baby. It has been discovered at Oxford University that babies breathe in the womb; they gasp, and sigh, and hiccup. When mothers smoke, the babies' breathing is immediately affected. Babies can be seen to gasp in the womb, indicating that they are short of oxygen. Further, mother's poor eating habits can create malnutrition and starvation.

The whole foetal environment, in fact, can be a poor one, no different than that of a neglected five-year-old – except that it is less obvious. The very same biochemical changes will occur in both the foetus and the five-year-old, and the damage is the same. The difference is that the foetus can't run home to mother because mother is the danger, and 'home' is menacing. What the foetus is learning is that the 'neighbourhood' is dangerous.

The foetus is learning from experience rather than from words. It is continuously communicating chemically with the mother; indeed, when the baby is ready to be born, he or she releases certain hormones which signal readiness. The mother, in turn, also releases hormones which facilitate birth. When there is stress, however, the signals do not operate properly. Too many stress hormones can change the immune system of the mother, and, in turn, that of her baby. The stress hormones can also cause increased uterine contraction and produce premature birth. One might assume that prematurity is at the base of a number of physical problems later on when, in fact, the problems are a result of a complicated chain of reactions arising from high levels of stress hormones. High stress levels in the mother cause both prematurity and immune system damage, leading to later disease. In this way, the hidden neighbourhood produces the basis for later hypoglycemia, diabetes, colitis, and even cancer. One can have a bad foetalhood more crucial than a bad childhood.

During the nine months of life leading to birth the system

is the most fragile and naive; because of this, the impact of trauma is the greatest. After twelve weeks of gestation, the foetal nervous system is fully organized and can fully react to, code, and store trauma. This ability means that the imprint begins very early in foetal history and can affect all systems, particularly those that begin to be organized in the first months of life.

Evidence of just how the foetus can suffer has been shown in ultrasound studies of a thirty-four-week-old foetus: its eyes were all scrunched up and its mouth was wide open as though it were screaming. If it were indeed a scream, there was surely no one to hear it.

The foetus may not think, but it certainly reacts in terms of its capacities. When there is trauma, when mother is anxious or depressed, when she drinks or smokes, there are physiological changes going on in the foetus that are neither benign nor transient. The mark they leave is in terms of continued changes in such things as cellular functioning. The memory is 'held' by these changes in the various systems.

Thus, the immune system may be shaken and altered long before we see the light of day. Immune disease may not become manifest until decades later. Indeed, it may never manifest itself as overt disease if the childhood is a healthy one.

Evidence of the way that the early imprint alters physiology is found in the work on lower animal life by Kandel.[1] What his work has shown is that both the number of receptors and level of neurotransmitters are changed permanently due to early experience of fear. There were profound and enduring changes in synaptic strength as a result of this fear. Further, it has been found that a class of tranquillizers, which are essentially valium receptors (benzodiazepine) in the brain are modified as a function of stress and anxiety.

---

1. Kandel, E.R. 'From Metapsychology to Molecular Biology: Exploration into the nature of Anxiety'. 1983, *American Journal of Psychiatry* 140: 1277–1293.

Current research unmistakeably indicates that possibly the very genetic structure of cells in the central nervous system is changed as a result of early imprints.

Again, it is not simply that there are changes as a result of early experience, but that these changes are the ways the memory is engraved. To relive the memory and connect to consciousness is to alter those cellular changes back to normal. The neurotic not only has a different body but a different brain. Any treatment of neurosis, therefore, must be able to address itself to those brain changes. Loving, liberal do-goodism is not sufficient in a psychotherapy. You don't love neurosis away.

We must give up the notion that memory is synonymous with the thinking mind, and that memory is what can be verbally recalled or cognitively remembered. Every cell in the body holds memory. That is why we see such major changes in the function of cells after the imprint is relived and resolved, and why there are important changes in brain function and in the output of hormones. This is particularly true about the reliving of preverbal events when there was no chance to recall them in normal ways. This is why we must never neglect the birth trauma and pre-birth trauma in considering immune function and serious chronic disease.

How to Be Neurotic in the Womb

The reason that we must consider foetalhood when we are considering illness and disease is because it is life – nine months of the most crucial kind of existence where almost every event leaves an indelible mark, where the substratum for neurosis is laid down. You can be neurotic in the womb.

You don't have to act neurotic to be neurotic. As long as there is sufficient imprinted pain and dislocation of function there is neurosis. If the dislocation is in the foetal cells and their functions, rather than in the 'mind' and behaviour of the young child, it is still the same neurosis. So you cannot point to yourself and others and decide whether or not you are neurotic. That is why psychological tests, incidentally, are not sufficient to test for neurosis; they can only measure the psychologic aspect. If the predominant reaction to imprinted pain is physical, the psychologic test will be inadequate and inaccurate.

Aaron

My mother died of breast cancer shortly after my birth. She was sick while she was carrying me and she was in deep mourning for her father who had just died. She was married to an angry, crazy man, and she was under great stress. It must have been very difficult for her to give birth during that time. It would have been better for me if they had not made the effort to keep me alive because I was dead on arrival – DOA.

I am a child of the twentieth-century, born of sick parents into a sick country, into a sick world, where I have known only one law – survival. All I have done in my entire life is try to survive, nothing more. I never expected any more. I died inside my mother a long time before I came into this world. The promise which every living organism feels, which I felt at one time, the promise that everything was all right and that everything was going to be all right, was already broken. For in there, inside my mother, it was not all right; as a matter of fact, everything was very wrong. She was sick with cancer, grief and anger. My development in her womb was not normal, and there was nothing I could do about it. I lived in an unfriendly environment which would not let me be. I've always felt 'I've got to get out of here. Something awful is going to happen if I don't.' That has been my feeling all my life.

How the Birth Trauma Changes the Brain

Dramatic evidence of the effect of events on a carrying mother for the offspring is illustrated in recent research by Marian Diamond. What she found in her animal research (and basic biology for animals and humans is roughly the same) is that an enriched environment for the carrying mother, (where the animals have toys to play with and are allowed a lot of freedom), changes the brain of her *offspring*. The baby's cortex is thicker, it learns better, and one might say it is more 'intelligent'. Psychological events in the mother can change the physical structure of the foetus she is carrying in her womb. What's on mother's mind can change the physical brain of the child.

When mother is miserable, it is reflected in the hormones which mediate her feelings. The stress hormones not only indicate stress, but also determine how much energy mother is going to have, how much sugar is in her blood, how sexual she is, how well the baby is carried, if it is going to be miscarried, and finally, how efficient her immune system is. We know that the higher the stress level, the lower the immune efficiency. This is translated to the foetus, who is then born with what may be subtle sub-clinical immune deficiencies or vulnerabilities that only later stress will make manifest.

How the neonate responds to trauma at birth depends on his earlier environment. If the mother has smoked continuously, depriving the foetus of oxygen, an anaesthetic given to the mother at birth may seriously affect the newborn who is already vulnerable to oxygen deprivation. Robert Bauer, former head of UCLA infant research, found anaesthetics in the system of newborns. They were lethargic and did not suck very strongly. There was a kind of passivity in these new babies.

I have seen many hundreds of patients reliving various kinds of birth trauma over the years. These patients, from some twenty countries, have gone through certain reliving episodes which cannot be faked. This has been demonstrated, for example, by the way the feet and toes are locked in certain positions, whether it be a Japanese or a Swede undergoing the reliving. We have made electronic measurements of the pulse, blood pressure, body temperature, and brain waves during the reliving session, and found that all measurements rise enormously. In some cases, the amplitude of brain waves doubles, the pulse rises to 200, and the blood pressure to 220, the temperature some two or three degrees in a matter of minutes – all this in a person lying fairly still, but in the grip of memory.

Such a memory clearly has a force. It is always there, even when not triggered. Its processes are hidden under layers of effective repression so that the acute result is not evident. Even with no awareness on 'top', the immune response shows diminished effectiveness and is processing the pain unbeknownst to consciousness.

The greatest stress reactions we have observed and measured occur during the birth trauma. Since stress and the immune system work in see-saw fashion (when stress is high, immune functioning is low and vice versa) we assume that the birth trauma has a profound effect on the immune system.

We can only reflect on the amount of pressure created by the birth trauma by watching patients relive experiences. It is humbling to realize what the body can store so quietly under a calm exterior for many years. To hold that kind of stupendous pain and be unaware of it is a testimony to the strength and effectiveness of our repressive system.

Prototypes

The Principle of Prototype Origin

It has been found that early experience 'fixes' the neural connections that will last a lifetime. Certain experiences will stabilize and reinforce certain connections while others fall away. What remains are those that are most critical for survival. This is the principle of the origin of the prototype. The fixed connections that originally facilitated survival continue to endure due to a kind of developmental principle of natural selection.

Each day of foetal life hundreds of thousands of nerve cells are grouped, specialized, and developed into the organs they are destined to become. Certain cells are destined to become brain cells, while others will become the liver, the spleen, arms, and so forth. When the mother's system is toxic, when she is under stress, the foetus will absorb the toxins and its physiology will be distorted. The fragile new cells in the process of organizing into complex anatomical structures and intricate connections of neurological networking are especially vulnerable during this time.

The Trauma Train: Agony As a Permanent Fixture

The distortions in the foetus that arise with trauma in the mother, tend to be fixed. They endure as prototypical distortions. The pain surrounding birth is imprinted as a prototype (an original model on which something is patterned) that affects a variety of related behavioural traits. Prototypic behaviour means that a certain trauma imprinted in the developing brain and physiology causes a kind of response to that pain which will remain forever as an engraved tendency or pattern, on both physiological and psychological levels. The imprinting of very early pain accomplishes two major alterations within the system. It sets up a lifelong 'pool' of residual tension, and directs and shapes behaviour and physiology in certain particular ways. Both pain and the entire repertoire of responses and defences to that pain are stamped at the same time as a unified imprint.

Thus it is with a neonate who has been heavily anaesthetized as the mother's dose of anaesthetic passed through the placental barrier and infused the baby's system with a dose that is hundreds of times too powerful. The newborn will be rendered suddenly passive and ineffective, perhaps even unconscious, and will have both the pain of the experience and its following response of passivity stamped in as a prototype that affects both physiology and behaviour.

The prototype is fixed because of what I call the 'trauma train'. The trauma train is a metaphor for the sequence of events throughout birth that terminates in a certain characteristic way. It has been my observation that the way in which the birth ends is engraved as a prototypic reaction, as though the body were screaming 'cut ... print!' It all depends on the send-off at the station at birth. If it's the wrong train we're on, to paraphrase another author, 'every stop we make in life will be the wrong one'. The tracks leading out into life have been literally derailed and we're on a side trip, being taken we know not where for reasons we do not understand.

The trip is inexorable and there is nothing we can do to get off the train. No one knows how to stop it. The secret lies in going back to the start of the journey so that we can find a clear path that has long been clouded over.

If the newborn is drugged and half dead during the birth process, the train is going to go very slowly; it won't have much steam and it won't get very far. If we're sent off in the fight mode, still fighting to get out and having been successful in doing so, the train will forge ahead overcoming obstacles, bumping into everything and clearing the path aggressively, with plenty of energy available. For those who get off the train in the passive mode of a drugged birth, the energy output has to be reduced in order to stay alive; the train they are on is fleeing from the memory of a near death. When the going gets rough in this mode the first thought is of complete surrender – suicide. This is not the case with those born in the active mode, who are always busy charging ahead.

I have just mentioned the 'cut ... print' phenomenon at the end of the trauma train. Thereafter, it is as if some devil is in charge of us. This is why we can have nightmares at the age of thirty-five and forty in which we are losing our breath, being smothered, being strangled – all of the original birth sensations. The unconscious does not work capriciously; it doesn't manufacture nightmares out of some diabolical whim. It uses the wherewithal of the imprint to produce images and sensations that plague us throughout life.

The way we finally emerge from the canal, the end of the trauma train, dictates personality tendencies in a broad way. If the foetus is heavily drugged during birth and cannot do anything but try to breathe, a life saving response, stamped in, will be that of passivity, resignation, futility and despair. None of these qualities are conceptualized until the development of conceptual tools much later on. The trauma will alter the physiology, however, and that alteration will be re-represented on the higher levels of consciousness. It will be registered on the inchoate neocortex. It is thus years later when the neocortex is fully developed that we will have the capacity to name the feeling: futility.

What we cannot do is name its source. Because the representations of the early trauma are impressed on a not yet fully developed cortical consciousness, the result is like a faded Xerox copy that is almost undecipherable. Only feelings brought to consciousness can make the message stand out again. Still, it is the re-representation that allows for a connected feeling decades later. One simply follows the ideas of futility, the feelings of despair all the way down to their roots.

What the trauma train does is shape response tendencies that form the basis of personality. Thus, there will be either repressive tendencies (as in the trauma above) or expressive ones (when battling to get out ends in success). Later in life when there is conflict or stress the first survival reaction during the trauma train will again be enlisted, as those extraneous neurons no longer useful fall away. Thus, for those who had to keep reactions to a minimum to survive, as in being strangled by the cord, one of the later responses will be shallow breathing, leading to a shallowness of affect. The later general tendency is keeping things in.

It is no wonder that when this child is upset at the age of

three he might hold his breath (a recapitulation of the original trauma and the response that was life saving). Later on, he will hold in his feelings when conflict arises. Then someone will discover that those who get cancer tend to hold in their feelings. They will have therapy to encourage expression. But all the expression in therapy will not change the basic tendency set up in the trauma train. Holding in (feelings) and the development of cancer as a repressive disease are part of the same syndrome, emanating from the identical early event. In general terms, cancers are the result of repressive tendencies, in contrast to heart disease which tends to be an expressive disorder whose provenance is a more active, aggressive trauma train experience. The tendency towards either repressive or expressive behaviour encompasses every aspect of our being.

Prototypes and Survival

The prototypic response to life endangering events was not neurotic originally. It only becomes neurotic when it persists into adulthood and is inconsistent with current reality. It is then neither life-saving nor appropriate. Bronchial constriction is appropriate when one is drowning in fluids during birth, but the asthma it may create as a response to an argument between one's parents later in life is not only non-adaptive, it may be life endangering. As a general rule, prototypic responses turn into their opposites and become self-destructive later on because they are out of context and not in accordance with current, external reality. The aggressive driving behaviour, for example, that got one out of the birth canal at the beginning may, as an imprinted prototype, make one die prematurely from overwork.

To see someone with lifelong claustrophobia come out of a birth primal reliving being crushed and smothered is to understand the original terror of that phobia. One sees at once the power of the unconscious imprint and the true feeling of a fear of dying. This kind of person may well be the kind who later cannot be 'pinned down', who will not be confined to any time commitment as anything with limits, anything precise, becomes something to avoid. To see someone terrified of leaving her house – someone whose world has been narrowed down to a single room – and watch her relive the terror of leaving the womb, lays bare the force behind such a phobia.

Those who do not want to put themselves in anyone else's hands, who can never tolerate a boss's authority, who want no limits, no barriers or restrictions, are acting out an imprint. This imprint may be based upon being totally help-less and at the whim of mother's physiology and anatomy during birth. Under such circumstances one 'learns' that when one's life is in somebody else's hands one can die. It is an unconscious process often reinforced by later life circum-stances.

Prototypic behaviour is the memory of the beginnings of neurosis. One can sleuth after the many convolutions of neurosis and only fog the prototype. The entire superstruc-ture of one's personality rests on a prototype, but it never works in reverse. Changing attitudes, symptoms, or one's behaviour never changes the prototype. The prototype is a physiologic fact, not a theoretical construct.

The logic of the prototype is inherent in the phenomenon itself. It clarifies, makes sense of, and makes disparate events coherent. It ties symptoms to origins; ideas and behaviours to beginnings. Experiencing the prototype allows a fifty-year-old to finally rest, because he no longer has to be making something happen as he did at birth. An insight based on reliving the early event will immediately feel right because the higher level representation of the event will seemingly lock into place. It is an insight that no one else can offer, because an insight is no more than the top level awareness of the feeling it is connected to below.

The ways in which the imprinted trauma can form person-ality are myriad. For example, take the baby who, in the process of getting born, is battered and bruised, smashed and crushed – all for no apparent reason, at least to the baby. What may be imprinted is a kind of physiology of injustice; he has been hurt without reason. This underlying quality will become manifest only if the feeling is reinforced in later childhood, when the child is rejected, unloved, or criticized without reason. There may then be an abiding desire to correct the injustices. She will cry for the maiden who is banished because she loved the wrong man. She will be interested in the hero who brings justice to the populace. In short, she will plug unconscious primal needs into all the events around her. As an adult, such a person may act very litigiously, perhaps even becoming a lawyer to right the wrongs of society. But the driving, motivating force will be a sense of injustice, first experienced in the most primal of all experiences – birth, and then guided into shape by childhood events.

We must remember that the catastrophes that happen to a fragile foetus or newborn are happening to an organism with a wide-open sensory window, who receives all impulses and all pain directly and can put nothing between her and what is going on. The newborn cannot call a friend and talk about how unjust the experience was. He can't go to court, hire lawyers and try to rectify the experience via a proper verdict; he can't send the parents to jail; he can't go to the store and buy a pack of cigarettes and smoke it away, and he can't go to the refrigerator and eat it away. He just suffers. When the baby is born crying, doctors regard this as normal. The screaming newborn screams because he has been traumatized. Screaming is not a normal result of birth.

The roots that connect the birth events to later adult symptoms and behaviour are often labyrinthine. What is insidious about these roots is that it is as though one has gone on a journey far away from one's home base and erased the road as it is being travelled. There is no recollection of one's starting point or, indeed, how one got to his present situation. It is years later that the person finds himself in a doctor's office complaining of palpitations, angina, chronic fatigue or high blood pressure, the origins of which are a complete mystery to him and the doctor.

Our behaviour and our symptoms are not random, meaningless events, but are the end result of a history. If we take an ahistoric approach to the development of symptoms, we will be as lost as the person who has erased the road behind him. Symptoms are an end product.

Treating the symptom is valuable and necessary; one must treat an ulcer as one must treat the pain of a migraine, but let us not confuse treatment with cure. Unless one addresses the generating sources, one is only alleviating symptoms, and symptoms are not the same as disease. They are merely the means by which the disease is manifest.

The function of a symptom is to bind and absorb the energy of the imprint. To abruptly remove a symptom is to leave a person bereft of an outlet. One patient who came to us had been treated for impotence at a Behaviour Therapy clinic. After some months of therapy they had somewhat successfully treated his problem and he could get an erection from time to time. However, soon after, he developed two other symptoms; a kind of narcolepsy, falling asleep constantly, and a case of herpes. Removing the symptom put him under greater stress. The pressure went somewhere else, as it must. Evidence of this is found in the work of Ronald Glazer, Ohio State University, who showed that even the added stress of a final exam was enough to produce herpes. Sometimes the mind can absorb the impact with a well constructed belief system; other times the energy will move against the body. The organism is at all times a compensating system, balancing the internal pressure as best it can.

The following case history of an epileptic illustrates the above. This patient, in his own words, explains better than any expository prose the dramatic impact of birth and its vicissitudes upon later life.

Bill

I'm almost certain I suffered a concussion in the birth canal. At first everything was so smooth and rhythmic, then WHAM! The womb went rigid and slapped my head. As an adult, I had a car accident and broke my sternum. I have relived that accident like some photo unrolling until I was totally conscious of what happened and the extent to which it recalled the trauma of my birth. After those feelings, I began to heal rapidly, much more rapidly than before. Somehow feeling pain has something to do with healing that same pain.

The birth scene was, I think, my prototypic seizure. It was, like the first stages of death a result of helpless anoxia. It was totally appropriate to the situation. The birth scenes I have relived were many times more traumatic than my accident. The hundreds of seizures I've had in my life were just unconscious attempts to react fully to the initial deathly horror of my being oxygen starved at birth. No wonder I had a pre-seizure feeling on the tip of my tongue. Something was really on the tip of it. A feeling. It is no mystery why I always passed out when I began to recognize what it was. Merciful unconsciousness saved me from knowing something that was too much to know and feel.

Over the past few weeks I have repeatedly felt myself regaining consciousness, halfway out of the birth canal, beginning to breathe. In my feeling everything seemed to be violence and discord. I slurped air in great hiccups. I wriggled to free my arms and head, but mostly I just lay and gulped air. I sucked it down like fluid. My cries came out sporadically as whoops and wails. The electric buzzing (what I believe was my first seizure) happened with my birth. As I sucked air, my body tingled (the same tingling I get with my seizures) and then coalesced into agony, sensations of suffocation and concussion. I've slept poorly all my life. My nightmares were full of those same early sensations of suffocation (dreams of drowning and of huge waves keeping me from breathing) and I see how those early sensations were always trying to get out and be free. I was really having those early feelings and sensations in my sleep. I woke up before it was too conscious. I had a tough time falling asleep because those same feelings made my head race constantly. I was full of thoughts that wouldn't stop.

Since seizures were appropriate to the way I really felt they never seemed outlandish. These feelings may sound mundane or bizarre to some people, but to me they are the explanation for the way I felt each day of my life. If I could be conscious of what knocked me into unconsciousness over and over again there was no reason to seize and make myself unconscious.

There is a continuum of disorganization from seizure through the physical sensations that is often reported by people who have seizures as they near birth feelings. Sensations literally fragment and dissolve when a seizure begins; a cry becomes a disembodied knot in the throat, the knot breaks up into mobile shards like broken pots, to something like smashed glass and then to a fine fuzzy sort of electric buzz. This is the mediating agent for the plethora of symptoms that haunted me.

My symptoms changed like a chameleon. If my arms didn't hurt, it was my head. If that didn't hurt, it was my belly. If nothing hurt it meant that something strange was afoot. On such occasion I lost my balance for several days. Symptoms melded into one another within seconds. It makes it difficult to know which symptoms to describe as 'physical' since panic could shift from a stomach ache to a knot behind my right eye and then a knife-like sensation between my shoulder blades.

Seizures were not manifest until I got the message that I wasn't to call for help, complain, or show any signs of imperfection. When my mother was screaming in my face, virtually any response could be dangerous. When I banged my elbow and couldn't call out at age seven, I seized. After being asked whether my brothers and I should go to an orphanage I seized on a regular basis.

I've had trouble with both colitis and constipation. The two may not seem to go together, but that's the way it is. All my symptoms seem to be episodic – first I hold everything in and then ... the old prototypic pattern.

My headaches went away with my feelings of birth and the lack of oxygen. I think I had no way to discharge the accumulated poisons; since then I've had an obsession to purge myself one way or another either by confessing or having the runs. Stagnation! That's the word. I can't stand it. Drives me nuts. Not getting it is the same as stagnation and being poisoned to me. So I have always been driven. It is a relief to get rid of those impulsions.

I could feel the knobby grains of asphalt stuck to my cheek and brow. The playground was empty. What had happened? I sat up: no one had to tell me that I'd fainted. But here there was no trigger; no stubbed toe, no hard tackle or cut finger. Who faints without cause? Perhaps I was just sensitive. My mother told me I had a hyperactive imagination. But I hadn't imagined anything! Something was wrong with me, always had been.

When I sat in the empty schoolyard after passing out, these sensations passed from my brain like a musician's fading chord. For moments during the day I lost track of what I was saying. In mid-sentence I'd stop. As though entranced by the window sill I'd stare. I was saying ... what? I laboured to breathe. For long moments I would actually forget to breathe, and start only with difficulty, approaching that native rhythmic pleasure as a problem in logic. If I move my chest, so, and drop back my head, air will come in. Painful assaults from knees and wrists. Irritant sensations up my ribs and spine. I felt like a lizard was squirming in my chest. It moves when I move and I feel its weight when I'm still. I have always been miserable.

I loved the bath. I wanted to float in it, to be covered and filled with it yet not to drown. A jellyfish ... they're 95 per *cent water. So is the ocean. Pure mindlessness. I wanted to drift. I've lived my entire life that way; all consequences and no decisions. The maths numbers swimming in my head, the pretty girls I could never talk to, the voiceless, preverbal blank I drew when I tried, that emotion without form, sensations that will not emote. I had always been apart from my cohorts, from my family, shielded as though by plexiglass housing which only parted for catastrophes and shortly after.*

Between me and the world was a cosmos, a cosmogony of pain. Sensations of breathlessness and alone which I could not transcribe. Neil Young sang it: 'It's these expressions I never give that keep me searching for a heart of gold, and I'm getting old.' Emotions swallowed in my throat – a tide, a river. A veritable montage. All seemed to be welling ON me in that very moment in the bathroom as I stared out at my face in the mirror.

In the transition of death a man sees his life. There are no holds barred, no reason to struggle. Deathbed testimony is law. From where in my suburban middle-class life had all this come? I saw hours and days as though seconds. And I saw death as though it had occurred. And always the pain: alone and never, never anyone to help. No one knows and no one hears.

What does it matter whether you play football or ride the breakers when you see the centre of your life corroded, eaten by death, by misery? What matter how it got there, whose fault. It was already there. At the beginning of each struggle I had already lost. What sense to make love to a living, flesh and blood woman? At some moment she must awake and find this diseased man – this corpse – between her legs. Not evil, perhaps well-intentioned, but a little off. And what do intentions mean in a dying man? What good are apologies? It is all futile. Just a boy who needs so much it seems foolish to call him a complete organism. And there, standing in front of the mirror, planting both hands on the bathroom sink, I stood before death.

I had chosen volumes of literary masters to speak for me ... I wanted so to live. Plato, Rabelais, Miller and Nietzsche. I trotted out Marx, Darwin, Rimbaud and the Founding Fathers but in the end I succumbed, I submitted. I no longer asked for help. I didn't speak to my mother. When I had to cry I did it privately, in some dark place. I abstained from sex, good company and dances. I never asked for anything – never a ride home from school with a friend. I never imposed. No one ever to take care of me.

I was afflicted with knowledge. Dostoevski, in Notes From the Underground, *attributed his epilepsy to being 'hyperconscious'. The knowledge sears. Nobody. Forever. Why couldn't someone have come to me earlier in the day? Must it always reach this point? Was this less trouble than a friendly smile?*

In my early feelings I was pawing the air begging my mother to let me go out on the front porch. I want to see the sun, mama ... I'm dying. Over and over bloodcurdling soul-satisfying screams. I wanted her to sit with me on the porch, to take in the sun, the fresh air for one time.

Everything related to seizures. I would stumble into the Primal Institute confused and hurting. I would talk and then feel. As feelings approached so did the seizures, but I could turn it back to the real sensations and not pass out. My head would roll back in spasms of pain. My eyes rolled in their sockets: idiot terror, death and then the therapist would say, 'Say the feeling! It's a feeling. Say it!' My tongue came alive and I just said, 'Mama'. 'I can't stand it!' There was nobody in this world to help me. HELP! I screamed over and over.

Those horrible moments of my infancy and childhood were immortalized in flesh and blood in my system and constantly replayed. My old seizures were useful handles to spring me from bucketfuls of pain. Each piece of the memory a call to freedom, a call to heal. My old pains swept through my chest like broken glass. I could guess the proximity and severity of a Primal to come by the strange prodromal (pre-seizure) sensations on my tongue and in my bowels. Now instead of seizures I had the same strength, convulsive feelings. I had my own electronic meter. I could spot where I was between seizure and feeling.

The smaller and more highly charged the fragments, the harder the magic words would come, the more spacy I would be and the closer I would come to seizing. It was then that I needed more direction towards my feelings. With finely dispersed pains the memories might be too much, too draining.

I think of men who know of these experiences without resolving them; Dali and Artaud; of Freud's hysterics whose attacks were an exact imitation ('imitation' he calls it) of the birth process. The moral: collapse and cure are different even when the cure involves a sort of collapse. Since as a teenager I could not ask for sex, my orgasmic convulsions were transmitted actually (seizures). Who has thought of prescribing sex for epileptics? To my knowledge only Shakespeare:

> *Iago: My master has fallen into epilepsy. This is his second fit today.*
> *Cassius: Rub him about the temples.*

I know now why my pre-seizure sensations often start in my cock. Circumcision. Let them cut my knee, my leg, anything else. Anything! Christ. Cut like a Christmas turkey. The second time I felt this I went vegetarian for a month. Nobody wants to lose his balls. Listening to my mother's description made me clasp my hands over my crotch. It is supposed to be a civilized operation instead of a mugging. But just picture this: you're thirteen, your penis is all swollen and bandaged. You're moaning and lying in bed with sticky crap all over my dick and itching. Nobody comes and there is a rash. Everything is sore. I was left as a victim as a battered drunk lying in an alley. My wounds festered and I cried body and soul for help that never came.

Most people I knew wondered why I lacked ambition. Why I did not take my righteous place, a member-in-fair-standing of upper middle-class USA. It wasn't a matter of morals or ethereal transcendent. I just 'knew' it was no use.

All of the preceding events contributed to my epilepsy; each by raising the pain load, raising my brainwave activity and cutting away the opportunity for love, sex, desires, any active response. It was useless. Any of the things that happened to me could have been avoided had my parents not been nudged, harassed, barricaded into an antediluvian two-car-in-every-garage parenthood. I bore no relation to their own needs. Need must be fulfilled, perforce; I should have ever been conceived, let alone born.

I first passed out in the womb at birth. Later in life, when I felt hopeless, I'd reproduce my whole seizure/dying scene to the point of wriggling through the same convulsions. I now come out of feelings mouthing insights; that's why the seizures, that's why the hours staring hopelessly at a maths problem. That's why this and that's why that.

People are called unconscious who are influenced by verbal suggestion. No matter what the form of anaesthesia the body feels pain and love on some level. There are concoctions and procedures to sever feeling and quiet complaint; but there is no drug to abrogate the truth. We all block pain; cells withdraw from it, lawyers rationalize it and professors change the subject. It is natural and good to avoid a thing that will harm you. I think pain alone motivates healing. It's true in my case. I began to stop my seizures when I felt what had happened at birth.

A good number of unhealed are the epileptics. I was one. My seizure response was totally appropriate to the situation. The hundreds that followed were just semi-lucid attempts to respond to that initial deathly horror. So it has been with every psychosomatic symptom I've ever had.

Madmen do not invent their suffering. All the helplessness, hopelessness, the disease and amnesia ... all *responses to a prototype; all honest attempts to heal. I have returned to the event of my birth repeatedly over the last couple of years. I bear no wonder that I used to become unconscious with impending awareness of such an event.*

In the beginning there was only the womb; the garden of Eden, the cosmos. The golden womb of succour and nurture; a paradise. It was my golden age; a paradise I never forgot. Then the womb contracted and I couldn't breathe and I later had migraines. Funny these birth feelings. When I skip them there is a migraine. If I do them they can even be pleasant. As Janov says, 'A pain that doesn't hurt'.

What happened to my mother? She said once that her water broke at home. Another time she said that she stayed in another room contracting so as not to wake up 'your father'. She held back from going to the hospital and I was born forty-five minutes later. They have her a shot of demerol. Whatever happened it was totally inappropriate. Would that the humans of this world – those civilized folk – leave off making babies. Leave it. Barring that let every mother be granted love during her delivery and after. Let her not be wheeled about overlit sterile wards on a tray while her husband paces in a waiting room. Let someone hold her hand and make her feel she is not alone in this world. If the hospital won't allow it then damn the hospital; find another. The theme of my life as been 'no air'. That's what I said about saints and icons, my schoolteachers and parents; they gave me no air. All those prim bastards who think I lived by rules. It was never any use conforming. A lifetime of headaches and nightmares; sensations of anoxia spread cell by cell like ink through a blotter. It spread deep within me; around my lungs, the bones of my arms and forced my toes in. There was no use fighting; I've fought enough for one life. Enough for a platoon. I used to masturbate pretending to be squeezed through a tube of toothpaste.

I never lifted a finger to cause anything. I wonder at the

*reliving, at the feeling of it all. I am buffeted by waves
without synchrony. Magellan's voyage could have given
him no greater sense of wonder of the miracle of all this. In
the womb I am no more. The partitions of my body have
taken on a life of their own. It is a basic simple life like a
colony of sponges. Now in my feeling I'm alive at last; a
lifetime spent in agony has come to an end. I want to live,
to breathe, to see beauty free from the dark morass I've
inhabited all of these years.*

9

The Birth Prototype
and The Later Personality

Just imagine, if you will, that you are nine months old, lying comfortably in the dark, all cosy and warm and safe, and suddenly for no reason you are jolted about roughly, your head and body are crushed into a narrow space, and you're administered a heavy drug. You need all your wits about you to try to escape. You begin to gag and smother because of the fluids forced into your system. When you finally get out, hardly able to breathe, you find yourself in a cold, barren room; a giant appears, swings you upside down, smacks you hard enough to make you cry in pain, and then places you all alone in a box somewhere with bright lights shining in your eyes. *Welcome to the world. You have just been born.*

The birth trauma is surely one of the wonders of the world. Although it drives civilization, it is never detected. If someone points to it, he or she becomes a pariah. It is part of the general 'conspiracy of the unconscious'. Millions die from it but no one can say what 'it' is. Why is the nightmare there? What is it doing there? How did it get inside of us in the first place?

The Sympathetic and Parasympathetic Modes

Earlier, we talked about the birth prototype – a design for a personality which becomes imprinted in the course of a traumatic birth. The profound implication of the prototype is that it is the first determinant of personality. Once that personality is formed we have a system that constructs the world to match its metabolism, and a metabolism controlled by the prototype. What the psyche does thereafter is create a world which can rationalize altered metabolic processes set in motion earlier on. It is a constant attempt to make rational in the present reactions that were appropriate to the early trauma. If the trauma sped us up, then we create an adult world full of activity and busyness.

The nature of the birth trauma, for those who experience it, skews the system for a lifetime in one of two major directions towards what I call the *sympathetic* and the *parasympathetic* modes. Both are modes of metabolic regulation governed by the hypothalamus, and each is controlled by a different aspect of the autonomic nervous system. The sympathetic mode energizes, expands, mobilizes, and galvanizes the system; the parasympathetic mode conserves, rests, cools, and heals.

Let's look at each of these in greater detail. The sympathetic system is the work horse: it alarms and alerts, increases the activity level of all organ systems, raises body temperature, and increases vital functions such as heart rate and blood pressure. It increases urine production, produces bowel spasms, and churns up the viscera; it regulates peripheral blood flow so that in anxious situations the hands and feet become cold and the face pale. It is this system that triggers the secretion of the steroids or stress hormones. It mediates nervous sweating, dry mouth, high tension muscle states, taut face and jaw, higher voice, and it is the agency for impulsive behaviour. It keeps us focused externally rather than being reflective.

The parasympathetic system is the energy saver. It is dominant in feeling, deep sleep, and relaxation. It is called the anabolic system because it helps repair. It dilates certain blood vessels so that the skin is warm and the eyes and mouth are moist. It helps relax muscles and lower the voice.

Parasympathetic responses are predominant during rest, recovery, during healing and, most importantly, during feeling. In a therapeutic session, we can watch the radical shift from sympathetic to parasympathetic functioning as the patient drops into a feeling. The pulse, body temperature, heart rate and certain brain wave patterns all skyrocket (sympathetic mode) until the person is no longer defended and begins to feel. Then there is a shift towards the parasympathetic system as all of these signs drop below their initial values. It is how we know a feeling has locked in.

The traits which make up the dimension of parasympath/ sympath are highly complex and exist along a continuous spectrum. Everyone is a unique blend of these characteristics. Although these traits are normally distributed, certain persons fall towards either end of the spectrum. Very pure types are rare indeed, each of us being a combination of both. A truly healthy person has a proper balance between these two states. But this balance can be upset by early traumas, dating back to womb life, so that one mode may predominate in a manner over the other for a lifetime.

The importance of the sympathetic/parasympathetic model is that it provides us with a biological base for understanding the unitary relationship between personality, physiological development, and later disease. It enables us to leave abstraction and metaphor behind us. We no longer need to talk about id force as the core of personality development. Rather, we can talk about the precise ways in which the brain and nervous system react to and encode life events, and how those reactions became physiological and psychological states.

The Imprint of the Trauma Train

How does the birth trauma end? Is the neonate in the sympathetic or parasympathetic mode? Did the trauma end while the struggle was still going on? Did it end after hours of agony, or naturally and smoothly? Did the baby come out still fighting, or did the baby come out bereft of all fight? Did he learn to give up? Or did he learn to struggle on through, despite the obstacles? Was there too great a dose of anaesthetic? Breach birth? Overly long labour? Did the baby get off the trauma train almost dead from drugs, in need of being revived by ice water, more drugs, or smacks? Was the baby born by Caesarean? These earliest life-saving responses are imprinted, and will be used over and over again in future stress situations, because they are what the system in its first major life and death crisis did to survive.

The mode of birth helps determine the kinds of disease we suffer from later on. If it is a struggle and fail syndrome at birth, where despite all efforts birth was not easily effected after a monumental struggle, certain physiological processes and a sense of despair will be imprinted. Because traumas associated with birth are immediately repressed and remain deep in the unconscious, inaccessible and imperceptible – they can, over many decades, in small increments, finally culminate in catastrophic disease. The prototype may determine not only the boundaries of our behaviour, but the configuration of our physiology as well. It determines whether we will have a hyper or sluggish general personality type.

When the birth trauma is such that the neonate has no alternatives, when there is nothing he can do to change his state, as for example, being strangled on the cord, the parasympathetic system will dominate. Aggressivity would be life threatening. The systematic reaction will be one of defeat and despair. Paradoxically, giving up is part of a survival effort. Fighting and struggling would be life endangering. The parasympath will be the one to suffer from immune diseases later in life because the basic prototype tendencies will be to hold back and hold in, repression, in a word. With that goes a deep despair, as well. Since I have noted that the immune system processes feelings, we shall find this feeling of defeat there (the real meaning of psychosomatic; where the mind intersects with cellular tissue), not as a conscious experience but in terms of diminished immune cell functioning; cells now follow the personality type and function in a less aggressive and active manner.

By contrast, the sympathetic personality has all systems on 'go'. The mother who was locked up tight and could not release her baby had a foetus fighting for his life. The imprint of this fight remains so that he later becomes driving, ambitious, unaware of, or indifferent to obstacles, optimistic (because the birth outcome was indeed optimistic), relentless, pushy, aggressive, never despairing, never depressed, and never defeated. He is a candidate for a heart attack, not cancer. If he had despaired he would have stopped fighting, and that would have meant death. So despair is not in his vocabulary. In adult life he never gives up. He keeps on struggling no matter what the odds.

The sympath is 'burning up the streets'. He is not in the energy-conserving mode, as is the parasympath; he is clearly in the energy burning mode. Eventually, though, he is going to 'run out of gas'. His pulse and body temperature are higher. He is more into sex because all the impulses are coming up and out. He acts out. The parasympath acts in. The sympath is in the expressive mode, while the parasympath is holding back, holding down, and keeping in.

If there were one central difference between the two modes it is that the sympath has learned to try in order to survive, while the parasympath has learned *not* to try to survive. To put it differently, for the former to try means life; for the latter to try means death (where serious activity during birth was lethal). All later childhood traumas will only compound the basic feelings occasioned by the birth trauma. Thus, the parasympath under a small amount of adversity gives up trying for love, while the sympath nearly always tries for it. The parasympath gives up on life much quicker than the sympath, and he is not as likely to finish projects because not finishing avoids the catastrophic core futility involved in the finish of the original trauma. He is quicker to see death as relief, because it was; and is therefore more likely to consider suicide. The parasympath will struggle against adversity but the minute he senses that he is overwhelmed he will give up. The dialectic of his treatment is that before he can feel that he can really make it he must feel the deep feeling, 'I can't make it'.

Philip was in many respects typical of the sympath type.

Philip

My birth was a long, eighteen-hour struggle. I felt that there was no way out, but I could not stop struggling because to stop was to never get out. I was frustrated and scared by this long wait, as I did not know what was happening.

I was born angry. My head was misshaped and bruised at birth, and I've always felt sore in my neck and upper torso. I was always afraid of physical hurt but I still played sports in order to get attention. I could not play well due to my fear of being hurt (again).

I was a head banger and a crib rocker. I know now what that was because I had been banging my head to get out from the start. Whenever I was frustrated, I just resorted to what I did originally to find relief and freedom. In order to stop my banging, I was tied with a sling under my chin to immobilize my head so I could not bang it. This way I had to relive, again and again, the original pain of my birth of being caught by the head. I've had pain in my joints all of my life, I guess from trying to get free. I had treatment for rheumatoid arthritis starting at age thirty-four.

I've also had reliving sessions in my feelings where a hand is grabbing at my face and two fingers are in my eye sockets. Once I felt this pain, my lifelong headaches just above the eyes disappeared. If I get an occasional headache, I know that feelings are coming up, and when I feel, the pain goes away.

My married life was crazy. I always felt 'tied down' and wanted to be free, yet I did not want to be alone (having

*been left alone and terrified just after birth). The act of
going to bed alone in a dark room was always painful and I
always fought against it. I needed to drink in order to fall
asleep. Again, that primordial aloneness must have left me
with a memory of terror that I never got over. Now I can
enjoy a good night's sleep, and anyone who has had sleep
problems knows what a blessing that is. It is so nice to
wake up and enjoy mornings.*

Despair: The Root of Disease

The parasympath has fought and been defeated by insuperable odds. He or she develops a 'what's-the-use' attitude
because what *was* the use? If the immune system could talk,
it would say exactly the same thing. So it is not as vigorous,
not as ready for combat; it despairs in its own way. For the
sympath, fighting for what he needed meant survival. Any
later obstacle is going to provoke that fight. For the parasympath, fighting meant no survival. If the mother had a large
tumour and the baby could not get out, there will be the same
feeling of confronting insuperable odds. Even later in life,
when those odds are not so insurmountable, events will be
responded to in that way, not only psychologically but
physiologically as well.

The conditions for parasympathetic suicidal preoccupations are exactly the duplicate of birth – high agitation,
seeing no way out, trying but failing, and giving up. The
imprint of death, despair, and defeat are everywhere in the
parasympath and lead the way to later catastrophic disease. It
is now part of the physiology exactly like those India-ink
granules I discussed earlier. Noxious stimuli became part of
the physiology of the amoeba. And they became part of us;
first to render them innocuous, and secondly, to store them
until they can be felt and integrated.

The parasympath, in his general attitude of doom and

despair, attempts to validate *now* a reality that *was*. It is an attempt by the mind to make real externally what really exists only internally. It is thus an attempt, as in all neurosis, at coherence, cohesiveness and harmony, albeit a neurotic harmony. What finally kills the parasympath are the events that gave rise to the feeling: 'Nothing I do will be good enough, I really don't deserve to live.'

If leaving the womb was traumatic for the parasympath, then change means disaster. This prototypic experience is going to dictate a kind of conservative, cautious personality who is wary of abrupt change, who cannot alter his schedules easily, and who needs to predict everything in advance. If, later on, we discover that conservatism is associated with a certain disease, it would not be surprising. This is not to say that conservatism causes disease. It is simply that both are based on the same imprinted reactions.

Under stress, the parasympath is hypoactive, and tends towards low-blood pressure, slow pulse, low body temperature, and low thyroid. The good news is that if the parasympath can avoid catastrophic disease such as cancer, it is likely that he will outlive the 'sympath' simply because of his low metabolism (assuming that the parasympath has led a fairly healthy life).

Everything about the parasympath seems rather sluggish. Speech patterns are slow and sometimes laboured. Thoughts are carefully measured and weighed.

The parasympath has come close to death when coming into life with no possibility of struggle. (The fear of feeling too alive, exuberant and joyful, can stem from this paradigm – doom follows life). There isn't the kind of 'struggle and succeed', as in the sympath. Rather, the struggle is aborted very quickly as, for example, massive anaesthesia pervades the system, rendering it unconscious and near death. It is 'struggle and fail'. Later on, when there are obstacles the person will tend to give up because she has no experience with tenacity and success. Her pessimism will outweigh any later encouragements. Her cautious, grim, conservative approach, where possible catastrophe awaits behind every decision, might be suitable for an accountant, but will not enable her to take the kind of steps necessary to finish a project in a vigorous manner.

She is looking forward to a doom that has already happened, a doom of which she is unaware. She sees hopelessness everywhere. She is staring her past in the face and does not know it. This is the key element that makes for catastrophic disease. It is why animals who are trapped without alternatives fall ill. Their situation was hopeless.

No Exit for the Neurotic

The parasympath is on a darkened train with the windows sealed shut, each compartment isolated from the other, with no real destination, no real sense of direction. This is the way he feels: alone in the dark, shut off, lost, with no options or alternatives, defeated. The train labours to its ineluctable destiny. It has become the 'agony train' that one climbs aboard at birth with no exit signs because there were none originally. The parasympath is nearly always more aware of his pain than the sympath.

I recall one woman who described the parasympath feeling as that of being in some kind of cocoon – a hard shell from which she could not break free. She the second-born twin. She had trouble getting out and spent a lifetime feeling stuck. After the feeling, she said, 'Now I can move and be free.' Most of her life she was a prisoner of a gloom that surrounded her all the time. She said she felt like a 'mangled mess' who never had a chance for life.

Some time ago I was having trouble with a young therapist who was too aggressive and pushy with his patients, forcing them to go too fast. All exhortation was in vain until he felt the feeling ... 'when I feel stuck and I don't know what to do, I push.' No more complicated than his birth feelings which were intruding.

Victoria is an example of a parasympath.

Victoria

I woke up the other morning feeling that everything was too much for me; even the thought of going out to make breakfast or do errands for the day was too much. I felt so overwhelmed by everything so that I couldn't get out of bed. I wanted to cry, and tried to get in touch with the feeling. The first thing that I said was, 'It's all too much for me. I just can't do it.' Then I cried for a while, and as I was crying I remembered what I had dreamt during the night: my husband and I were on vacation and we were going to motels that were out in the country. As we went into the rooms I would get a feeling that there was a danger there – nothing specific – just a very subtle feeling of danger that someone or something was going to hurt us. It felt as if someone were lying in wait for us – a sense of impending doom.

As I cried about the dream, I remembered how terribly frightened I have been all my life – how I would check my room every night by looking under the bed, in the closet, and under the skirt of the vanity table, as well as having a light on in the room (even at the age of twenty-one). I still lay in the bed rigidly waiting for someone to come and get me and hurt me. This feeling led to scenes with my mother where, when my father would go away on business trips, she would make a rope out of neck ties so that we could climb down from the second storey in case someone came to murder us. She also put a stack of old plates on top of the table by the window, to be thrown down on the cement below to wake the farm manager, in case the murderer cut the phone lines. Then she would lock the bedroom door and we (Mama, my brother and I) would sleep in there together. I was always so terrified; if Mama were so scared, then there must be something so big and frightening out there that it could really kill us. She seemed so big, and if she *were scared, who could protect us? I couldn't wait for my father to come home and bring some sense of security with him. My mother was such a hysterical person; she was terrified of everything – authority figures, money, the world in general – as if everything 'out there' were potentially dangerous and hurtful. Her fear was very infectious.*

As I cried about all the things I had been frightened of as a child, I came to a feeling of being born in which I couldn't breathe, and then just after birth when I was left alone. My mother expressed her fear and panic in childbirth by screaming uncontrollably and by banging her head against the bedpost. Her terror was communicated to me, and at birth the feeling of fear was further compounded by being left alone when I so obviously needed to be comforted and held. I didn't know then that anyone would ever come to me; I felt a sense of timelessness and eternal aloneness. My father said that as he looked through the hospital glass window I was screaming the loudest, and that he could easily hear me over all the other babies.

This feeling so neatly describes why I always approach something new with the immediate and all-encompassing reaction of, 'No, I can't do it. I'm not ready.' My first experience of 'new things' was totally frightening: my mother not helping me to get born because of her own fear and terror, and then not being held after I was born. As I grew up, my mother continued to reinforce those original fears of mine with all her real and imaginary fears.

No matter what the new situation is that I'm up against, no matter how well qualified I am to do it, I always feel that I can't do it. This even carries over to when I am doing something well that I know I can do. Now I understand the reason. Doing new things puts me face-to-face with my birth and childhood feelings of aloneness. When this feeling is pushing up, I feel that I can't do anything, despite all the evidence to the contrary and people telling me that I can.

That need for reassurance, which never succeeds in

reassuring me, is very early pain rearing its ugly head. The reason that no words of truth can reassure me out of that feeling is because it is a birth feeling and there are no words for birth feelings. It seems like I have a core feeling of fear and insecurity that is one of my most central feelings. My therapist once said that when I am in that state of asking for reassurance, it's as if I am grasping out all around me, but nothing that is said reassures me. He's so right; I feel as if I am falling into space and no one is there to catch me. My mind compulsively goes over whatever problem I am having, trying to make sense of it, where there is none. Even after I have understood how to correct a mistake, I am still not satisfied, and continue to think about it obsessively.

No words of reassurance help, only feeling the original feeling makes the obsessive worrying stop. That is why I have always said that feeling a birth feeling is something that I embrace happily, because the mental torture that I suffer while obsessing is the true agony for me, not the traumatic feeling. I really feel relived when I can make a feeling connection because I know it won't be much longer before I can find peace. All my life I have said, 'I just want to rest'. My body never rests. I am constantly vigilant, with a startle reaction second to none, and only after a birth feeling do I feel truly relaxed and sane. So, 'I want to rest' is a physical statement as well as an emotional one.

After I finished feeling all this, I couldn't wait to get on with the day, and eagerly went about all my errands. The doom had lifted. In fact, I refinished a mirror in my bathroom that I had lived with for four years in a most deteriorated state. An interior decorator had previously told me that it couldn't be refinished, and I had just accepted his verdict. But now, by questioning several people at a paint store, I discovered that there was, indeed, a way to repair it. In the past, I would have never done that; I would have accepted his pronouncement as incontrovertible fact. I now see that feeling frees me from the constraints upon my

> *imagination which have held me back from all forms of creative endeavour. Before feeling, it seems that everything is too much for me; after feeling, I am freed to do anything I want to do, and with ease.*

The above case is indicative of what I call 'compounding'; that is to say, the birth trauma was compounded by very similar circumstances with her family later on. She had a terrifying birth, was alone and terrified after birth, and then had a mother who was hysterical and afraid all the time as well, which got transmitted to her.

I also recall the case of a girl who had been held back at birth by the nurse until the doctor arrived. Struggle as she might, there was a hand to make sure she would not get out. Her vital signs during the reliving leapt skyward until they reached a critical point where she seemed to give up the struggle. The pressure on the system at that point was nearly fatal. In addition to her high vital signs, she experienced a feeling of futility and despair – the groundwork for later serious disease. Here is an almost pure example of the struggle and fail syndrome often leading later to such afflictions as manic-depression; first, all systems are in a frenzy, manic, and then exhaustion and the failure of struggle (depression).

The early traumatic event of struggle and fail is the causal link contributing *both* to despair and, later, cancer. It is this vital early element that has been left out of most calculations in the attempt to understand cancer. We must remember that the human system is never capricious; it never manufactures symptoms out of whole cloth. Despair doesn't arrive out of the blue, but is a result of precise early events.

The girl discussed above had a heavy course in college and though she tried to keep up she found herself falling behind. The current situation triggered off the past and it all became too much for her. She gave up. She then fell into a deep depression. No one knew why. She was classified by the college clinic as suffering from a form of *mental* illness, namely 'severe endogenous depression'. Endogenous in this case meant, 'We do not understand where this depression comes from but it seems to come from inside for no apparent reason.'

The resolution of her deep despair and depression required the reactivation and reliving of her early life-and-death struggle, which included all those near lethal vital signs. It was those signs, incidentally, that told us she was unmistakably locked into an old memory. Here again the dialectic: she was depressed because current life set off an early unconscious imprint that produced depression, and then in order to ameliorate the problem we had to again evoke the past memory, this time consciously, to resolve it. Same memory, different ending.

After the feeling, when all those signs diminished, the insights began. She was able to see how against even the slightest odds, her body reactivated the memory of insurmountable barriers. She reacted by caving in and giving up. Just as importantly, the resolution of the memory changed her blood flow, her muscle tone, and her hormonal output in such a way that her entire body configuration changed, including the texture of her hair and her complexion.

When there is a birth trauma that leads to the struggle–fail syndrome, the body feels defeated even though it has no cortical apparatus to conceptualize this feeling as yet. That despair is being processed in its own way even though the precise feeling never rises to consciousness. Immune cell impairment is but one way that Primal despair is translated cellularly.

To *feel* hopeless is not to be repressed. Serious illness comes from the *repression* of hopelessness, not its experience. What comes from feeling the hopelessness very early on, however, may be death. So choose your weapons; you can die as a baby feeling catastrophic despair, or you can repress it and die from it later.

I am sure that if I told someone the reason he developed cancer at the age of fifty was because of what happened at birth, he would be sceptical, cynical, and disbelieving. How can you believe in something you can't see, feel, smell or touch? It's like asking someone to believe in the tooth fairy.

The Act-Out of the Birth Trauma

The act-out of the birth prototype is not easily understood. Let us review: Every very early feeling is compounded and represented at other levels. Childhood events do not necessarily bring different feelings so much as elaborations of the earlier feelings. The need to be drawn out, to communicate, to be given time, to be allowed freedom all are part of the first-line birth events. Feeling unwanted, unworthy, ignored are likewise part of this elaboration and compounding. Almost everything we do in adult life is a replica of the early imprints; what I have described as the 'act-out'.

The question is, 'Why do we constantly act-out the compounded birth prototype?' Why do we constantly want no obstacles in our way? Why are we anxious when waiting in a long line? Why do we chose those that make life hard for us? Why are we terrified in each new encounter, and why are we so afraid of change? Why are we afraid to be in anyone's clutches? What we do is to duplicate the earlier traumatic environment over and over again and live the past in the present without cease. Why?

First, because the earlier event was never felt and therefore was repressed, leaving a residue of tension which must be worked off and released. It must be constantly discharged for homeostasis or balance. Just tapping the feet and hands is a form of discharge. Constant talking and sex are other forms. The person must discharge enough excess tension to normalize the system; to bring it into an optimum productive level. Secondly, the entire panoply surrounding the imprint – the lead-up feeling and defense, the feeling itself and the body's reactions form a gestalt which is constantly transported into the present for healing. It is an attempt at mastery and resolution, albeit symbolically. Thus, the act-out is an attempt to re-create the earlier trauma with a hopefully different ending. Yet, because there was no different ending originally, we manage to re-create the exact conditions with the same ending. So we are constantly creating holes to climb out of. We begin to succeed and do something to ensure failure (the analogue of the birth process, compounded). Or we almost make it and then quit. We cannot stand any form of restriction or constriction. We keep everything uncompleted because completion (originally) means disaster, etc.

Thirdly, the act-out ensures unconsciousness because it keeps the focus in the present and thus aids the forces of repression. When we isolate a person and prevent his usual defences the old feelings come up immediately. A person who suddenly falls ill and cannot act-out is thrown into his past and he begins to feel anxious and tense, usually not knowing why. So, in a great paradox we act-out to keep the past alive and dead at the same time. We keep the past going in the present and repress the real context so that it won't fragment consciousness. Full consciousness, remember, can mean death. We need to be aware for resolution, yet awareness in the primal sense means disintegration.

The act-out involves implicit hope because in the original trauma there is almost always a deep hopelessness. We repeat earlier birth patterns because those patterns saved our lives. It is not a choice we make; it is automatic. To attempt to change the act-out, in effect trying to alter neurosis, is an attempt to erase history; and that is not easily done.

The central reason that we duplicate the environment from the past onto the present is that the old environment exists in the brain and body *in exact form all of the time.* We react to it because it is there and we do what we must to make coherent and rational a constant brain–body state. We keep on the move, keep busy, feeling that we love the excitement of constant action because movement unconsciously means life, and no movement means death. We never feel that original context because we keep on the move. To be housebound would mean to come close to the real feelings and with it terrible anxiety.

The valence of the imprint is the strength of the act-out, and even though there are childhood aspects to it, the act-out (read, neurotic behaviour) cannot be fully resolved until the basis for it all lying deep and remote in the unconscious is resolved. One can reduce the force of the act-out by feeling things that occurred in childhood but the act-out persists. It will just take a greater stimulus to set it off. When the deepest level traumas are relived and resolved we can say that neurosis is over.

Does all of the above mean that no experience, not even an intense therapeutic one, can change neurosis? Yes, that is what it means; because no experience can penetrate the shell of repression, below which lives an environment of immense magnitude. The inner imprint is a constant environment that we react to first. It predominates over any other experience. Unless the new experience is life threatening, and unless it occurs early in life, demanding a new kind of response, there is nothing that can change neurosis – except – except unblocking repression and liberating the imprint. Again, the neurotic act-out was formed in response to a near-death event. Unless another event is strong enough and early enough the first survival mechanism we learn will be the first refuge of defence.

Compounding the Prototype

Primal Therapy is not only about birth. Birth tends to start neurosis on its way. It gives it its direction. Certainly, a benign or even supportive and loving environment is going to attenuate the impact of the pre-birth and birth traumas. A parasympath who grows up in a cold, austere, unloving home suffers from compounded pain. Because of the general personality prototype, he will respond by giving up even more.

If the parents of the sympath child are weak and ineffective and the child is aggressive and demanding and gets away with it, then he is going to be even more belligerent, more assertive, and more aggressive, and it will pay off. These tendencies will be further reinforced.

Why is it that 'sweet' people get cancer? Because they have largely given up on their own needs. They defer to others and try to please in every way possible to get even a semblance of love. They become very inoffensive, innocuous, pliable, undemanding, people. When this is compounded by the kind of school that repressive parents are likely to choose (such as military or religious school), the child will be repressed even further. He has almost no chance at all. By the time the child is ten years of age, he is a highly repressed individual. He is also a candidate for depression and immune diseases. The young body has the resources to combat this for many, many years, but as one grows older resistance fails.

A normalized balance between sympathetic and parasympathetic functioning is important for good health. When patients relive pain over time, thereby normalizing their metabolism, they demonstrate better health and a more balanced system. It is not done by an act of will. It happens automatically. The system has been 'righted'. The emotionally disturbed have often been called 'mentally unbalanced' and now we understand why.

Maryanne

As far back as I can remember I've been depressed. I was always withdrawn in school, never had many friends, never felt any great joy in anything and never had much energy. My father left my mother when I was six for another woman. They had two kids and he kind of forgot about me. He left me with a crazy mother whom I couldn't talk to at all. It seems like all of my life I've been waiting for my father to come back and have been carrying around a depression because I sensed that he wouldn't.

At my sister's wedding I fell into a deep depression because my father came. I hadn't seen him in three years and he barely said hello to me. I knew it was all over then. I've felt how hopeless it has been. I never had anywhere to go with my feelings so I kept them in all of my life. The more I get them out, the more I beg my daddy to come back, the better I'm beginning to feel.

I think I've been depressed from the start of my life. I was held back because they couldn't find the doctor when I was being born, and I've felt the futility of trying anything ever since. My pulse has been extremely low (around 45) all of my life and I think that is part of my not having any energy. I found it an effort to walk anywhere, like I'm dragging my body around. I think that everything shut down when I couldn't get out and somehow the exhaustion I felt in the birth struggle has dogged me ever after. That exhaustion and shut down just made me give up when my father left. I guess I was angry but I never expressed it; what was the use, he wasn't going to come back. 'What's the use', was my theme song.

The Sympath as Optimist

The adult sympath is clearly an optimist. He was from the day of his birth, and he had reasons to be. One might say that optimism either prevents cancer, or that once cancer has taken place, optimism helps produce remission of symptoms. But the truth is, it is not just an *attitude* of optimism but rather a *physiology* of optimism. Optimism is the psychological aspect of an entire agressive–assertive physiology. The cells, in their own way, are assertive and optimistic. They, too, are hard working, success-orientated and energetic, and in their conglomerate, shape a specific kind of personality. All of these varied reactions, physical and psychological, are the ramifications of the prototype. Drive, movement, and subsequent success are the hallmark of a sympath. Julie is a sympath who exhibits these traits.

Julie

When I was in Los Angeles, I couldn't wait to get out. I was feeling very overwhelmed by the situation I was in – my work, and my personal life – so all I could think about was getting away on a trip. But when I finally got away on the trip, I kept having the feeling that I had to get out of where I was – just as I had felt in Los Angeles. At first, there would be a sense of relief when I arrived somewhere because I had, in fact, acted out the feeling and got away. But after I had been there for a very short time, the feeling would come up again, and all I could think about was wanting to get away. So I would go on to the next place and after a short time, the feeling would come up again, and I would want to move on.

The feeling is the one I had at birth, which is, 'I have got to get out of here.' It's a terribly compelling feeling that drives me. I just want to go from place to place to get away from that bad feeling.

Yesterday I was in a tourist office buying a ticket, which meant that I was moving on, and I had a great sense of relief. But when I got home I realized, 'Well, I've done that', and then the feeling came up again. It seems like there is nothing I can do to get rid of that feeling except feel it. The minute I get to a new place, I'm okay for a while. And then the minute I am settled into that new place and routine begins, I am driven to move on.

It's the same with any kind of routine job; that's why I have always avoided anything that was routine. There is no movement in routine. A routine is a dead environment and that is what it must be like in the womb before you get the urge to be born. I've got a feeling that parasympaths probably respond much better to routine because they don't like change so much; maybe for them, change is the danger. No change for me was the danger.

The thing is, when you run away from something, it is always there when you get back, and actually, it is there when you get there as well. The more I move, the more the feeling moves with me. I am sure that if I had gone on being driven, I would have collapsed from a heart attack at a very early age.

The pressure is really a physical sensation. I am probably unconscious in some respects, but I am sure aware of the pressure. It is like you are driven in your body; that's why I can never sit still. I always have to be doing something. In the kitchen, I'm getting up, doing this, doing that, always moving. I guess moving meant life for me; at least it meant survival. What's awful about my situation is that I can't stand peace. Peace gets to be like routine. There is so much turbulence inside me that I have to get out and drive somewhere in order to get peace. The only peace I seem to know is in movement, so I can never relax and just rest.

Manic-Depression: The Origins of the Cyclic Personality

Manic-depressive neurosis is one of those mysteries that has become so unfathomable as to be laid to rest in genetic fields – attributed to inherited characteristics against which the sufferer can only take drugs such as Lithium. There may be some genetic factors, but my experience in the successful treatment of this problem has led me to doubt it.

I think that manic-depression (wide swings from manic excitement to the depths of depression) derives from a basic prototype of extended struggle with near success followed by abject failure of struggle at birth. A common example is struggling to get out against a tumour and the resultant Caesarean section. Or, the baby being held back during labour by a nurse who was waiting for the doctor to arrive. What this kind of birth does is stamp in a cyclic personality. The difference between this problem and the typical parasympathetic response is only one of the amount and extent of the struggle period – phase one. The manic-depressive has had a longer period of struggle at birth before catastrophe struck. The depressive parasympath did not have a chance for an extended active-manic phase.

Later in life, particularly when life is harsh and stressful, the cyclic prototype kicks in. First the person is engaged in wild struggles, uncontrolled impulsiveness, flights of ideas, cheque-writing and shopping sprees, writing reams of manuscript, etc. This is followed by utter despair, hopelessness, lack of energy and a feeling of 'what's the use?' These two phases are aspects of the same imprint. They mirror exactly what happened in the birth struggle. In the first phase there is activation, struggle and hope, where the person is desperately running from the possibility of death. The second phase is touching death and the terror of that experience. As one of these patients put it, 'I'm always afraid of feeling too good because disaster follows. I get a mild anxiety when I'm feeling great.' Another patient expressed the same apprehension differently: 'I try and try and then everything turns to shit.'

Because the imprint is ultimately a series of electrical impulses, manic impulsiveness is an electric overload driving the person here and there and everywhere. It is these amassed electrical charges occurring at a time when the cerebral cortex was still not fully formed, that produces a person later out of control. In the manic phase there is a dispersal of ideas which are scattered hither and yon because there is no cohesive neocortex to keep them in rein. The fact of constant upsurging massive first-line pain does not allow for the buildup of a cortical mind that is strong enough. Sometimes the person is lucky enough to develop a belief system to corral the flight of ideas. Indeed, the function of a belief system (particularly a mystical one) is to structure the fragmentation. This belief system will of necessity be inflexible and unyielding to fact because it is pressed into service to contain a rampaging force. In this sense, illusions are the medicine against feeling.

When the manic person spends his energy in the first phase and it avails him nothing (as it did originally) he slips into the depressive phase. He is now in touch with the imprint that he was running from in the first place. Death is now imminent. There is despair and futility and depression. Both phases spring from the same event. They are part of a single disease. Yet it turns out not to be a disease at all but rather a variation or exacerbation of the struggle and fail syndrome of the parasympath.

The reason that the birth imprint shapes all later reactions is, I repeat, because it is a life and death struggle that happens before the baby has seen the light of day, and it is a memory of survival.

Manic-depression differs from the usual depression in its inability to contain and repress on a continual basis. The depressive has suffered global repression and it works; there is no unleashing of the primal forces. Indeed, what characterizes depression is the absence of outlets. Manic-depression is very much like what happens in the sleep cycle; first there is a mind racing and an inability to fall asleep, then deep sleep characterized by deep repression, then repression diminishes and one rises to the dream level with agitation, thrashing about and wild dreams.

Manic-depression has been a mystery because its roots lie so far in the past, so unseen and unknown that heredity has seemed to be the only logical conclusion. The manic-depressives I have seen have almost invariably had the kind of birth trauma that I have described. It is a reversible affliction.

There is one neurosis – hundreds of manifestations but one basic cause – imprinted pain.

Marie

I am a twenty-five year-old woman. For years I attempted one task after another; I was convinced that I was 'chosen' to take on great projects that would better the condition of life around me, or that would make me a better person. 'Doing something with my life' was a mad, driven crusade that I began as a child and continued into adulthood in more subtle ways.

In high school I was an officer of every organization I could belong to; I wrote editorials for newspapers in order to be a 'good citizen'. To be 'artistic' I studied piano, singing, and dancing. In college I became a feminist, a mystic, and an organizer of a revolutionary theatre group in order to 'advance enlightenment'.

Most of my projects have failed. Even when they succeeded I always ended up being depressed, because I was never satisfied. I knew that I lived cycles of great activity followed by periods of depression, panic, or illness. The more obvious this became, the more I realized that I had no control of my life and would never be able to do anything I wanted until I could stop repeating myself. All this followed my birth – great activity – little success in making it – falling back into despair, wanting to give up and then trying again.

Jesse

I feel like I finally found out about the origin of several of my symptoms, including vertigo, nasal congestion and bronchitis. Along with getting rid of those symptoms, I have finally discovered why I hesitate and stand back all of the time. I've always felt like it's easier to get things done by being good and waiting patiently. I feel like ever since my birth, I have been afraid of any conflict that would arise if I were assertive.

I was a first-born child and my mother told me that my birth took a long time. I started to be born around 11 p.m. My mother said that she was very sleepy (evidently drugged), and the nurse had to keep waking her up to tell her to push. It is not surprising that I have had feelings about never getting any help from my mother from the very start of my life, and that I gave up trying in the birth because of this. Ever since, I seem to have been waiting for something to happen. Now that I have felt my birth, it seems like waiting was the only alternative I had to forging ahead and feeling the pain of not being helped. My first neurotic shutdown happened before I was born.

I am usually led to my feelings by specific symptoms that start to come up. One time I was working in a tall office building, thirty storeys high, and I had to run errands on different floors by using the elevator. I had always felt uneasy about elevators, but now the feelings became overpowering. I would imagine the chute of dark air under the elevator and feel so afraid that I was going to plunge down all the way to the bottom. I was terrified that the elevator would break and that I would get dizzy and sick, so much so that I would have to hold on to the sides of the elevator.

I began to feel like the fear was coming from somewhere else. One day in therapy I began to feel so alone when I remembered being left in a mental hospital by my father when I was twenty and how crazy it made me. The feeling went back to being a baby and screaming with terror. My body was rigid and awkward as though it were expressing the terror too. I then began to feel like I was falling backwards into a black void. This was the most terrifying sensation I've ever had. I was dizzy and totally disorientated, and I cried and screamed until finally the feeling subsided. During the feeling my legs went up over my head and when I finished my legs were halfway up the wall and I was practically upside down. I knew then what the feeling was. After I was born, somebody held me upside down and then I suddenly realized that my fear in the elevator was the same feeling.

It is interesting that a few months later I began feeling something slightly different. I developed a huge swollen gland in my neck that was so painful I had to go to an emergency ward. The doctor didn't know what had caused it, but a week later I began feeling like a tiny baby and I relived having fluid in my throat that was suffocating me. I cried and cried and retched; there was something in my throat that shouldn't have been there, and then the mysterious lump went away.

I've always had a stuffy nose until I had those feelings of trying to breathe when I got born. Now, for the first time in my life, I can lie in bed just breathing and enjoying the sensation of air rushing into my lungs. My lifetime stuffy nose has gone away, and so has my bronchitis.

I now know why under times of stress in my life (when my brother died and my father left home, for example) I would get an immediate bronchitis attack. I guess these experiences triggered an old birth trauma where I was trying to keep from dying with all that fluid in my windpipe.

Leslie

I consider myself a night person; I hate the day with its strong daylight. I usually get up in the morning as late as I can and go to bed very late so I can enjoy as many of those evening hours as possible. Every day starts in the same manner. Waking up in the morning is the worst moment of the day. I feel very bad and defenceless every morning, as if I have a long struggle ahead of me to pass the day and finally reach the evening where I know I am going to feel better. As the day goes by, I feel better and better. When night finally comes, I start feeling really good and safe. I reach a peak at bedtime – that moment when I slip into my bedsheets and feel the warmth and security of my bed gives me so much joy that I have feelings all over my body. Then I become very relaxed and sink into a forgetful sleep.

I never knew why each day of my life began like this or even that there was anything unusual about it until I felt a couple of birth feelings and became more conscious of how tremendously the imprint of my birth is affecting my everyday life. What I felt was a long and agonizing struggle. Incredible pressures smashing my head and back.

My mother wouldn't help me at all. I was stuck inside and could count only on myself to get out and live. So I did all the work myself, pushing and pushing for several hours until I completely exhausted myself, at which point I gave up because there was nothing else I could do and I was nearly dead with exhaustion.

I eventually got out alive. I'll always remember that one feeling when I am lying on my back, sucking my thumb and slowly going to sleep. The struggle is over. I made it! I'm out and I'm alive. I'm safe and now I can relax and let myself go to sleep and forget it all! That moment felt so good!

So I go through each day exactly the same way as I experienced my birth. In the morning the struggle is yet to come; my birth is beginning and I'm apprehensive. The closer I get to that moment when I can relax and go to sleep, the better and the safer I feel. As the evening comes and bedtime approaches, I feel more and more relaxed and safe. More and more myself, too. Later on, this pattern was reinforced by the fact that every evening before bedtime Daddy would give my sister and me one entire half hour of his valuable time, playing with us and telling us stories. That was the only half hour of the day when he would take care of us, and we really looked forward to it every day.

All of this made me a night person. It is truly amazing to me how my birth experience has had such a great impact on my everyday life, and also on the way I react to pain. When I am overwhelmed by pain, I become depressed and exhausted. Then I have only one desire – to get into bed and sleep it away!

The Predictability of Neurosis

The prototype helps make us predictable. It explains a host of behaviours and symptoms which, when taken as an ensemble, seem to be aspects of the same early experience.

For example, it is my observation that the way we get up each day is exactly how we first met the world at birth. Each and every day we re-create our birth in the manner in which we wake up. The parasympath meets each day as though she's just come out of an anaesthetic. She sleeps later, barely drags herself out of bed, and gets going much later in the day. She is a night person.

The sympath bolts from bed, ready to go. He becomes conscious and alert much more quickly than the parasympath. The sympath meets each day as though he's just been given five cups of coffee and a dose of amphetamines. In other words, the sympath is still very much galvanized, as he was at birth, and the parasympath is very much in a fog, as he was at birth. That is one reason why one of the hallmarks of the parasympathetic state is confusion. The parasympath never quite knows his own mind, never quite knows what to order until he finds out what everybody else orders, never quite knows what to do with his life. When we have examined the characteristic behaviour and personality of our patients we can fairly well postdict the kind of birth they have undergone. Contrarily, knowing the details of a person's birth is fairly predictive of the personality we shall encounter.

Michael

It was the day before I was going to leave therapy. I began to have feelings about how safe I have always felt in this room, and cried about not wanting to leave. And a strange new thing began to happen to me. It was as though everything went black and quiet and I was curled up in a ball, barely aware of anything. This safe feeling triggered a hellish process. I seemed to be in the womb, and my move to leave set off my birth process. It was a horrendous chain of events of agonizing pain; it seems like it was all bumpy and grindy, trying to get out.

I realize now why I had been so afraid to leave anything, including the Primal Institute. The Institute had been a place where I had been calm, safe and understood, and my move was like some terrible anxiety about waiting for some calamity to happen. I didn't realize that the calamity had already happened. After I had this feeling, I realized that it was not going to be very difficult to leave and that I could cope with leaving very easily. I know I am more relaxed now in a way that was probably impossible for me before. I can't emphasize enough this good feeling I have because it is the first time in my life I have ever felt calm and tranquil. I have a feeling that I wouldn't have lived very long, carrying that much pressure around in me all the time.

Jennifer

I have slowly begun to feel (after sixteen months of therapy) an early feeling which I believe rules my life and is at the basis of my neurosis. It is a feeling of constantly having to fight for my life – that I have to fight all the time to stay alive. It is a present-day reality for me to have to fight in my everyday life just to stay on my own two feet. My 'natural' (I should say neurotic) inclination is to just give up and not fight. It has constantly been that way for me. The cycle goes: fight, get nowhere, give up, want to die, not want to die, decide not to die, and fight again, get nowhere, and so forth. The cycle goes on and on. Along with this is the feeling that it doesn't matter what I do – I don't get anywhere, so why try, why fight? I might as well give up and die. But I want to live, desperately.

The more I take care of myself in the present the more I feel this feeling. Taking care of myself makes me feel how hard my aloneness is, and how there is no one to help. Getting my life together means starting to really live in the present and to feel the feeling of fighting to live as an old feeling.

The farthest I go back to feeling that fight to stay alive is to the age of one (except for a slight birth feeling I've had which I will speak of later). I feel like I am lying in the crib just waiting for my mother. I wait, and wait, and wait, but she never comes. And I want her so badly. After waiting for a while, I start to choke and gag, breathing heavily, and I feel like I am going to die if she doesn't come for me.

I feel so empty and I need something. I need my mother. I need to be taken care of. I feel this feeling in bits and pieces at various times. Often it is when a migraine is starting. Other times it is after I have an orgasm from sexual intercourse. Most times, the stronger the orgasm, the stronger the feeling. It seems as if pleasure brings instant pain. I often find myself holding back from fully enjoying the orgasm because of the pain it so often brings.

I still don't think my life is in good enough shape to feel the utter pain of this feeling. The migraine pain is pushing on me most of the time, telling me my pain is there.

So the stage I am at now is just being very angry at having had it so hard my whole life. I hate the fact that I have to fight to live. Lately, when I wake up, I have what I call an 'angry headache' within fifteen minutes. It is located in my left temple, eye, neck and shoulder. It is a similar pain to the migraines which I get on my right side, but a bit less intense. The first thoughts that enter my mind are, 'Here we go again, fight through another day'. I am angrier since I went on vacation to the Caribbean and had three wonderful days where I didn't have to fight. I just lived. And I realized what I missed out on my whole life. I think that once I get past this tremendous outrage, I will go deeper into the feeling on the way to resolving it.

Below the feeling of fighting to live is another feeling which I have experienced only slightly. I have gone back to the feeling of being stuck when I am being born. I have to fight my way out of the birth canal. Finally, my head is out, but the rest of me won't come out. This feeling is such an analogy to my life: my head is out – I'm always thinking, thinking – but the rest of me is inactive. My body doesn't feel connected. I so often live in my head, and only recently started to feel my body as part of me.

Back to the birth feeling: I feel stuck and my neck hurts. It hurts even as I write about this. It feels as if someone is pulling on my neck and it's very painful. My head is swaying from side to side and my voice lets out small wails of being very scared. Again, I am fighting for my life and it feels as if there is no help. I even have to be born on my own. My mother does not help me out. That has been a constant all my life from the very beginning – no help, fight on my own.

Why are very early traumas so directive of personality? First, this is not simply a *theory* about the effects of trauma. We have measured the effects of the birth trauma, both during the reliving process and later. We have reversed all manner of serious illness after patients have relived these earlier events (see my *Primal Man* for research data).

What is amazing about prototypic behaviour is that it is so enduring. It is as if all the intervening years, the decades of time, have not made a bit of difference. It goes on its merry way, dictating behaviour as if no other experiences ever occurred. Does experience change people? Once the prototype is set down, experience doesn't seem to have a significant impact. It either attenuates the potency of the prototype or it is reinforcing – but there is rarely any profound change. Personality, once formed, seems to have a rock-hard durability.

If there were a mass collective unconscious as Jung proposed, it most certainly would be due to the birth trauma. These traumas and those inside the womb are the most invisible, pervasive, the most damaging, and the most unconscious-engendering of life's events. We are constantly directed by them and have no idea that they even exist. One has to work under pressure, waiting until the last minute; one cannot stand any restraints, or will not recognize defeat – all birth analogues.

What lies in the unconscious is a reality that is so difficult to perceive, accept and understand, yet it is the most pervasive fact of our lives. It has brought about the 'plague of mass unconsciousness'. The other apparent plagues such as cancer, heart disease and mental illness simply follow. Now there is something we can do about it.

Judy

All my life I have felt my life slipping away. I've also tried to throw it away. At fourteen I worried about being an old maid of fifteen so I married at nineteen. Then I worried that I would be an elderly twenty-two before we could afford a baby. I had my first at twenty-one. We couldn't afford her. We couldn't afford the tiny coffin she was buried in. I worried about turning thirty and forty. Thanks to Primal Therapy I'm not worried about fifty. I do cry about the years stolen from me, but I don't panic. I tried to commit suicide twice. And, I'm still suicidal enough in a passive way that I can lie on the beach with my body drenched in sizzling sunshine, gently caressed by the occasional wind-blown salt spray and think what a beautiful day this would be to die. So nice to die on a day when I feel good.

I have a large head. My mother was barely five feet tall and she gave birth to an eleven-pound baby after a labour that went on so long we both should have died; I know I nearly did. I wanted to give up, but I couldn't. I nearly drowned in the fluid that had cushioned me. I suffocated while my head was pounding against my mother's pelvis. From that I got a pain in my neck, head and shoulder – a pain that sometimes makes my arms tingle to my fingertips. Even the small of my back hurts. The autopsy done on her after her death by abortion showed a sprung pelvis that never closed completely after my birth. Her family recalls that she walked 'funny' after I was born. I don't know how long it was after my birth before she walked at all.

I did finally get born by my own efforts; there was no one there for me; there was nothing there for me. All I had was my poor, unconscious mother. I was alive, and I had nothing. I feel hopeless a lot. If the tunnel with the daylight at the end is only a metaphor, why am I crying as I write these words?

Chris

I've only had birth feelings recently but they seem to explain a lot to me. I've caught a glimpse of the answers to a lot of questions I've been asking myself for the past ten or fifteen years. I am beginning to understand why I am the way I am. My birth was Caesarean and my mother tells me I didn't want to come out. I think and feel that I tried my best and hardest to be born but my mother tensed up and held me back. I must have tried so hard that I think I nearly died. Knowing the way my mother is, I am sure that her body tensed up out of fear and anxiety.

Everything has always been hard for me. The smallest tasks were frequently overwhelming for me (and sometimes still are). Physical situations are always extremely difficult. My body hurts very easily and it recovers from physical stress very slowly. I get overheated very easily. I sweat profusely and I hate it. I feel that my body is already working hard enough in just day-to-day living. When it comes to a job, I am straining myself physically and mentally to just 'make it'. (Maybe I've never fully recovered from being born.) I wet my bed almost every night until I was fourteen years old. I never understood why I did it or why my mother humiliated me for it.

My body has always felt weak, tense and tired. I think I am constantly stuck in birth feelings; therefore, I have no energy left to do anything else. There have been times when I feel like an old, worn out man ready to give up and die. I think I nearly died at birth. I have had a few dreams where I am suddenly facing certain death. I am usually falling, and the feeling so overwhelms me that when I wake up my heart is beating furiously and I am sure that what happened in the dream is true and real.

When I feel about my birth I am struggling in pain to get out. The only way I can relieve the pain is to scream my guts out in agony. I squirm, kick and shove my body head-first against the wall and my spine arches and tenses against the pain. I know now why my neck and back are always so stiff and tense.

I used to have a dream when I was very young that someone was sitting on my chest. The pressure in my chest comes back occasionally and then I know it is the birth pain coming up. I used to think I had an ulcer or something – the pain was so great.

I can remember as a teenager in high school always wishing I could start everything all over again: class, school days, assignments, school years, relationships with fellow students – my whole life! I wished that I could do it right this time. This hope was the only thing that kept me going. Instinctively, I knew that better parents and better circumstances would have made a world of difference. Unconsciously adopting this attitude, my miserable life was doomed to failure. Everything I tried to do failed miserably. There came a point when I just gave up even trying because I always expected the outcome to be the same. The story of my life is based on my beginning. My birth was hard – my whole life has been hard.

What is amazing about prototypic behaviour is that it is so enduring. It is as if all of the intervening years, the decades of time, have not made a bit of difference. It goes on its merry way, dictating behaviour as if no other experiences ever occurred. Does experience change people? Once the prototype is set down, experience doesn't seem to have a significant impact. It either attenuates the potency of the prototype slightly or it is reinforcing – but there is rarely any profound change.

If there were a mass collective unconscious, as Jung proposed, it most certainly would be due to the birth trauma.

Birth and traumas inside the womb are the most invisible, the most damaging, and the most unconscious-engendering.

What lies in the unconscious is a reality that is difficult to perceive, accept and understand, yet it is the most pervasive fact of our lives. The plague of mass unconsciousness has resulted in catastrophic diseases such as cancer, heart disease and mental illness. Now there is something we can do about it.

PART TWO
The Forms of Neurosis

10

Stress, Anxiety, and Tension:
Symptoms of Disease

Stress, anxiety and tension have a lot in common. In fact, anxiety is the key form of stress in our lives; and tension is what we do with anxiety. On the phylogenetic scale anxiety comes long before tension, is more primitive and comes from a different area of the brain. Is there normal anxiety? Do we need a bit of anxiety to succeed in life? We shall examine these symptoms and their origins from a rather different perspective from the conventional view.

What is Stress?

There is a great deal of discussion about stress today. Job stress, marital stress, parenting stress, and financial stress are all given thorough treatment in both popular magazines and scientific journals. Unfortunately, stress itself is rarely defined. When we use the term stress we are usually referring to something that makes us 'nervous' or puts us under pressure. Stress is really a mind-body response to events which cause alarm and put a person on a state of alert.

Hans Selye, an authority on stress, has identified three stages in the stress response: (1) alarm, (2) resistance, and (3) exhaustion.

In the alarm stage, a person recognizes the stress and what

211

appears to be causing it and prepares for action, to either fight or escape (the well-known fight or flight response). At this point many of the familiar indicators of stress are experienced. Irritability and hyper-excitation, pounding of the heart, dryness of the mouth, trembling, and grinding of the teeth are such indicators. People under stress are easily startled. They suffer from insomnia, perspiration, the need to urinate frequently, diarrhoea and indigestion, and muscle pain in the neck and lower back. And this is only the beginning of the list. The damage to the body which occurs in the first stage of stress can be repaired. But the pain associated with the alarm stage can form an imprint just as any other trauma can.

If the stress continues, the stress response moves beyond resistance and into exhaustion. Now the body can no longer repair the damage, and chronic stress-related disorders are likely to occur. The long term deleterious effects of stress are being elaborated constantly in medical research. Stress, for example, now appears to play a role in elevated levels of cholesterol. Stress also inhibits immune functions, increases susceptibility to virus-related diseases, and facilitates tumour development – all matters we will raise again in the context of our discussion of disease and the immune system.

The Fight or Flight Response

The first stage stress response of fight or flight is an attempt to ensure survival. It makes the system 'combat ready'. If fight is possible the response mode is aggression. If fight is not possible, then the mode of response indicated will be flight, fear and escape.

What is rarely discussed and less understood is the primary internal stress that resides within the system at all times – the enduring stress of engraved pain. Imprinted pain can keep the body on alert even when there is no external reason for doing so. Stress hormone levels can rise, along with blood pressure, body temperature and heart beat. Immune surveillance is diminished. The system is responding to an event from the past as if it were happening in the present. And, in a real way, it is.

Suppose baby sister sees Daddy administering a severe beating to older brother. The feeling, inarticulated, is that 'Daddy is violent'. 'Daddy can kill'. 'Daddy can kill me if I get out of line'. Thereafter, there will be continuous fear and apprehension, and specifically fear of father, whom the baby senses as a violent threat.

At this point, gating and repression begin. Noradrenalin pathways inform the entire brain of the need to mobilize in the face of this stress reaction. Serotonin, another class of inhibitory neurojuices, and endorphines rush in to try and hold down the pain. The person is now under imprinted stress. The outside has become inside. Fear of Daddy and his violence do not go away, both because the terror is so great, and because Daddy himself remains. He is there every day as a reminder to stay in line, to hide feelings, and to passively obey.

If there are enough terrifying situations in baby's life, if Daddy really turns his violence against her, and if mother is weak and of no support, repressing transmitters cannot do an effective job and baby will become a nervous apprehensive child, frightened of almost everything. Such a child will suffer from what we earlier referred to as 'leaky gates'; defective repression.

Stress means that the system is under assault, whether it be via an attack from a dog, a reprimand from mother, or the administration of too many inoculations at one time. The body will prepare for fight or flight, and all of its sub-systems will gear up for this eventuality. The dog who bites us, the heavy traffic that makes us late, and the authoritarian teacher are all temporary stressors which we recover from relatively soon. Even a stressor like an unpleasant job is likely to last no more than a few months. But a teacher, for example, who is severe and unrelenting when we are attending our first class at the age of six can leave a lasting stressful impact. If the child does not have the wherewithal to handle this kind of traumatic stress, it is likely to be imprinted and to affect all later learning.

The principle that current stress mobilizes imprinted past stress was clearly embodied in our earlier example of the woman who received many inoculations at once. Her body regularly developed a fever based on an attack from long ago. The inoculations revived the imprint of trauma which had to be relived; the original situation was reawakened as the body attempted once again to master it.

This is what happens to trauma. It forces us to deal with it one way or another throughout our lives. One patient, for example, was a stockbroker who gambled heavily and obsessively on the market, even when he did not have sufficient financing. He had to win, and he tried even when the odds were against him. Unconsciously, for him to lose was to die. His obsessive gambling was simply a symbolic substitute for his past imprint – the near-death experience at birth, accompanied by the same panic and frenzy which now characterized his speculative behaviour. Gambling didn't put stress on him; he put stress on the gambling.

The loss of a boyfriend now can be catastrophic when coupled with the loss of a father at the age of six. The defence system can no longer cope with its doubled load of stress, and fails to hold down the pain. What ensues is active anxiety, tension, depression, inability to concentrate or function, and, in general, a collapse of the normal personality.

It is rare that current stress alone will have such an impact unless it is of such extraordinary power that it can be equated with the life-long potency of imprinted stress. Certainly, if an adult lost all of his family in a car accident, the power of that event would be enormous, and could put him under the kind of chronic stress I am discussing. If one's childhood history is rather benign, it is unlikely that any current adult stress will cause a breakdown of the system into neurosis.

Pain is the key stressor. Not all stress is composed of pain, but certainly, all pain is stressing. An adult who is deep into a childhood feeling of utter hopelessness, or of never being loved, is in great danger. This is because for a very young child, love means life. Children cannot simply go on sensing hatred and feeling unloved at the ages of three and four. When these truths threaten to enter consciousness everything is mobilized against this. Under these conditions, it is imperative to remain unconscious.

The Stress Syndrome

Most of us can function on a day-to-day basis when we only have to deal with the pain of our past stress. We do it with smoking, drinking, tranquillizers, and so on. But when something devastating in the present resonates with something in our past, we suffer from the 'stress syndrome'. It is then that it is recommended that one leave one's spouse and leave one's job to go to another city, because the current situation is seen as the whole cause of the breakdown. In reality, the current situation probably has a valence of three as opposed to a valence of ten from the original trauma.

Imprinted stress is the most insidious form of stress because it is intangible. It cannot be seen, smelled or felt. It cannot be pinpointed or found in any one cell. It lives its life stealthily gnawing at our foundations like termites, destroying the structure of our house, so that we imagine we are fine right up until the structure crumbles.

People who are sick look sick. The reason they look sick is because they are under stress from a virus, a bacteria, a tumour, or whatever is stressing the system. Looking sick is part of the stress syndrome. Neurotics can look sick too, but because of a different stimulus. They are not invaded by viruses. They are invaded by pain. Consider the following:

Sick at Heart: Roseanne

I used to be assaulted by terrible anxiety attacks. Since the age of fifteen, I have lived in the dreaded fear of having a heart attack. Every time I had the anxiety attacks I would feel panicky, weak, sweaty, and become pale and sometimes faint.

There are no words to describe the loneliness and helplnessness I felt in those moments. I would feel that there was no hope left for me. I was bound to suffer. Those attacks became the symbol of my hopelessness.

I don't have the attacks any more, and the reason is simple. I don't build up overwhelming stress and anxiety. If something hurts me now, I cry or get angry. I react to it and let it out instead of keeping it in like before. My chest used to be a pressure cooker. My unexpressed feelings would create so much pressure in my chest that I would actually experience the symptoms of a heart attack. All those feelings inside me trying to get out, pushing against my chest and making me feel 'I'm going to die ... without love'.

Now I let the stream out. It has felt so good to cry about my father – the need for him to talk to me, to touch me, and help me, all the things I had been deprived of. Every time I cry about my needs I get more in touch with myself and I become less tense. It sounds strange, but the truth is that feeling the pain actually helps me to reduce the stress, strain and awful anxiety in my life.

The Nature of Anxiety

Whereas the stress response is a feeling of being constantly under pressure, anxiety is an immediate, diffuse, debilitating fear, an anticipation of some impending danger and a feeling that one cannot deal with even the smallest of things. Of the two, anxiety is the more acute, the more immediate, and the more harrowing.

The symptoms of anxiety are clear. There is the terrible, amorphous feeling of nameless dread; a sense of impending doom together with a racing heart. There is also a wobbly, shaky feeling, accompanied by chronic sleeplessness. There may be 'butterflies in the stomach', choking and smothering sensations, and feelings of being crushed. There is often the feeling that one is going crazy. The system is totally galvanized, and nothing seems to calm it.

Although anxiety is the central focus of many psychotherapies, it is perhaps the least understood of all psychiatric phenomena. Carol Tavris, writing in *Science Digest* (February 1986, p. 46) says that anxiety disorders 'may be the most common mental health problem in the United States today'. The National Institute for Mental Health believes that anxiety is the number one mental health problem for women, and number two for men. Clearly, the incidence of anxiety has reached epidemic proportions.

What professionals seem to know about anxiety with any certainty is that it can be diminished with tranquillizers and pain-killers. This is a clear indication that anxiety is somehow related to pain.

When we turn our attention to the question of the physiological character of anxiety we find that recent research has provided some interesting clues. Pure terror seems to be organized in several places low in the neuraxis, including the aforementioned locus ceruleus. Deep in the brain stem is also where we believe that early traumas are registered. Electronic stimulation of the locus ceruleus produces what seems to be an aggravated anxiety attack – pure, nameless, ineffable terror. It is a state without words.

Anxiety is an instinctive mechanism for survival. It is a form of terror, a terror that has no rational stimulus in the present. Clearly, it comes from the past, often without warning. The question is, 'What is it?' To understand anxiety we shall have to quickly review early imprints.

Anxiety is primarily a visceral reaction involving the heart, lungs, colon, stomach, and urinary tract. These organs are known as mid-line responses and are the first to mature during development in the womb. Events in the womb and during birth are registered in the nervous system that controls these visceral organs. That is, we react with the most adequate nervous system available when trauma strikes. What is available and is fully adequate during our womb life is the mid-line nervous system; i.e., the first line.

We know that the typical anxiety reactions are early because of the visceral reactions, such as 'butterflies' in the stomach, difficulty in breathing, palpitations, the need to urinate frequently, dizziness, diarrhoea, and hyperventilation.

Anxiety is a first-line phenomenon. It begins its existence as a reaction to real events that were life-endangering. It feels exactly like what the foetus and newborn were feeling originally. It is global and nameless, because the foetus and neonate do not have words. This is coupled with a feeling of impending doom. Anxiety is no more than the precise response to the early trauma now filtered.

Anxiety will occur later in life depending on three factors: (1) that life experience is so damaging that the overall defence system is faulty and it cannot contain the early terror, (2) a person takes drugs, such as LSD which interfere with a cohesive third-line functioning, so that the defences cannot hold back that very same terror, and (3) something in the present resonates strongly with an original feeling (as, for example, an original desperate helplessness).

The anxious person anticipates doom. The doom is looming *now* as an imprint because the person has no knowledge of the memory at is at a loss to understand what he is suffering from. The doom is ancient history. One thing is certain: a present feeling always has an origin somewhere. We just need to find where.

The reason that anxiety is a survival mechanism is that it warns and mobilizes the system into action against a perceived threat. The terror that is at the base of anxiety is *always there.* It is only when the defence system weakens that it manages an occasional trip to the surface. That is why some painkilling drugs manage to handle anxiety effectively.

What these drugs do, by and large, is alter the transmission ability of the neurons to send messages of pain to higher centres. They usually affect the reticular activating system down low in the brain, which is in charge of alerting the entire brain to danger (discussed in a moment). The drugs cut the message off 'at the pass' and thus the mind is not flooded with impulses over which it has no control. The drugs affect the lower centres but have a profound affect on thought processes; this is one more way we know about where the force that drives the cortical, thinking mind comes from.

Another way we know about the source of the racing mind, bizarre ideas and scattered thought patterns is when the patient relives those very early traumas and all of that automatically ceases. With it goes the periodic, sudden bouts of anxiety that have plagued the person for years.

In our therapy, when early pains are rising towards consciousness, there is almost invariably an anxiety attack. The terror involved in anxiety is *consciousness*. Early conscious connection meant feeling the complete abject terror. That is why, when feelings are on the rise, producing an anxiety state, there is often a heartbeat of over 200, a blood pressure also over 200, and signs of an organism in great danger.

A newborn strangled on the cord is terrified. There is no comprehension, just pure terror. He reacts with the capacity he has. The heart is pumping, the temperature is rising, hormones are churning, all of which we see when we lift the lid of repression in our therapy. This is a state of anxiety. That is how we know what anxiety is and where it comes from.

All anxiety is free-floating at the time of the trauma; it is neither conceptualized, nor understood. There were no possible defences against it. Death lay just beyond. Later, with the capacity to focus and symbolize we can channel anxiety. It can become a phobia – a focused anxiety attack. Too often, the phobia is then treated as if it were the real problem.

Phobia clinics abound in the United States. Phobia is a

problem that can be controlled by avoiding the situation. And that current situation is nearly always a symbol for the original trauma. Thus, the fear of elevators (the fear of being contained, crushed, squeezed, having insufficient air, being unable to see out, etc.) is a way of manipulating an original trauma symbolically. That is usually the *raison d'être* for phobias.

A very traumatic birth process with long labour may show itself in the form of a fear of leaving any comfortable place; hence the later phobia of leaving home. It is a fear of 'going out'. The thought of leaving home makes the phobic person react as if an electrode were placed on the locus ceruleus.

In everyday life, this kind of phobic-anxiety is controlled in small imperceptible ways, such as not going out to meet people, not trying new things, not leaving the situation you're in – be it a job or a marriage – no matter how painful. This is because unconsciously there is more pain involved in leaving than in staying. Leaving triggers off the original primal event with all of its terror. Not being outgoing can be an aspect of this same problem.

I once treated a jet pilot for a phobia he developed in cloud banks. When he put himself back mentally into the clouds he became terrified. He could not sense motion. He spent hours and hours reliving a birth trauma where not being able to move (he was blocked by a tumour in the canal) meant death. Cloud banks simply triggered the old fear.

One could have analyzed this terror for months on end without relating it to its true cause. Birth was never even suggested to him, (who could have dreamed that up?) but the technique of mentally placing himself back in the cloud banks elicited an early sensation that was pure dread. Giving himself over fully to that dread put him back into the original terror.

One should not treat a phobia as a thing unto itself any more than one should treat a dream that way. The story in the dream is the mind's way of explaining the fear. Artists use images to paint their fears. The same is true with phobias. What is important to understand, however, is that the feeling in a dream or phobia is always right. The story is symbolic. Go after the feeling, not the apparent focus.

Anxiety, Repression and the Defence System

While it is the early subcortical brain mechanisms which are involved in the origins of anxiety, it is the neocortex that provides its appreciation and its awareness. If it were not for the cortex, our reactions to both anxiety and stress would be purely instinctive. Instead, we have the capacity to block the danger signals and act as if we are not in danger. When we deaden ourselves against anxiety, we lose the capacity to feel, and thus we lose some of our humanity.

Anxiety is a danger signal. It is not neurotic in and of itself. There is no 'anxiety neurosis'. It is an appropriate fear wedded to a memory. When that memory comes too near to awareness so does anxiety, and primitive visceral defence mechanisms are mobilized. In fact, feeling anxious is the opposite of neurosis. It is feeling the actual terror, albeit out of context. Placing anxiety in its original context is resolving.

Anxiety, as we can see, has a double function. It warns and it is also the visceral component of the early terror. When the combined pain of current stress and past imprint are too great, the serotonin-endorphine supplies become exhausted and we experience anxiety directly and consciously. This warns us that our defences are crumbling. The signal is to 'take a pill to enhance the endorphine stock'.

There are backup systems which protect us from feeling anxiety. What we know to be neurosis is comprised largely of these defences. More specifically, these backup systems aid in the repression of pain and gating. Most people can usually compartmentalize their terror and hold it in storage down deep in the neuraxis. They don't have to think about it all the time. The anxious person, however, has lost this capacity. His warehouse is filled, and then some. The terror travels, finds outlets, and is channelled. Meanwhile, it is the worst of feelings for the sufferer, because he doesn't know what it is, where it comes from, or how to stop it. He just feels awful most of the time.

Those who don't repress well are sometimes known as 'anxiety neurotics'. They're just not good at being neurotic. If you take a well repressed individual and give him an injection of naloxone, which antagonizes the inner painkiller, endorphine, he will immediately become anxious. Naloxone doesn't produce anxiety. It undoes gating and allows us to feel what is already there. If you gave a normal person a shot of naloxone I doubt if he would experience anxiety.

What this discussion indicates is that once the repressive process is weakened, the system tends to return to its *normal* state – fearful and terrorized. The anxious one does not have to be made aware. The fear intrudes into his awareness constantly. The problem is to make him unaware – to cap the fear and put it away for a while, or make him conscious – allowing the terror in bit by bit for resolution.

What Sets Off Anxiety?

It often takes a present stimulus to set off the old imprint and its anxiety. At other times no stimulus is required. This happens when a person's life has been unusually harsh – when a child has been unable to develop defences to protect himself. It also happens when someone has taken drugs, such as marijuana, hashish or LSD, which interfere with psychological defences. The chronic use of such drugs weakens the gating system in the brain, and permits the escape of memories ordinarily deeply repressed.

I saw a Vietnam veteran who suffered chronic anxiety states for fifteen years after the war. He came close to death on the battlefield, an experience which reawakened memories of almost drowning in a bathtub at the age of one. After the war, he took LSD at least fifty times. At that point, his system no longer had the means to defend against his combined terrors, which seeped up constantly.

He was vulnerable to combat neurosis because it reso-nated with a past event. That doesn't mean that combat itself has no effect. Not everyone in combat suffers equally, however. The more combat resonates with past life-threat-ening events, the greater the toll it takes. Combat can leave one very shaky and nervous for a long time afterwards but it will not shape a new neurosis.

We mustn't forget about critical periods. Trauma during those periods generally shapes personality. A great trauma later on can make one anxious for a time, but it is not likely to produce a new neurosis. There is the notion, for example, that Hollywood and its pressure destroys some actresses. I think it is far more likely that destroyed people seek that environment because their need is so great that only millions can fulfil it. That atmosphere serves to reinforce their neuroses.

Anxiety and Obsessive Compulsive Neurosis

We have all heard about the man who has to wash his hands forty times a day; someone else who cannot step on the cracks of the pavement; someone else still who has to check the locks in the house twenty times a day. These are all examples of obsessive-compulsive neurosis. They are repeti-tive behaviours that are seemingly out of control.

Obsessive-compulsiveness is really not a special category of neurosis. It is only the way it is manifest. All neurosis is obsessive in the sense that we repeat patterns over and over again throughout our lives without being able to control them. The smoker takes a cigarette every forty minutes all day every day. The nymphomaniac or satyr is constantly in search of a sex partner. A person acts shy time and time again, no matter what the circumstances. The difference is that these behaviours expand over time and are not the controlled, ritualistic, transient behaviours of the obsessive.

The obsessive has managed to find a well-circumscribed behaviour, no different from the sexual pervert who has found a ritual that offers him release. The ritual depends on two factors. The first is life circumstance – growing up with a fanatical mother who insisted that the children wash after touching the dog, the door, the chair, etc. The second is that the ritual must reflect back to a basic feeling; i.e., feeling dirty (in the broad sense of the term) and the need to feel clean constantly. An obsession that 'sticks' is one that manages to reduce the tension level. If you feel unsafe and afraid you check the locks and it makes you feel less afraid. As fear mounts, you check the locks more and more. The ostensible fear is of intruders. The real fear is from growing up with parents who never made you feel safe.

To understand obsessive-compulsiveness we need to return to the fact that very early trauma is not only registered in the low neuraxis, but tends to move towards consciousness at all times for resolution and release. We're always trying to be normal. One of the key structures in the brain stem that activates is called the reticular activating system. This vigilance or alerting system gathers all of the sensory input, both from outside and from the input of the imprints, and sends it to the cortex, first by way of the limbic system. Until it arrives at the limbic system the voltage it deals with is nonspecific; it is a quantity of energy or activation. The limbic system gives it emotional content.

The reticular activating system has long projecting fibres to the neocortex so that as soon as very early trauma begins its move to consciousness, the high level mind is aware of being uneasy, agitated and uncomfortable. It is a necessary state because the lower mind is saying, 'get ready for the assault'. Anxiety begins its life.

As the pressure of the imprints mounts so does the reticular pressure. It moves against cortical inhibiting forces. We now have a clash between inhibition by the frontal cortex (feeling hopeful) and the ascending impulses of early pain in the brain stem (feeling hopeless). Obsessions indicate a failure of inhibition. If you give drugs to quell the reticular upswell, you manage to reduce that conflict and the person feels more at ease. If you don't, the person is forced to intensify his obsessive acts or thoughts to try to contain the rising force. The cortex is pressed into service with greater and greater urgency.

There is a hierarchy of mental as well as physical symptoms. The symptoms seem to follow the evolution of the human being. Pure anxiety is a first-line affair. Phobias, the use of imagery to contain and capture the pain and terror, is second-line. They rush in to stop the overflow of Primal energy from early trauma. When phobias fail we may find obsessive ideas – third line.

These are increasingly sophisticated ways to handle the same pain, not different diseases. Finally bizarre notions and paranoid ideas are enlisted on the same level when obsessive ideas strain the defence system beyond its capacity. It is the shift from neurosis to psychosis. It is the evolutionary shift from primitive anxiety mechanisms to the latest in man's brain capacity – paranoia. Paranoia is an advanced form of thinking.

Here we see how neurosis is a defence against psychosis in the same way that symbolic dreams help prevent terrifying nightmares. The anxiety-ridden person usually cannot manage to enlist symbolic dreams to defend himself against the nighttime anxiety attacks which are nightmares; in the same way during the day he cannot manage to have a well structured defence system. Nothing he did in life 'worked' to allow him to escape anxiety and nothing he does at night will work either. A well-put together dream means, by definition, that structures are in place to symbolize feelings. It is no accident that schizophrenia is rare in epileptics. So long as one can discharge built-up pressure in a massive way, then the top level consciousness doesn't have to stretch itself into the bizarre to cope with it. We are going to discover that nearly everything we deal with is but one disease. It just travels.

Every level of conscious development has its own peculiar

kind of symptom; this is true in the physical sphere as well as the psychologic. The difference between diarrhoea and arthritis is a long phylogenetic leap.

In a phobia an image of a snake is enough to set off an anxiety response. You don't need any image at all for anxiety, which is a non-imagery, non-verbal state. Imagery is a later development to fixate the anxiety in time and space. Phobias are largely the property of the second-liner whose whole development seems to have been arrested before the intellectual stage. The phobic can avoid his target and not feel anxious. The obsessive is not so lucky. The anxious obsessive must avoid himself; not so quickly done.

Those who are able to develop past adolescence without overwhelming anxiety can manage to live in their head and produce obsessive ideas. These basically third-liners have less access to their feelings than the phobic. The second-liner, living on the level of images and dreams is more musical, artistic, less philosophic but more emotional and less controlled than the third-liner. The advantage of being a second-liner is that he can learn foreign languages easier. He can hear the nuance of sound and the musical tone in a language. He surely cannot learn maths as well as the third-liner; and certainly never physics.

The second-liner could just never get a good third line going due to the constant assault on it by lower level imprints. The obsessive is trying mightily to use thinking to control and cage a monster that doesn't submit easily to containment. Flimsy ideas, no matter how repetitive, are a weak match for massive imprinted lower level trauma.

As obsession-compulsion intensifies (because the impulses moving upward are incredibly strong) but finally ceases to work, we have a decompensating defence structure which can ultimately lead to psychosis. Now we have bizarre notions as the cortical mind is stretched to the maximum by the mounting early pain. It is not a difference in kind. It is using the same cortical apparatus to handle the pain and terror. Because there is a total breakthrough of early material the psychotic is plunged into the remote past. The disparity between that past, and present reality, is greater, leaving the impression of a strange mind.

We can illustrate all this through electroencephalographic (brain-wave) measurements. The resting brain-wave pattern generally reflects the activation-inhibition struggle. A new patient can show an EEG of nearly two hundred microvolts, and months later bring it down to thirty. Clearly, the activation and pressure on the cortex is far less. When it is high, one could expect obsession and compulsions, just as one could expect other symptoms of overload, from epilepsy to tics. Anything that stimulates brain-stem activity, from caffeine to amphetamines, puts more pressure on the cortex, finally resulting in a possible psychosis. The upward pressure of early pain tends to use up serotonin.

Serotonin is a key chemical agent in the armory of repression. It is spread throughout the brain but there are clusters of serotonin-producing cells along the mid-line of the brain stem. From there they travel (sending networks of fibres) where needed, not the least of which is the limbic system.[1]

There is a drug called Ecstasy or MDMA which is rather popular these days. Those who take it find that they are truly in ecstasy. Why? Because they can feel again. They are euphoric because they are finally in touch with themselves. The drug releases enormous amounts of serotonin, and lowers inhibition. The problem is that in very high doses it can kill serotonin cells; and in very rare instances it can kill the person. Ecstasy does allow some great insights because the defence system is interrupted and there is access to the feeling level. Despite these insights, and despite the profound change the person thinks he has undergone, the change is temporary. The pain has not gone away; one has simply bypassed it for the moment. There is a way to accomplish all

---

1. For a discussion of how serotonin works please see *Science News*, Vol. 136, article by Ron Cowen, Receptor Encounters, Oct. 14, 1989 No. 16, pages 248–250.

this in a natural way; for if you don't you've got to go on taking drugs such as Ecstasy. If done naturally you recapture yourself permanently.

Serotonin's role in inhibition is found in diverse research. One interesting study done at the National Institute on Alcohol Abuse and Alcoholism in Finland found that murderers were very low in serotonin. These people had minimal inhibition going on and all of their impulses were acted out. If they could have had a good obsessive ritual going for them they might not have killed. Alas, the general harsh life many of them led, did not allow for the development of obsessions. Violent suicide cases also had low serotonin supplies. And it seems to be low in Alzheimer cases.

I have often wondered if early first line pressure over decades on critical brain cells had something to do with Alzheimer's disease. One has to first see that pressure in action during Primals to understand what it might be doing to brain cells.

I would speculate that what might happen during a traumatic birth is that the neurotransmitter apparatus that produces serotonin and endorphine is damaged or compromised in some way. Thus, later on it cannot produce what is required for effective repression. The person deficient in inhibitory neurohormones, given an unloving early environment, is the one who is likely to be a candidate for chronic anxiety attacks later in life; not to speak of serious mental illness. It is a double bind: the trauma that damages repressive transmitter output is also the same trauma that requires more repression throughout life.

What most tranquillizers do is 'smooth' out the person deficient in opiates. These drugs are taken to allow a person to 'feel himself' (literally), since one effect of them is to allow the person to enter the feeling zone (where the real self lies). Tranquillizers bring the opiate levels back to optimum. They help transform a chronic malaise into a state of relative comfort. If a person is deficient in thyroid it is not opprobrious to take thyroid, but if the deficiency is in painkillers there is a certain queasiness about taking them. It is taken as a mark against character.

The so-called 'addictive personality' is someone who has found a drug (be it alcohol or hard drugs) that helps him feel 'normal' again; helps him feel at ease and relaxed, perhaps for the first time in his life. If he never tried these drugs he wouldn't be called 'addicted'. It is a great discovery for this person to find something that makes up for a chronic physical deficit; something that finally can make him feel half-way decent again. There is this notion that once an alcoholic or addict always one. That even one drink, for example, can set off the addiction again. And that's true. So long as there is a physiologic deficit of the serotonin/endorphine supplies the body will need something. There is a real need for alcohol or drugs. To be more exact, the real need in childhood which went unfulfilled, has been transformed into a real need to quell the pain of its deprivation. When the pain is removed and the system equalized it is no longer a problem. That is easier said than done; for not every person can again normalize once there is a damaged or dysfunctional repressive system. Happily, however, most of those I have seen can normalize.

In the absence of the removal of pain the best that can happen to a suffering adult is to try to fulfil the lacks in his childhood; to find a support group which is understanding, tolerant, with whom one can express one's feelings and problems. A family substitute, if you will. It is even more helpful if the group provides an ideational system that bolsters the defence. It really doesn't matter about the content of the ideation so long as it reassures, bolsters, supports, makes the person feel not alone, helps him to think that there is a higher power who will help him, etc. Those beliefs must run counter to the unconscious pain – 'I'm all alone, I've never had any help, no one cares, there was and is no one to support and guide me'. Those are the real feelings resulting from thousands of childhood experiences. That is why so many of the support groups embrace religious tenets.

Often, the religious ideation alone is enough because one can *imagine* that there is someone watching over, that 'I am in his hands', that he will take care and help, etc. Needs force the imagination of fulfilment because fulfilment is the only thing that can ease a chronic malaise. That is the function of belief systems; they manufacture a fulfilment that doesn't exist to balm the unconscious need. They attempt to normalize.

The very feelings that result in a depletion of the repressive chemicals – no one cares – I'm not loved – are hopefully countered by opposing notions that will bolster those same juices. Attendance at support groups with its special ideation is as addictive as the drugs previously taken. It must go on for years because the basic unfulfilled need is always there unfelt. Same addiction, different form. There is simply no way to fulfil an old need in the present. The 'therapy' these addicts get in groups is implicit in the same way that someone can go to an analyst for years trying to fulfil old needs by having a person there on call who cares, understands, listens, empathizes and focuses on the patient first and foremost. The person goes through the motions of understanding, developing insights, analyzing dreams and adopting special lingo and therapeutic ideation while on a lower level trying to have real needs fulfilled (symbolically). What is truly addicting in these therapies is the semblance of fulfilment within the therapeutic situation. The therapy will be as interminable as the unfulfilled need.

The impulse neurotic, low in inhibition, seems to act out in many ways including criminality. He impulsively reaches for drugs because he needs an immediate fix. His system, as with all neurotics, is trying to stabilize. It needs repression. He is put in jail for trying to kill his pain. We put people away for taking drugs which often have the same effect as tranquillizers because they are not prescribed by the right people.

No one takes drugs such as heroin if they don't need it. They need it because they 'need'. The 'IT' comes later when real need is long buried.

The newest 'hot' drugs for the treatment of this obsessive

disease, which, I repeat, is not some special disease, but only an indication of the state of the gates, are serotonin enhancers. Their true function is to strengthen neurosis, not produce a cure. Obsessives are trying to have a good neurosis but they can't quite make it. Prozac is now being given to patients at one million prescriptions a month. It seems like half the population is on drugs these days.

The obsessive-compulsive is attempting to control his anxiety. If he did not carry out the ritual and did not bind the upcoming energy, he would be naked before the onslaught and find himself overwhelmed with anxiety. His racing thoughts, as he tries to fall asleep, are the way the mind races away from the pain. It must do this because there is so much nonspecific input all at once that there is no chance for full integration. When we take those same high level valence early pains and integrate them, we see, at the same time, a lower resting EEG, (a calmer brain) and diminishing obsessions.

What should be clear is that you cannot talk someone out of his obsessive ideas (or his phobias) because they have nothing to do with the rational cortex except insofar as it is the handmaiden of the impulses from below, obliged to do their bidding.

Sylvia

I have always lived by lists. I have a general one for use day by day, and another one for weekends. Despite this seeming organization, I am a messy person. I never feel 'caught up' or that I have it all together. My purse is jam packed with 'essentials' which I almost never need but can't let go of. Because I never was taken care of as a kid, my father left us and mom went to work, I never developed a trust in myself. I don't trust myself to remember and I'm terrified to make a mistake; so I compile list after list, but usually manage to lose or misplace them. At least, lists reassure me.

I am upset if someone comes early or unexpectedly. It disturbs my routine. I don't easily adapt to change. I need warning – like I didn't get when I was born, experiencing excruciating pain. I need to feel in control of every situation.

My preset ideas take precedence over my feelings. I need to have a certain regimentation and will stick to something no matter what the inconvenience or discomfort. I hate and love rules. I detest unstructured social situations where I might meet strangers and don't know what to say. I fear that I can't gauge how I or they will react (and then I feel stuck as I was originally at birth, and later in my crazy home).

My constant worry is not being able to take care of things properly. It is part of the helplessness I felt as a child. In school I worried all of the time – about losing my books, umbrella, keys, etc. I needed my mother to help me and make me feel secure. She was away at work, leaving me feeling like it was all too much for me to take care of myself. I was too little.

When I receive instructions it must be absolutely clear and precise and in logical order. I always have to start at 'A' if I'm interrupted. When my teacher told me something nice I felt desperate, like I couldn't hold onto his words. So I wrote them down and kept them in my purse. For weeks I had to take the paper out and look at it and feel good. It was like getting a shot of love each time. Obviously, I was holding back feeling so bad about myself. I see now how many of my hundreds of rituals are designed to keep those bad feelings and my anxiety away. I never had anyone at home to reassure me. My rituals, at least, serve that function.

I love exams in school because I can look at the grades and 'know' that I'm good and not bad. That's why I was teacher's pet. Everyone else hated exams. Not me.

When I'm alone my mind works overtime going over my latest schemes to make life better. I worry about it so much that I hardly notice it. It's a way of life. If someone hurts my feelings I obsess about it constantly; what I should have said or done, what I'm going to say. I go over and over the shortcomings of my boss, which is identical to what I did with my mother. I felt disgust for her for abandoning me, and at the same time needed her desperately.

The clearest example of this resolves around romance and sex. If I develop a crush on someone I spend my waking hours thinking about him, working out hundreds of fantasies of how we will be together (gazes, hugs, kisses, romance and sex). I now see how these fantasies are spun out of a longing in my body to be held and loved. It's half pleasure, half pain. It goes to the longing I had for my mother when I was little. As my needs come up I get more and more obsessive in my thoughts. I flirt outrageously during these times. I literally feel like an animal in heat.

I needed love from my mother with every cell in my body; as early as the crib I could feel it. And no one ever came to soothe me. I have to set up situations now where I can re-create the feeling of longing I had for my mother; so I obsess about men. Now my need has become erotic. The more I feel my early need, the less I obsess erotically about men in my life. My need becomes what it is, a need for my mother who was never around.

I think I had all of these basic feelings and then my household was so compulsive that I learned to channel them into obsessions. Dinner was always on time or my father would be irritable. He would open my bedroom door each morning and say, 'five more minutes'. Then, 'time to get up', then, 'one more minute', etc. Everything at home was regimented, including vacations, birthdays and holidays. My Dad would be ready first, then according to his schedule he would stand at the bottom of the stairs and count to ten slowly. We had to be downstairs by 'ten'.

I see how chaotic I feel inside. Trying to make some order outside reassures me. I think if there is chaos outside it is too much for me. Part of me feels so out of control that

*I have to control everything. I feel like if I don't try to keep
it all together I'm going to fly apart. My birth and my home
life was pure chaos. I needed stability and routine; so I
make it everywhere I go. If I take a tranquillizer that stops
all those feelings from coming up I can briefly feel like I'm
together. When the pill wears off I obsess to keep myself
together.*

*Happily, I am no longer the obsessive I used to be. In
most situations I can be spontaneous and don't get freaked
out by unpredictable things. I don't need routine to make
me feel stable and lists to make me feel secure. I have felt
the real reason I felt that way.*

The Nature of Tension

Tension – a tightness in the muscles and joints, tautness in
the chest, a stiff neck and tension headaches – is a later
development of the nervous system. Traumas that make us
tense occur later in our development. We are anxious before
we are tense. Tension is largely a body-wall phenomenon
related to a more highly evolved nervous system.

People in anxiety states rarely learn to use tension as a
defence. Their musculature is less involved; the pain is less
'bound'. Tension binds and absorbs. The anxiety-ridden
person is looser, or at loose ends, fragmented and in pieces.
She lacks the structure that tension offers. She is sometimes
known in Freudian circles as an 'hysteric'.

The tense individual is 'uptight', all bound up in himself,
and overly contained. The anxiety-ridden person is much
more vulnerable and dependent, since the imprint which
gives rise to anxiety occurs so very early.

The anxiety victim is more open to his needs because his
entire structure has been shattered very early by overwhelming terror. He has not had an opportunity in his development to generate a mechanism against that need.

In tense states, needs are being held back by tensing up

against anticipated pain, just as we tense up before a shot in the dentist's office. The difference is that psychologically we never leave the dentist's office.

Those who are tense are going to act in more mature ways than the anxious individual. First, because he is more removed from his childhood self and, secondly, he can structure up and perfect an act. He is less spontaneous, more conservative, and more cautious. The anxious person is awash in impulses barely contained. The anxious one trembles and shakes; the tense one shakes inside. As one anxious patient put it, 'I feel all raggedy'. The anxious one looks like a wreck; the tense one does not. Tense people seem to be in control, and they are – of themselves and their feelings. Too much control and too little access to feelings are characteristic of tense people. They are easier to treat in conventional therapy, where structure is very important, but more difficult to treat in Primal Therapy where structure works against feelings.

The anxious person suffers different symptoms from the tense person. The anxious one starts life more colicky and more prone to stomach distress. He ends up with ulcers and colitis. The tense one is arthritic, has tension headaches and back problems. He is always dislocating his knee, elbow, or shoulder. The focus is usually the body wall. The tense one grinds his teeth at night; the anxious one has nightmares.

In therapy, we help construct defences for the anxiety-prone individual, and dismantle defences for the tense one. Anxiety states need structure – which is just what the tense one does not need. The tense one is too focused. If he is a scientist, or a mathematician, he is immersed in his work to the exclusion of all else. The anxious one cannot concentrate and stay with things. He is scattered all over the place. That is because the early catastrophic input literally fragmented any kind of defence apparatus, and left him with a lack of cohesion. One is too glued together; the other is unglued.

Pain: The Antidote to Anxiety

Access to early imprints finally gives the therapist a window into the source of states of anxiety and tension. It allows us to pinpoint how and when the neurosis began. It allows us to search below the level of ideas into generating sources.

Feeling pain is the plain and simple antidote for anxiety states. It has been a systematic and predictable resolution for anxiety in many thousands of patients. This axiom has held too often for too many patients for this to be a matter of doubt.

We must remember that in our research, the patient is lying still on a mattress. The only thing that is happening to him is memory. We have measured those who thrash around without a specific memory – a state known as abreaction – and have not found in them the changes we predictably find in those who relive specific painful memories. As the painful memory approaches, the patient suffers until he drops into feeling. Then the parasympathetic nervous system takes over. Just before the feeling occurs, he is in the pre-primal phase known as an anxiety attack.

What usually happens in conventional therapy is that a person comes to a session full of anxiety after having, for example, shopped in a crowded department store, or having made a presentation in class. Often, medication is begun to suppress the symptom. There may be attempts in conventional therapy to deal with the current situation, e.g., the anxiety about presenting a class paper. This might help some because it is dealing with the third-line representation of the actual terror. But at best it is palliative. Even though the therapist can find many ostensible and plausible explanations in the present for the anxiety, it doesn't follow the feeling to its roots.

Nightmares are nearly always accompanied by anxiety. The source is the same, day or night. It is a breakthrough of the real feeling, which may be, 'I am smothered, I am dying', (translated as, 'They're trying to kill me') 'I am being crushed, I am helpless and hopeless' which springs directly from the imprint. I don't know why we need special names for anxiety attacks in the dark; they are still anxiety attacks. They still occur for the same reasons. The nightmare simply offers a circumscribed story to accompany it.

The brain is quite logical, and in therapy allows us to bring the pains into consciousness in sequence from the most current, most innocuous, down to the most remote and most noxious. By the time we are confronted with the earliest and most threatening pains, a good deal of integration and strengthening of personality has already taken place. The danger of rebirthing and other such procedures is that they deal with the pain in reverse order. They are interfering with the normal defence system that should at all costs be holding down those terrors.

Relaxation makes anxious people anxious. *Omni* magazine (November 1986) noted that 'relaxation may be hazardous to your health'. Researchers, including David Barlow, director of the Phobia and Anxiety Disorders Clinic of the State University of New York, found that patients seem to get anxious when it is suggested that they relax. One woman 'was doing nicely, and beginning to relax, and then, much to our surprise, and certainly to hers, she had a massive panic attack of full blown, unadulterated terror', during which her heart rate doubled in a minute.

After examining several patients with the same syndrome, Barlow began to see a general tendency. More than half of his patients began to experience terror when they began to relax. What is becoming clear is that when we ease our defences, we feel in danger. When the neurotic relaxes (his defences), everything bottled up surges forth. So now, instead of anxiety being the threat, relaxation makes us anxious, and relaxation becomes the threat. Tension then becomes the normal state of 'relaxation'. No wonder so many people cannot take a vacation.

Anxiety as a Survival Mechanism

We must keep in mind that the memory we are dealing with in anxiety is the memory of survival; that is why it does and should endure. It is a danger that we adults carry around nearly all the time. Unfortunately, at the same time, what we did to survive now threatens our existence.

Without some kind of repression, a newborn with a wildly racing heart rate, as happens to our patients during the reliving, would eventually expire. Some newborns have evidently suffered what seems to be cardiac arrest during the birth process. During reliving in therapy they have the beginnings of what seems to be a heart attack. However, if they lived the first time, they'll live the second.

It is not improbable, incidentally, that a six-month-old left alone in the dark in his crib can expire from undefended trauma on the ascent. He may die from a current terror, which has triggered off an early trauma at birth, particularly if there is no adult close by to soothe and calm him. Being alone in the dark and terrified resonates with a trauma months earlier with its lethal effects. His terror is unattenuated. He is in a general alarm state with no help, no support and, above all, no comprehension of what is happening. The survival mechanisms continue unabated until the system gives out.

Conclusion: The Age of Repression

In the absence of war, economic depression, and other major catastrophes, the age of anxiety seems to have given way to the Age of Repression. We are more comfortable with our neuroses because society rewards neurotic values and its great ambition and drive. We see more obsessive-compulsives, because obsessiveness seems to be the cultural mode. Driven, successful people are rewarded. It is only when the drive gets out of hand that we become concerned.

The passing of the age of anxiety is, in a way, the loss of our innocence. Repression is apotheosized, while neurotic energy is diverted into the goals of success, prestige, honour and other symbolic goals. We have stopped feeling anxious because we have stopped feeling.

11

Malignant Despair:
Repression and the Immune System

The overall impact of our research on repression, our own and that of others, is that we are on the verge of a new era in understanding disease in which the line between so-called mental or emotional illness and physical illness can no longer be meaningfully drawn.

The term 'malignant despair' surely has a baleful connotation, but it is useful and properly descriptive in the sense that it points to the theme of this chapter. This theme, which sees depression as a malignancy of the mind and cancer as a malignancy of the tissues, are two sides of the same coin.

Primal Research: How Psychotherapy Changes the Brain and the Body

Our research indicates the role of repression in disease. During the past fifteen years, we have done three separate studies of vital functions in our patients. We have measured the core body temperature with an electronic thermistor, and monitored blood pressure and pulse of our patients. All the vital signs dropped after eight months of therapy. The average body temperature, for example, dropped almost one degree, with a decrease occurring in 65.5 per cent of all patients. 'Normal' body temperature may not be 98.6. Blood pressure in our hypertensive patients also dropped on an average of 24 points, while heartbeat slowed down by 10 beats on average for all patients. On average, a decrease in pulse rate occurred in 58.6 per cent of all patients.

Of course, diet and exercise are also going to change blood pressure; and leading a healthy life in a non-polluted environment is very important. But let us not neglect the psychological factors, because in patients who have undergone no change of dietary regime or patterns of exercise, we are still able to reduce blood pressure simply through the reliving of repressed pain. Body temperature, in particular, is the key index because it reflects the overall heat-effort of the body, as it relates to repression.

Blood pressure and pulse also rise when a deep feeling is imminent, and fall when that feeling is resolved. If all of the person's vital functions remained high, yet the person claimed to feel relaxed, we would be very suspicious. Repression is an active, energy-consuming process. Repression never lets up because pain doesn't. Repression is trying to keep us alive. If we get sick and die in order to survive, then so be it. Repression got the species to be where it is, made us into human beings and helped us to develop a cerebral cortex with all of its logic and rational abilities. It isn't about to abandon its job, and it can't be laid off. It's got full time tenure.

The Fever of Neurosis

There is almost nothing noted in the literature that connects pain with body temperature. It is an invariable rule that the deeper the pain and the earlier its imprint, the higher the body temperature during the session. Reliving primal sequences around birth will nearly always drive the body temperature above 100 degrees. With the patient connected to an electronic temperature gauge during the session, we can literally watch the progression of pain on our dials as the patient goes from childhood pains to reliving very early perinatal birth pains. There is a dramatic shift in body temperature when this takes place.

The fact that body temperature rises significantly during a reliving session is less mysterious than it may seem. The feeling that makes temperature rise so dramatically is there *all of the time*. We have a 'governor system' which continuously dampens the rise in temperature. When repression weakens, the pain is activated and the body goes into a frenzy trying to keep it away. This work to repress is reflected in the heat of the system. When you take pain out of the body the whole system cools down and the drop in body temperature usually falls below its starting value, indicating a system at rest. This is one key way we verify the relationship between temperature and repression.

When an infant starts to die in the womb, all vital signs are mobilized tremendously. In the reliving of this trauma the same functions are reproduced as part of the overall memory. The early situation is re-created in its entirety. It is *the mobilization against consciousness*; consciousness is the supreme danger. During a Primal session when consciousness starts to lock into the old feeling again we see life-endangering vital signs. The baby is truly in danger of dying with protracted signs such as these. The adult is not. The job of repression is to see to it that the link-up to consciousness is not made. Its task is to keep the connection from happening.

If the early traumatic event itself was nearly lethal in its origin, the vital signs will approach lethal levels. The muscles are tensing up for action, the blood is pumping at a maximum rate, and hormones are spilling into the system. Early on, a shutoff valve was turned on. Now in therapy the valve is inoperative, and the duplicate of the traumatic memory is in the foreground. Repression is no longer able to do its job; and it shouldn't. Feeling is taking over.

Repression has no age. It doesn't understand that it has grown old and that the person it is protecting is now a mature adult who can take those pains. It is living in the past, acting as though the person inside is still a baby and must be protected at all costs and indeed, it is protecting our baby-selves.

As soon as there is connection between the remembered past and the present, the body temperature starts to drop continuously. This rise and fall pattern of body temperature does not occur when a person simply screams, yells, or cries without connecting to a specific past trauma. It is one way we know that *connection* is the *sine qua non* of the entire healing, integration process. Dialectically, when connection is made it is turned into its opposite – feeling; and with that feeling goes integration and healing. But of course connection means both great pain and then healing. Isn't it a wonder that we are in panic to keep that healing from happening?. One must pass through the pain on the way to healing and not everyone can or wants to do that.

We have discovered that there are significant differences in the physiological concomitants during a primal between the parasympath and the sympath. Particularly during the birth sequence, the sympath has much higher vital signs until connection; while the parasympath seems to go into a para-sympathetic crisis much quicker, following the original prototypic trauma. We are currently engaged in research to see how widespread the differences are between the para-sympath and the sympath. It would seem from preliminary data that the physiological measurements during the primal follow the original trauma exactly; thus in some parasym-paths there is not a rise in body temperature but rather a dip, which seems to mirror the whole conservation of energy syndrome that occurred originally. We are using electronic instrumentation ordinarily found in operating rooms, for the most precise measurements possible, and are finding diver-gent scores between the parasympath and sympath. Whereas the sympath begins at 98.6 and can move for over an hour steadily upward to 102 or 103 degrees (along with other vital sign indicators), the parasympath falls into a feeling very soon in the session and her temperature *drops*, sometimes two to three degrees in minutes. Sometimes nothing seems to be happening, the content of what the patient is saying is rather benign, yet the temperature takes sharp rises. We know that a heavy feeling is ascending, even though the patient is unconscious of it. We don't have to wait long for its appearance. Sudden peaks in our measurements indicate intrusion from lower levels of consciousness. Temperature alone can separate the two distinct personality types. The sympath almost never has serious drops in measurements during a session. Nor does he have an overwhelming futility that invariably accompanies those measurements. When we watch an electronically measured parasympath in deep early feelings we can usually tell by the drops in vital signs alone that there is a feeling of hopelessness and despair. I have seen radical drops in vital signs, particularly core body temperature and blood pressure, while a patient in a parasympathic crisis is thrashing about in a session. It is unknown in the annals of medicine, to my knowledge, that temperature can drop several degrees during the time of heavy physical activity and remain there for some time.

What is happening in these sessions is that we are observing the run-off of the exact sequence that occurred perhaps some forty years before. We are looking at the current session and observing history. What this history is saying is that first, there was a monumental struggle and then as death came near the abandonment of hope and the struggle. So the patient, despite the fact that he is actively thrashing, is responding primarily to his history and that history dictates falling vital signs. This is what later act-outs are about – responding to history despite the current reality – wanting to give up when things get too much or when there isn't enough encouragement to make us want to 'keep going'.

Our analysis of personality can allow us to predict the course of someone's session and the way that the vital signs will turn. And a careful examination of the vital signs during a session can confirm for us the kind of person we are dealing with; predicting among other things, the kinds of symptoms we can expect (migraine in the parasympath), the ways of relating (aggressive and pushy in the sympath), the manner of handling stress (the parasympath freezes under stress), the general attitude one has to life (the parasympath is a 'what's the use' type), the state of the libido (sympaths have more sex drive), sexual dysfunction (parasympath men are more often impotent and the women are more frequently frigid), the patterns of sleep (the parasympath drags herself out of bed; the sympath is out the minute he opens his eyes), and the general attitude to life (the sympath is positive; the parasympath is a 'nay' sayer, telling you how things can't get done). The way one handles a session is the way one handles life and is based on the prototype.

The relationship of the psyche to physiological processes such as body temperature is illustrated in an experiment we performed at a London hospital. A patient was having a reliving session in one room, while peripheral body heat sensors attached to her were read in an adjoining isolated room. I remained in this isolated room examining the temperature graphs, and could tell by the needle movements alone when the patient started feeling, when the defences mounted, when she dropped into the feeling, and on what level that feeling occurred. I was also able to tell when the feeling ended and insights began, all without seeing the patient.

It was dramatic evidence of the biological concomitant of feeling. The therapist who was with the patient carefully noted the exact time of each of these occurrences, while I marked the charts as to what I thought was happening. In this experiment we could clearly see the unity of body and mind – the unity of psychological processes as they affected the biological ones.

Measuring Neurosis: The Index of Repression

We have developed an 'index of repression' in which we take

various parameters such as blood pressure, brain-wave function, pulse and body temperature (the vital signs) which form a grid onto which we place the patient's measurements to determine his general state. We are thus able to quantify the amount of repression in the person's system. We cannot measure pain directly but we can measure the *processing* of it. The conclusion is evident: the earlier the trauma, the more far reaching its consequences and the more devastating and enduring the sequelae.

This is true in both the mental and physiological spheres. That is why when we alter personality in our therapy, we also alter susceptibility to disease. A newborn who has eczema, colic or neurodermatitis is really being born with an unconscious immune system. Due to birth trauma, the immune system has diminished memory, cannot recognize its enemies, and cannot rely on its history to help out. Later on, that same child begins to develop learning problems, taps his feet incessantly, and is hyperkinetic – all aspects of the same imprint. What is less obvious is the destruction going on in the bowel, lungs, or nasal passages. Each time the energy of the imprint travels to a new spot, a different specialist is consulted – each treating the separate symptom as a different disease, each missing the underlying identical source of the problem.

When one realizes that we have been able to reduce stress hormone levels by fifty to sixty per cent via reliving experiences, one begins to understand how we can strengthen an immune system which depends on low stress levels for its optimal functioning.

There have been so many studies which have correlated diseases such as cancer with certain personality types; studies cite coldness in the home as one, suppressed rage as another, depression as still another. What may have been overlooked is how both states may have the same foundation. It isn't that rage 'causes' or leads to cancer. It is that being blocked in the womb may lead to both rage and cancer. Expressing rage does help in therapy, but unless it is expressed *in context* it will not be curative until the imprint itself is addressed.

Neurosis is everywhere in the system. We have only to look carefully at almost any biological process to find it. There are ways to measure neurosis; ways to determine just how neurotic we are. For example, we have taken infrared photographs of the faces of patients before and after feeling. In research conducted by Doctors Harry Sobel and David A. Goodman from the Neuroscience Center of Los Angeles, thermograms were taken (with a UTI Spectrotherm model 801), by a scanning infrared camera. The face was divided into eleven key regions and infrared photographs were taken of each of these regions on each person. After a significant number of months of feeling, the peripheral blood flow in the face increased significantly as a result of resolving pain; less pain equals less constriction and better flow. In most of the regions, the peripheral blood flow was increased in advanced patients. What seems evident from thermographic research is that there is an enhanced peripheral blood flow as a result of the resolution of pain.

In addition, Professor Leonid Goldstein of Rutgers University and Dr Eric Hoffman of the University of Copenhagen, have done two studies of our patients and have found a significant change in brain function as a result of reliving experiences.[1] The relationship between the right and left hemispheres changes, as does the relationship between the forebrain and the hindbrain.

Another study at The Brain Research Institute of UCLA[2]

1. Hoffman E., Goldstein L., HEMISPHERIC QUANTITATIVE EEG CHANGES FOLLOWING EMOTIONAL REACTIONS. Acta Psychiatrice Scandanaia. Fall 1980
Hoffman, Erik. THE SIGNIFICANCE OF THE RIGHT CEREBRAL HEMISPHERE ION HYPEREMOTIONAL ACTIVITY AS MEASURED BY QUANTITATIVE EEG: Third World Congress of Biological Psychiatry, Stockholm, Sweden. June 28–July 3, 1981.
2. Gardiner, M. DIFFERENCES BETWEEN EEGs RECORDED FROM INDIVIDUALS AT DIFFERENT TIME POINTS DURING A PSYCHOLOGICAL TREATMENT. Conference on Human Brain Function, B19 report, 42, 1976 pp. 86–102.

found a lessened overall brainwave amplitude in our patients after one year of therapy. There were less neurons at work and the brain was less busy. The task of repression therefore, has been reduced.

In several brain-wave studies we have found that repressed individuals have a lower resting EEG (alpha band) than those who have access to their feelings, including those who have frequent anxiety attacks. Indeed, anxiety means a less coherent top level consciousness. These measurements help us to predict the course of therapy. The patients with low waves will take longer to cry and much longer to get into deep feelings. Those who are beginning therapy and who suffer greatly also have the highest EEG voltages. Later, as a result of the therapy, nearly all patients have a lower resting EEG voltage. This means that repressive mechanisms become less necessary as therapy progresses. In the UCLA study of long term Primal patients it was found that the resting brain wave voltage of patients who had five years of therapy was one third of its starting value.

Because brain waves are highly correlated with the other vital functions I consider them as one more aspect of the vital sign syndrome. The psychophysiologic-'meaning' of the measurements obtained is that there are specific physiologic correlates to psychologic states. By looking at brain waves, in short, we can say something about personality, and vice versa.

One is reminded of the progress in measurement by the fact that one can spit in a tube (as done in our research) and have a readout from that saliva as to the level of stress hormones (cortisol), and thereby the stress level the system is under. When we correlate the factor with certain brainwave signs and other vital signs, we begin to have an effective index of stress levels and repression.

With the index of repression we have also been able to see what kinds of traumas carry the heaviest valence, and which make the most difference in contributing to later disease. It is not whimsy that makes us posit birth trauma or incest as the most serious contributors to repression, but research. Is it possible to relive a surgery at the age of five? In patients who do, we find spectacular rises in vital signs, during the session. It is the one way we know of the veracity of such an experience.

Because of our research, we are beginning to have an idea about what a normal biology looks like. We now have physiological standards with which to judge the psychotherapies of today. With our research tools, we will be able to ascertain how much pressure each individual is under. We will have predictive indices about the likelihood of later diseases; this will be true irrespective of how well a person *thinks* he is.

I believe, incidentally, that until those in mental hospitals and prisons are able to relive their traumas, the chance of their continuing their aberrant behaviour once on the outside is quite high. So long as they are victims of their childhood imprints the best conventional therapy can do is medicate, push down the pain forever and hope for the best. There is an alternative.

Until now when an illness wasn't clear as to causes we called it 'psychosomatic'. The notion of psychosomatic illness has been a basket into which we have dumped everything we couldn't explain. We used it particularly when we were unable to effectively treat a disease on a medical basis. 'It must be psychosomatic,' the doctor would say. No one had any idea what that meant, except that the patient somehow thought he was crazy or that the illness was his fault. That label somehow relieved the doctor of his guilt over not being able to cure the patient. Even if he were correct in supposing that the medical problem was psychologically caused, the exact factors were never enumerated because no one knew what they were.

The term psychosomatic was never used as a primary diagnosis, or as a positive approach intended to specify the psyche's contribution to a particular affliction. It was usually a sign of exasperation. 'I don't know what is wrong, so it must be psychosomatic'. No one likes to feel like a failure – particularly when it comes to treating a patient. The implication seemed to be, 'If I can't treat you, it must be your fault'.

What we are learning from our research is that neurosis is not a *thing*. It is not a behaviour or an attitude. It is a *concert of reactions* that provides the fundamental keys for understanding many of the defects or malfunctions in the subsystems. It is this fact which suggests the common physiological origins between so-called psychosomatic symptoms of disease and neurosis. What normal seems to be is the lowest level of repression consistent with cortical function – the state of maximum possible integration among levels of consciousness.

You are not normal just because you act normal, and you are not normal just because you have no obvious psychiatric signs. You may not be normal even if you answer every question on a psychological questionnaire in a healthy way, because the body has to take its test as well, and has to give the right answers to the tester, namely the machine. The machine is asking in its own way, 'Is your pulse normal?' and the answer, with a pulse of 95 is, 'Definitely not!'

Liz

On 4 October, 1977, an amazing thing happened to me. While at my doctor's office, my pulse was read at 72. For me this is amazing, because I have a history of a fast pulse: my pulse had never been read below 80, and it was normally in the 90s. Even 100–106 was not an uncommon resting pulse for me. I would often lie in bed at night and feel my pulse, which would sometimes rock my entire body. I was once in the hospital for routine thyroid tests. My pulse was read every morning for three weeks and it was consistently high (in the 80s and 90s immediately upon awakening and sometimes before I was awake).

So this reading of 72 was indeed unusual for me. At

first, I figured perhaps the low reading was a single isolated one that would not be repeated. However, on four subsequent visits to the doctor, the low reading continued. On 20 October, my pulse was read at 64 about 32 beats lower than my previous common readings of 96. Furthermore, for the past ten years my blood pressure had been elevated (135/85). This has also gone down to a low of 110/80.

I am truly amazed, excited, and relieved about my pulse and blood pressure. I can hardly believe it's true, except that it matches my overall feeling of having had a tremendous burden removed from inside of me. I can't believe how much all those feelings were continuously agitating my body. So much repressed anger, it was literally killing me, and feeling it is reviving me.

Repression and the Immune System

We used to think that the immune system was only related to allergies, hay fever, and possibly asthma, and that to be allergic meant the opposite of being immune. In other words, if we were immune to something, we were no longer allergic. Thus, a person with hay fever was allergic to various antigens, such as dust or pollen, because the immune system was not working very well.

Research has come a long way since those days; we now realize that the immune system is involved in nearly every disease in one way or another, and that it is the key system for understanding many diseases of a catastrophic nature.

We have known for some time that the immune system is made up of white cells, lymphocytes, that carry out a variety of different immunological functions. There are B-cells, T-cells, and NK cells, among others. In general, all these cells form part of a surveillance system that recognizes and attacks alien intrusions (antigens) such as viruses, bacteria, dust or pollen. Lymphocytes are highly specialized kinds of cells; some are involved only in recognizing the enemy, while others are 'search-and-destroy' cells.

These cells, for example, are critically important in fighting cancer. Once a cancer cell is recognized by either a B- or T-lymphocyte, the natural killer cells move in. Natural killer cells are the 'hired guns' of the immune system; they are, literally, our *bodyguards*. When they weaken or diminish, we are in trouble. Natural killer cells form the first line of defence in combatting cells undergoing a malignant transformation. They are on the lookout for possible cancer development and almost literally scoop up the would-be malignant cells.

Research on Stress, Pain and the Immune System

In our research, we wanted to establish the fact that therapy could indeed affect physiological processes such as the immune system. We first wanted to ascertain stress levels and then relate these levels to immune functions. The significance of the research was to show that psychological factors affect immune functions and, by implication, play an important role in major disease.

Our aim was to identify the biologic comcomitants of neurosis and its resolution. We want to be precise about what changes take place in neurosis and develop markers which allow us to quantify neurosis and to determine a hierarchy of severity. In what follows we shall summarize our findings.

We have done a number of hormone studies over the past years which indicate *inter alia*, that stress hormone levels are reduced as pain is reduced in the human system. We have carried this research forward to see if we could replicate the reduction in stress hormones, and further, to see what other changes might accompany alterations in stress hormone levels.

We have found that after one year of Primal Therapy there is a normalization of these levels. In the case of testosterone (the sex hormone) and growth hormone, those who begin inordinately high move lower, while those who began low moved higher. There has been a good deal of research indicating the role of growth hormone in healing and repair. Sympaths, those who are more aggressive and pushy, tend toward higher beginning levels of testosterone. Later in therapy as they soften, these levels drop. Parasympath men, lower in these levels at the start of therapy move upward later on. There seems to be an inverse relationship between growth hormone and stress. The higher the stress level the lower the levels of growth hormone. After Primal Therapy, as stress hormone levels decrease, there is an increase in growth hormone levels. At the end of twenty-six weeks of Primal Therapy there was over a two hundred per cent average increase in growth hormone level. During that same period of time, for those who could not get into deep feelings there was a significant drop in these same levels.

We have noted that for the past two decades there is soft tissue growth in our patients. Females have noted breast growth, for example. We believe that among other hormone changes, it is also related to alterations in growth hormone output. In our most recent research, we hypothesized that in our patients, as we had seen previously, there would again be a lowered level of the stress hormone cortisol after a period of Primal Therapy. We reasoned that these lowered levels would be reflected in changes in the immune system. We were particularly interested in the natural killer cell (NK) activity. We believed, in accordance with previous research done by others, that as stress hormone levels (and other indices of stress) were reduced, immune function and NK cell activity would be enhanced. We also measured imipramine binding in blood platelets, reasoning that higher levels of binding would be indicative of less repression, and that less repression would in turn result in better immune system function. The future implications might be that if NK cell activity and other immune functions are enhanced, there would be one possible prevention of a serious disease, such as cancer.

In order to explore some of these ideas further, we conducted a double blind study in conjunction with Professors Steven Rose and Sean Murphy of Open University in England, as well as with Professor Bernard Watson and Dr Nuala Mooney of Saint Bartholomew's Hospital of London.[1] We measured stress levels of patients and a control group (university students) by testing the amount of stress hormone in their saliva. We (Dr Andre Blank of my clinic) also took blood samples to study neurotransmitter functions namely, blood platelet-imipramine binding. We also measured lymphocytes, part of the immune system, to observe the relationship between stress levels and immune function.

The issue of imipramine binding is a complex one which is not yet completely understood. The chemical imipramine is the primary component of a mood elevating drug used to treat severe depression. The precise mechanisms by which imipramine has its mood elevating effect is not clearly known, but one of its distinct measurable effects is blocking the re-uptake of serotonin and norepinephrine in the nervous system. Both of these substances are thought to aid in the suppression of pain. Imipramine shares similar functions with serotonin in the sense that low imipramine binding is correlated with higher serotonin in the brain synapses; thus the lower the binding the higher the repression. Imipramine seems to modulate the serotonin system and enables the brain to be more sensitive to this neurotransmitter.

We know, for example, that electronic stimulation of lower brain structures facilitates the suppression of pain by increasing levels of serotonin. Animals low in serotonin are also quite agitated, and become calmer when serotonin is injected.

This led us to propose that the mechanisms of imipramine, owes its mood elevating effects to its effect on repression. We

---

1. Rose, Steven, Sean Murphy: Psychotherapy and Imipramine Binding to Blood Platelets, Brain Research Group. *Open University*, Milton Keynes, England.

reasoned further that the ability of the nervous system to bind, or metabolize imipramine should be positively affected by Primal Therapy.

Since blood platelets share a common embryological origin with brain neurons, we believed that by measuring precisely how well radio labelled imipramine was binding to blood platelets, we would also gain an idea of how well imipramine might be binding to brain neurons in the nervous system. Making such measurements before and after Primal Therapy would then measure the effects of Primal Therapy on repression.

The background for this, to reiterate, is the finding in other research that the binding is lower in depressives, and that the administration of imipramine as a pharmaceutical has a mood elevating effect. It is for this reason that the level of imipramine binding is also sometimes used as a diagnostic marker in the antidepression treatment process, with those at lowered levels considered depressive.

Consequently, our detailed subsidiary hypotheses were that: (1) Primal Therapy would reduce stress levels, (2) reduced stress levels would enhance immune function, (3) Primal Therapy would produce enhanced imipramine binding.

Research results tended to confirm all three of our hypotheses. We found that Primal Therapy brought about the changes we anticipated in imipramine binding. After six months of therapy, the Primal patients, who had begun with much lower imipramine binding than the controls, moved up to parity with these controls. Imipramine binding is clearly correlated with changes in psychological states.

In the immune studies done at St Bartholomew's Hospital, patients were observed along with a control group of university students. They were tested three months before therapy, three days before therapy, the first day of therapy, twenty-one days after therapy began, and six months later.

We found that the proportion of NK cells changed with time and within the patient group, and that these changes were statistically significant. At the six month level, the patient group had lower NK cell activity compared with the pre-study level.

The sixth month of Primal Therapy is what I call the 'point of no return'. It is when the patient has fairly well penetrated his defences, when he is the most anxious, and when he has not yet well-integrated upsurging pain. That integration begins to happen after about one year of therapy. Thus, my interpretation of these results is that, at the time when the patient is most anxious, the cells concerned with cancerous development are at their weakest.

The proportion of NK cells changed within the patients, but not within the control group. When appropriate statistical tests were applied to the data there was conclusive evidence that statistically significant differences existed between the five measuring periods. Since Primal Therapy was the central independent (treatment) variable which distinguished the two groups, it is appropriate to ascribe these differences to this therapy. This indicates that alterations in the psychological state have an effect on the immune system. NK cell activity within the patient group was lower after six months than at the beginning of the therapy – a time when the patients tended to be more structured.

When the patients were compared with the controls at different times, the control group had significantly higher numbers of T-cells present. This we would expect. A psychiatric population seems to have a lesser functioning immune apparatus. Unfortunately, we were not able to go on for a year or two to see what changes occurred after integration of pain. At that time we would expect to see immune system function enhanced beyond starting levels. This is a project for the future. Based on psychological evaluation, eleven out of twelve randomly selected patients in this case showed improvement. One subject who showed a decrease in psychological functioning also had a decrease in imipramine binding. These results were statistically significant.

What is important here is that cellular change occurred

through a psychologic treatment procedure; it occurred in the expected direction; and it occurred in correlation with improvement in the psychic state of the subjects. The patients had increased their levels so as to be indistinguishable from normals.

Here we found physiological correlations with mental states. Wellness and neurosis were found in the cells. In the future, in order to measure neurosis or wellness we can again look to the activity of these cells. To my knowledge, this is the first time that the efficacy of a psychotherapy has been tested on a cellular level. The results were significant enough to Professor Rose to justify the measurement of a number of psychotherapies in the same way. Based on this research, we hope to develop markers to measure the effectiveness of various psychotherapies.

Significance of This Research

In summary, our research indicates that (1) pain is central to neurosis; (2) dealing with pain alters neurosis (the majority of patients felt improved after therapy); (3) the alteration of neurosis includes specific physiological processes; and (4) we need to continue to look at immune processes in neurosis to discover how these two factors are related. I am convinced that these relationships will become more and more evident as we refine our research techniques.

The conclusion that progress or its lack in psychotherapy can be registered at physiological levels is ineluctable. It is based on a specific theory of pain and neurosis and on the hypothesis that pain and its relationship to the immune system is intimately related. As long as psychotherapy remains in the domain of the psyche as opposed to the body this kind of research will be neglected, and with it, a chance to see what psychological factors are crucial in catastrophic disease.

There is nothing wrong with isolating psychological factors

in the study of the outcome of a psychotherapy, as long as we do not deceive ourselves they are the whole story. What we need is a number of other biological markers (such as the hormone studies we have done), which in their conglomerate give us a picture of *profound* change in neurosis.

It is not sufficient for therapists to make *ad hoc* decisions about what criteria they will choose as a means of measuring changes in their patients. The criteria must reflect the whole gamut of physiological changes in the body. If we show that certain neurotransmitters are involved in neurosis, those criteria eventually have to be considered in measuring progress in psychotherapy. We can no longer construct a theory of neurosis that ignores biological markers. The more markers we find, the more specific criteria will assert themselves and the more precise will be our measurements.

What repression does is split the person literally in two. Unfortunately, those who are charged with treatment have continued the split and deal with the split as a normal state of affairs. The patient has been bifurcated – his mind extracted from his body for psychologists to study and treat – while in medicine the body has been extracted from the mind and treated as a viable, discrete entity.

Recent Research on the Immune System

Robert Ader, a pioneer researcher in the newly emerging field of psychoneuroimmunology, administered two different chemicals to animals: rats were injected with cyclophosmanide, a drug that suppresses immune function, and at the same time they were given saccharine-flavoured drinking water. Following a period of time, the same rats were given only the saccharine-flavoured water and *their immune function was suppressed exactly as though they had been given the original immunosuppressive drug.* In other words, the immune system remembered and responded as though the old environment were still there, just as the nervous system does.

The immune system has an extraordinary memory. That is why a childhood inoculation can have a lifelong effect against disease; the system remembers the original attack and mounts a permanent defence against it.

We have learned that immune cells manufacture the same endorphines that the brain does. Although endorphines have a variety of functions, it seems that an immune cell is able to manufacture something that kills pain even while it is dealing with immune functions. Thus, a child abused very early in life may remember not only with his brain cells but with his immune cells as well. In fact, almost every neurotransmitter that deals with stress and pain is manufactured by the immune system as well as by the brain. Here in the immune system we see the confluence of the psyche and the soma (body), the real meaning of psychosomatic. The nervous and immune systems are truly a single communication system, each sending their own message to the other.

In Switzerland, Dr Hugo Besedovsky has found that immune cells are not only receptive to the information from the brain but that the immune system itself sends chemical messages to the brain – in particular to the hypothalamus, the part of the limbic system which plays a great role in mediating emotion. Immune cells can 'call an assembly' and send 'delegates' in the form of chemical messages to the brain. They are not sending words to the brain, but they are sending information. If that information is 'shocking' and overwhelming the system begins to break down and develop severe disease. On any level of the system there is only so much information that can be accepted. After that the organ system is in danger. As we see in cancer that information often consists of despair and futility, feelings that are processed physiologically.

Malignant Despair

Dr John Liebeskind of UCLA has conducted experiments

with rats who were injected with cells of tumour tissue and then made to undergo periodic and inescapable shock to their feet. These rats were both helpless and hopeless; they had no options for behaviour that could ease their suffering. After enough of this experience, they developed tumours. The tumour's cells which were injected became malignant *when stress and despair was inflicted upon the organism.* The psychological state of Liebeskind's animals evidently lowered the immune functions causing these animals to develop cancerous growths.

In other research, Hans Selye put rodents on slippery mounds surrounded by water. He arranged the experiment in such a way that whenever the animals fell asleep, they would fall into the water. They became chronically fatigued and stressed, and they developed cancer along the pituitary-adrenal axis, (the pituitary is one central structure which stimulates the secretion of endorphines). This environment was too much for the animals. They were indeed helpless and defeated, and could do nothing about their situation.

These rats felt defeated or despairing for good reasons. They were subjected to a great deal of senseless pain and there was nothing they could do about it. The common theme of current research is unmistakable: despair, hopelessness, helplessness and feelings of defeat are the 'seeds' of malignancy. They make the system vulnerable to all other toxic sources in the environment. I use the word 'seeds' advisedly; because it is the deep rooted sources from a long past history. For too long we've been cutting away the weeds and imagining that we were solving the problem. We must look for these deep psychological factors in many current diseases, from Epstein-Barr Syndrome to multiple sclerosis. While they may not directly cause the disease, they clearly 'prepare the soil' for its erosion.

Rat research is not so different from what children undergo in some households. They don't have to be *made to feel* helpless; they *are* helpless. While cortical cells *express* despair, lower level cells process it. *It is the physiology of despair*. These cells are saying, in effect, 'Let's give up, there is no use'. Despair may express itself by a general lack of recognition of danger on the part of the immune system, or a lack of aggressiveness and inability to clone itself sufficiently to build a strong 'army'. These processes are the counterpart of the neocortex expressing the attitude, 'What's the use', I'm going to give up', 'I'm not even going to try', 'There is no point in anything'. Thus the brain and the immune cells function as a unit to translate despair into immunological dysfunction and psychologic hopelessness at the same time. Rats get sick because they are in hopeless situations. Human feel hopeless and then get sick and cannot seem to connect the two. Worse, they are often unconscious of their hopelessness.

There is a great deal to be learned about humans from these animal studies for humans. Lack of options was a very important element in the development of catastrophic diseases in the animals. So was the fact that they had absolutely no control over their pain. And indeed, when animals *do* have control over their pain, they are far less likely to develop cancer.

A Mayo Clinic study found the rate of cancer to be five times higher than would be expected by chance in people whose spouses had recently died. A woman of seventy who loses her husband has few options. She can no longer plunge into her work, her family, or night life. She certainly has no control over the death of her spouse, and she suffers because there is nothing that can be done. She is not likely, at her age, to find a replacement, or even to hope for one. Her grief is tumourous.

Research at the Mount Sinai School of Medicine in New York showed a sharply reduced immune response in depressed people who had been hospitalized for their depression. Widowers showed this same immune suppression during their days of bereavement. In addition, it has been found that recently separated women had very poor immune function when matched with a group of married women. For those who were married but who perceived their marriages to be poor, the same thing was found.

The Imprint of Malignant Despair: Hopelessness and Cancer

In the human system, despair becomes an imprint when the original trauma is insurmountable. There is no abused four-year-old in the world who can integrate the fact that his life is hopeless, that he will never be loved, and that there is no point in any struggle. It is intolerable that he would be fully aware of these feelings day in and day out for years.

There may be a scene in the child's memory that epitomizes this despair, but it usually is suppressed. Hand-in-hand with that suppression goes a change in hormones and cellular function. Thus, on one level, the child is unaware of his despair and dares not articulate hopelessness, even to himself, but on a different level the despair is there without words, creating damage until malignancy results perhaps decades later. And therein lies the problem. The distance between the original imprint and the eventual disease is so great that it makes detection almost impossible. In any case, it is clear from the studies done with rats that you don't need words in order to feel despair and defeat. Is it only bad things that are imprinted? Not at all. But it is the traumatic events that dislocate function, and it is in those dislocations that the 'bad' memories are held. High blood pressure, for example, is the way that the traumatic memory is kept alive, possibly the same blood pressure that accompanied the original trauma.

Vernon Reilly has conducted a detailed survey of the available scientific literature and has concluded that injury to the immune system clearly leaves a person vulnerable to the action of cancerous viruses and other newly transformed cancer cells. Thus, due to stress, pathologic processes that are normally held in check by the immune apparatus no longer are contained. Without an effective immune surveillance system, the possibilities of developing various kinds of cancer are increased.

In another review article, Ruth Lloyd pointed out that certain social conditions of defeat and despair have been shown to be associated with 'pronounced elevations of corticosterone and immunosuppressive adrenal steroid in mice'. This defeated feeling provokes increases in endorphine output, which in turn compromises immune functioning.

Eli Seifter points out several specific ways that stressors enhance tumour growth: 'They decrease the number of tumour cells required to establish a viral tumour; they increase the growth rate of some tumours and shorten the survival times of mice bearing certain tumours.' These conclusions are based on the statistical results of a variety of studies.

Thus stress is a major factor in the fostering of tumours as well as many other diseases. Indeed, the very stress of having a tumour makes things worse in every possible way. Seifter indicates that each of several kinds of stressors, whether physical or psychological, has the same effect as that of a tenfold increase in tumour growth. In other words, *stressed organisms behave as though they have a greater initial tumour burden than is actually present.*

Seifter believes that psychological stressors contribute to tumour growth 'in the same way that physical stressors do'. When mice are stressed with an injection of toxic compounds and then injected with tumour cells, the cells remain local (and benign) as long as their lives are stable. But as soon as their social psychological structure is disrupted, the tumour grows, extends, and metastasizes, and then the animal dies.

Sobrian has found that stress to a pregnant mother lowers immune functioning in the offspring. This seems to confirm the probability that a person's susceptibility to tumours and cancer has its beginnings in the womb. Damaged immunity may be ameliorated by a loving environment. George F. Solomon of Stanford University found that rats and mice that were handled and fondled were able to develop more anti-bodies and therefore combat disease better than those who were not handled.

As I have noted before, caressing and fondling of animals, and no doubt of the human organism as well, increases immune functioning. Research on cancer patients generally finds them to be somewhat 'cold' and rigid, with deep needs for affection which tend to be covered up. The parents of cancer patients tend to be stern, severe, and unaffectionate. Lovelessness can be fatal.

The Mind of the Immune System

The polio vaccine isn't able to say to the polio virus, 'Oh, yes, I remember your face; we have met before'. But it certainly does remember and respond to the familiar shape and configuration of the virus. The immune-triggered endorphine cells don't say, 'Here comes another of Dad's attacks; better rev up'. But they *do* rev up the moment the message of pain floods the body..

That cortical ideas and psychological states affect immune functioning is beautifully demonstrated by experiments that report how a person's response to poison ivy can be determined more by what the person expects and believes will happen than by the contagion inherent in the poison ivy plant. Subjects who were exposed to a harmless plant, but were told it was poison ivy, actually developed a poison ivy-like rash. Those exposed to poison ivy but told it was not, did not develop a comparable rash. The immune system is responding to what is in the *mind* instead of to objective reality. Put differently, the mind *is* our primary reality.

Until recently we believed that the brain guided the bodily sytems in a more or less one-way direction. Now it turns out that *intercommunication is total*: messages run in both directions with equal force and impact. The brain is immediately informed about intrusion by alien forces, whether they are viral cells or traumatic emotional responses to psychological events. An attack in the form of criticism, rejection, or abuse has the same final effect on the brain and body as a virus. Overwhelming psychological abuse is overpowering information. The system tries its best to reject it; that is when repression steps in.

Psychological abuse is an alien force in the sense that it no longer allows the system to be itself – to be normal. Rather, it produces a dislocation of all kinds of physiological processes with the result that the person can only again be herself when the abuse is finally integrated. Alien simply means that it is a disharmonious force that is not easily absorbed into the ongoing system. The abuse is treated like an unwelcome stranger.

To make this clear, let us take an example. A six year old boy hears his parents arguing. He looks out the window and sees his father loading all his suitcases in the car and driving away. He senses he will never see his father again. His mother comes into his room to break the news. She is inconsolable, weeping her heart out. She tells her son, 'You're going to have to be the man of the house now'. It is a trauma where the boy realizes that he can't be the child any more, cannot have a father, cannot depend on his mother and has no one to appeal to or lean on. In short, he can no longer be himself; his childish needs for a strong and stable parent will forever be unfulfilled.

Only a small part of this event and its catastrophic meaning can be integrated. The rest is shunted away from consciousness and held in limbic storage. The unintegrated part cannot be part of the self. It is not smoothly absorbed into the organism but held apart, as it were; and then it is treated as something alien. The immune system then treats that part of itself as alien and may later attack itself (the nonself); hence the autoimmune diseases. Thus, in multiple sclerosis immune cells attack the myelin sheath covering nerve cells and ultimately produce serious motor dysfunction. The real feeling is treated like an invading army that must be repelled at all costs. So long as the real feelings remain alien, behaviour based on them must be unreal. If the behaviour were real there would be immediate agony. Later in life when the stress is too much the person may adopt beliefs that aliens are set to invade. And they are; he just forgot who those aliens are.

One of the most interesting aspects of the immune system is that it seems structured in much the same manner as external behaviour. Human behaviour often proceeds as if a neurotic self or unreal self is acting against the interests of the real self. Analogously, the immune system has the task of differentiating between 'self' and 'not self'. It must be able to identify foreign cells as *not self*, and endogenous cells as self. There are diseases such as rheumatoid arthritis which are known as auto-immune dysfunctions – where the immune system makes the mistake of attacking its own cells as alien cells.

The fact that the immune system must learn to distinguish between proteins which are part of the body, and so-called 'non-self' proteins is most interesting. This suggests, as we have supposed, that some sort of cellular memory is critical to the effective performance of the immune system.

Thus, a sense of *self* is not just something that occurs in terms of personality; it is a process of the organism that reaches down to the most basic cellular levels. To 'lose oneself' or to 'find oneself' must also mean an alteration in those basic cellular processes as well. Those tiny microscopic cells carry the *self* around with them all of the time. And that is why I say that you cannot get 'better' in psychotherapy; you can only get back yourself, because when patients retrieve their deep hidden selves there are basic changes in the immune cells.

The brain and immune systems are so interactive that any kind of damage or burden to one will cause immediate alterations and abnormalities in the other. The immune system is equipped to replicate many of the brain's functions – somewhat like a second nervous system. When endorphines manufactured by lymphocytes are injected into the brains of mice, there is both an analgesic and a tranquillizing effect.

The immune system is able to manufacture substances that affect the processing of emotions and feelings. Thus, feelings not only affect the immune system, they are a part of it. There are pieces of feeling in those immune cells. This is the true meaning of a psychosomatic ailment: a stressful (traumatic) emotional state alters brain and immune functioning, which ultimately translates into disease. In these minute immune cells the mind and body meet as one. The mind is in the body and vice versa. Where is the mind? Everywhere in the system.

None of this is difficult to understand when we consider that animal life evolved a consciousness out of the most primitive cells. Human consciousness represents the most highly developed, complex, and organized form of cellular life. While the neocortex developed as a defence against adversity on one level, resulting in an attempt to understand and master adverse forces, the immune system developed as a defence against the body's invasion by foreign agents, parasites and microorganisms on a different level. Long before there was a cortex, there was an immune system that operated as a primitive consciousness. The immune system must be considered a level of consciousness which conforms to the laws of brain-mind functioning. When repression settles in the brain it also sets into the immune system. That is why psychological repression also diminishes immune effectiveness.

One reason the cortex evolved was to suppress the overload of harmful or threatening stimuli. I believe that before we used the cortex for complex thinking, we used it for *defence*. The highest level of cortical function is that of inhibition. It developed and took over when lower organization was unable to. Organisms had to become more 'conscious' of life-threatening environments in order to survive. The immune system provided a kind of cellular consciousness but it was not always equal to the task. That is why certain lymphocytes of the immune system react to stress or foreign invaders with biochemical properties similar to that of nerve cells in the brain.

So we can see the immune system as a diffused peripheral sensory system working in conjunction with the central nervous system, capable of giving and receiving information to and from the brain. Over time, the two systems have communicated so often and so strongly that they became a single network.

Once we establish that the functioning of the immune system is integrated with the functioning of the central nervous system, we can quickly see how imprinted pain, either emotional or physical, can render one unconscious simultaneously on cerebral and immune levels.

The Immune System as Consciousness

The immune system is a system of consciousness: it recognizes, encodes, remembers and responds. When there is a high enough level of stress, for example, the immune system no longer functions effectively; it no longer recognizes and destroys all of its enemies. Stress, in short, upsets perception by the immune system, just as it disrupts proper perception by the cortex.

The immune and central nervous systems both recognize stimuli and make appropriate responses. The difference is that the immune system takes longer than the central nervous system to react, and the cells of the immune system move around the body, while those of the brain and central nervous system are fairly stationary. You can condition the immune system just as you can condition the nervous system. Ordinarily, the immune system has an excellent memory system. Pain seems to 'fog' its memory. Thus the T-cells are no longer able to recognize the foreignness of an intruding virus, and mistakenly allow it to pass into the system.

What imprinted pain seems to do is produce unconsciousness on many levels of consciousness, including the immune level. It means that these cells are no longer able to recognize its enemies. Hence the system may attack itself. On the least harmful level, imprinted pain leaves the immune system in a chronically suppressed state, making some of us more susceptible to infections and colds.

The immune system, it seems, undergoes the same kind of identity crisis as we do psychologically, and in spite of its extraordinary memory for millions of antigens, suddenly finds itself faltering due to the surge of psychological pain. In its amnesia, the system cannot remember what happened to it before and therefore loses the memory that would combat disease.

While the number of cells is diminished by painful imprints, those that remain seem to 'run out of energy' as well; they do not make as many clones of themselves to ward off foreign invaders. Thus the immune army is heavily depleted and can't fight the battle.

It is very important for the natural killer cells of the immune system to maintain their vigour. There is sufficient knowledge now (including our own research) to show that pain and stress significantly alter the effectiveness of these cells. There is little doubt now that a vigorous natural killer cell system may indeed avert the development of cancer in humans. That is why it is so important that we understand the relationship of psychological states to the immune system. To say that cancer may be due to insufficient killer cell activity overlooks a vital step: *that lowered activity is a reflection of how early and how much pain was suppressed.*

Even if we were able to 'cure' a cancer by injecting powerful elements of the immune system such as interferon or interleukin II, we could not assume that the cause of the cancer was an organic, genetic insufficiency of these elements. It would be the same logic as saying that because aspirins cure headaches, the cause of headaches is insufficient aspirin.

I have noted elsewhere that inhibiting endorphines is a useful cancer therapy in animals. This does not mean that increased endorphines is the cause of cancer. We must ask ourselves why those endorphines are increased in the first place. Once we understand that they are secreted commensurate with the pain, the total picture becomes clearer.

Burn patients undergoing skin grafts are often given drugs to suppress immune reaction in order to avoid the rejection phenomenon (remember, the graft is alien). Those who undergo long-term immunosuppression therapy are far more prone to specific kinds of cancer. A common virus which would normally be attacked by these cells may finally end up as a tumour or cancer. This is one way we know that a competent immune system may serve as a preventative against cancer (in particular, in protecting us against virally-induced tumours).

The kind of person who is most prone to cancer is one who had a traumatic birth, usually of the parasympath variety, followed by deep repression, compounded by a love-less childhood. It is the very repressed individual who has everything bottled up inside, who gives himself no alternatives for action, and who is very fixed in his outlook and in his moral stance who falls ill.

Professor Marvin Stein of Mount Sinai School of Medicine in New York has clearly demonstrated that depressed patients have a less efficient lymphocyte system. These kinds of people tend to be inhibited and highly moralistic – mentally bound – so that they literally cannot find a way out of their problems. They retreat further into themselves, thus heightening their depression and their susceptibility to later cancer.

K. Achte has found that the closed up person suffers from the most rapidly advancing cancers. This study from the University of Helsinki in 1966 found that those who suffered most were the ones who did not want to know the truth of their condition. They rejected and/or repressed the information – an extension of what they were already doing internally. They tended to repress truth of their condition even when they were informed.

Clearly, repression is carcinogenic.

Lethal Loneliness

George Solomon states: 'We have come full circle back to clinical medicine: If noxious effects (such emotions as anxiety, grief, depression and loneliness) are immunosuppressive (suppressing the immune response), then it stands to reason that whatever psychotherapeutic intervention makes for a distress-free state of mind might be expected to improve immune function.'

Loneliness is clearly a feeling that can translate into immune system disease. Those who score high on the loneliness scale also have higher stress hormone levels, as well as lower levels of lymphocytes. The kind of loneliness, however, that is really damaging is not the loneliness of missing somebody at the age of thirty-two. It is catastrophic loneliness that is set up as an imprint in the first few hours of one's life. A child taken away from its mother in the first hours of its life also suffers from catastrophic aloneness.

Alienation and loneliness are not a single or unitary feeling, but are found in combination with many other related feelings, not the least of which is terror.

As we have seen in an earlier chapter, it is possible to enhance lymphocyte levels through Primal Therapy. Other techniques have sought to effect similar changes, but the results seem to be transient at best. Carl and Stephanie Simonton have developed a technique using guided imagery for the auxiliary treatment of cancer patients. They encourage patients to visualize immune cells gobbling up the cancer cells. Clearly, they are addressing lower brain centres with their imagery, which seems to have a temporary effect on the hypothalamus and on the immune system.

In similar studies, Nicholas R. Hall of the George Washington University Medical Centre has found that he is able to increase the number of lymphocytes circulating in the blood. Interestingly, as soon as the patient stops practising his imagery, there is a decline in the number of circulating lymphocytes. The idea is that, over time, by using positive

272 The New Primal Scream

controls, you can override the neuroendocrine feedback controls that lead to pathologic processes.

I frankly do not believe this. I think there is enough research now to indicate that pain and repression are central to changes in the immune system, that the immune system is a looming factor in the cause of some cancers and other catastrophic disease, and, finally, that one must address the generating sources of all these alterations in order to change the possibilities of illness.

Hall believes that positive thinking and overcoming negative emotions can make you well. First of all, I am not sure that there are such things as positive and negative emotions. I think there are emotions, *period*, and they exist because of real experiences in one's history. They are logical extensions of certain events, so that one doesn't *decide* to have a negative or positive emotion. I do not believe that there is a force in the present strong enough to override this history. Further, our measurements indicate that current forces are almost never equal in strength to past imprints. It is simply magical thinking to believe that through a variety of gimmicks, techniques, or special mechanisms one can combat serious illness. It is the apotheosis of the ahistoric and nondialectic approach, that does not see symptoms as the inevitable result of an internal conflict. Current manipulation of any kind neglects years and years of experiences that went into the making of that illness.

It is also likely that the element of hope in all of these therapies is effective for a time. Whether it is the hope of religion, mystical ideas, philosophy, directed imagery, and yes, even psychotherapy, it galvanizes the endorphines, allowing for some relief for a time.

The practice of imagining that little angels are hammering away at cancer cells may be effective because of the *hope* involved rather than because of the imaging process itself – a hope that is pushing against hopelessness and despair. That is probably why those who are most helpful and determined to overcome their cancer have a better chance of doing so. I don't think this is a very long-lasting event. What they are fighting against is a tidal wave of loneliness, defeat, terror, alienation and frustration – all feelings that demand expression.

Symptoms such as anxiety, phobia, obsessions, high blood pressure, colitis, are all warning signs. They signal unfinished business, telling of unfulfilled needs and hidden hurts. To artificially remove them is to deprive the system of important warning signals. It won't be long before the system finds another alarm to ring. These signs are critical in the psychologic economy of the individual; for they are a reminder of a missing link, something that we need to make us normal and healthy. Odd, symptoms as a warning for health; but they are.

I do not want to take an unnecessarily negative position towards people who have cancer and who do have hope, because I think that hope in the short run is helpful for surmounting some kinds of cancer. Joan Borysenko of Harvard Medical School has found that those cancer patients who do best maintain a strong degree of hoping, convinced that they will recover. Those who fight cancer do better than those who give in to despair and helplessness. But I think that despair and helplessness are *already* characteristic of patients who develop cancer. A defeated feeling not only accounts for the fact that the patient does not survive, but may account for the onset of the disease in the first place.

It is possible to 'buy time' with certain techniques so as to make some changes in the immune system. That seems to be evident. But when we remember that even with massive electric shocks, time after time, we do not change the imprinted memory, we realize what it would take to finally change that imprint, even just a fraction.

I believe that enhancing the state of self-deception ('I'm happy when I'm really sad' or 'I'm calm when I'm really angry') finally aids the forces of repression, and we now know what *that* does. Our physiology is not easily fooled, and eventually we shall be stricken down by our own reality.

Repression as a Fatal Disease

One clear example of the effect of the repression of pain on catastrophic disease was a psychotic woman referred to me by a hospital. It seemed as though she was having continuous birth experiences in the hospital without being aware of it. This included being in the foetal position with many infantile postures, the inability to verbalize, and so forth. We could not take her (because we do not have in-patient facilities) and so referred her to another psychiatric hospital, where for many months she was given massive does of tranquillizers (up to 600 mg/day of thorazine).

At the end of one year the woman developed cancer. Four months later she died. Reasons for her death, in my opinion: a lack of love, a terrible isolation, years of depression, loneliness and solitude. As long as she was simply *in agony* she was mentally ill; but when the agony was chemically repressed, she died of that repression in the form of cancer. They took away her suffering and offered death in exchange. As long as she could suffer acutely, she survived. The woman simply (or not so simply) exchanged mental psychosis for cellular psychosis (cancer). The imprints had their day.

Will a positive attitude help? There are at least two schools of thought about this issue. Researchers at the University of Pittsburgh School of Medicine studied 75 women with breast cancer. Those patients who were apethatic, listless, and lacked vigour had fewer natural killer cells and a poorer prognosis. Those who were most manifestly distressed at the enormity of their disease, and whose anxiety later dropped off, maintained high levels of natural killer cells throughout. Most interestingly, those who appeared calm and well-adjusted from the beginning, who neither focused on the disease nor talked about it, together with those who 'staunchly denied their disease', did not fare so well. The researchers concluded that the 'brave approach' is not very helpful.

The brave approach was also studied by scientists at Yale

and at the University of California, San Francisco, who found that so-called brave patients do indeed have lower natural killer cell activity. Raging against death, at least initially, seems to be a more helpful approach.

The answer to catastrophic disease isn't going to be found in the cells alone; it is going to be found in the carrier of those cells. It is very difficult to find loneliness and despair in a single cell. Yet despair and loneliness are obviously lodged there in some way. But the cells only reflect the total individual. If we don't know the history of that individual, no cellular analysis is going to yield the answer.

Stress, despair, futility and loneliness are not always obvious to an observer. There are those who are so totally unconscious that they dissemble automatically. They would deny stress even when pointed out to them. Though everyone carries it around, stress is like some grand secret that is not to be acknowledged. The endorphines are like disappearing ink. The load we carry doubles us over, but the endorphines blur our vision so that we see nothing. The paradox is that even when one is dying from it, no one can see what 'it' is.

Measuring the Effects of Early Trauma

Could it really be that very early traumas are so important? First, this is not simply a *theory* about the effects of trauma. We have measured the effects of the birth trauma, both during the reliving process and later. We have reversed all manner of serious illness after patients have relived these earlier events. This is true in both the mental and physiological spheres. That is why when we alter personality in our therapy, we also alter susceptibility to disease.

Previously, these patients had seen all manner of specialists for a variety of diseases. Each specialist treating a different symptom as a different disease, each missing the underlying identical source of the problem. They were, in effect, chasing the imprint hither and yon.

I'm not strong enough to stand the remedies;
it's all I can do to stand the disease ...

Molière

12

Illness as The Silent Scream

Discussion

Unhappiness is lethal. Psychological anguish is mortal. Hidden pain and unconscious suffering are the killers.

Why do we get sick? Because we are already sick and don't know it. Neurosis is the key illness of our day. It has so many manifestations that it seems like dozens of ailments. It is the most intangible and insidious of diseases because it has no single location, no focus, no smell, no look, no obvious structure; to make matters worse, the person is not only unaware of his illness but will deny its existence when confronted with its possibility. Once the neurosis sets in, however, it is only a matter of time until symptoms appear, either physical or mental.

The better hidden this illness, the more damage it does. The most arcane, hence unbelievable, of events such as those that occur in the womb or around birth tend to do the most damage because they are falling on a naive and vulnerable brain. These events are the culprit in many catastrophic ailments, such as cancer, yet the distance between the occurrence of cancer and the trauma at its origin is so great as to seem almost beyond logic.

It is diabolic and unjust that that which makes us suffer the most is usually the most difficult to find. The treatment process is difficult because the truth of the condition – the connection between a past trauma and a current illness – lies

277

only within the patient, not in the mind of an expert. Indeed, the truth is constantly trying to express itself in all of us only to be beaten back by the heavy hand of repression.

We must remember that the repressive system has been perfected over millions of years; even the lowly earthworm has the mechanisms for repression (in its manufacture of endorphines). We need unconsciousness to keep society going, and we need an accommodating social system to keep the unconsciousness going. It is this pervasive unconsciousness that shall finally be our undoing. The legacy of the perfected endorphines and gating system will be to banish us from this earth.

The body neither lies nor exaggerates. It is the tabernacle of truth. The memories of the body are not approximate; they are precise. As is the damage they do.

The screams of the body are muted by the symptom which absorbs the energy of the trauma, filters and purifies it. How many people are being treated for hypertension, for example, a silent killer, with no reference to their history? We have seen in our research how imprinted pain has a direct relationship to blood pressure levels.

If we do not take into account a person's history, it is all too easy to go astray in diagnosis and treatment. The patient is then treated as an ahistoric entity who has this or that symptom, whether migraine or compulsions, with no antecedent roots and thus, no context.

There is still the tendency to confuse the symptom with the disease. Hence, the suppression of the symptom is taken as tantamount to cure; bury the symptom and imagine that the ailment no longer exists.

In our therapy, when we transform a symptom into its reality, from its silence into its screams, we see what role pain is playing in the illness. The ailment, I repeat, is neurosis.

Clearly, symptoms have their own reality and must be treated. The problem is that specialists become experts in the detailed minutiae of the specific afflictions. They learn more and more about the symptom and less about its origins and the humans who exhibit the symptoms.

Ironically, an effective treatment of the apparent disease may still shorten our lives, for it is the treachery of neurosis that undoes us. So we have lower blood pressure, but more pressure somewhere else. The doctor treating the disease is looking at the end product of something perhaps begun at the age of six months. So here the doctor is confronted with a forty-year-old sick patient whose cause lies in the 'antipodes of his unconscious'. That unconscious spouts forth a silent but continuous energy force. The patient then has blood tests and various cells examined in an attempt to understand the ailment, when in fact hidden historical forces have already deformed the cells many years ago. Worse, repression has rendered the early traumas forgotten. So now we have deformed cells that have been altered by events that cannot be remembered nor acknowledged.

The doctor is at a disadvantage. He can see hypertension before him. He cannot see a six-month-old infant crying it out in the crib, all alone and terrified, nor a child of five all bottled up by critical, tyrannical parents. In a sense, the doctor is not alone; even the patient himself cannot see that child. Even if those early traumas were recognized and understood, it would be difficult for a specialist to comprehend that they have stayed in the system over decades of time and completely unchanged.

As if that weren't enough, the traumas of which I have spoken may not be dramatic events at all; indeed, most often they are not. They are day in, day out, lack of affection or a constantly tense mother and angry father; small events which accumulate into major traumas after years. 'Have you had a happy childhood?' the doctor asks. Too often, the repressed patient answers affirmatively. Consider, therefore, what a monumental task faces the doctor. It is enough work to treat the symptom. He or she would be most happy to at least see the symptom disappear. Imagine the work entailed in treating the whole individual. Worse still, to treat his entire history.

The Unity of Pain and Symptom

Because pain forms a unity with its symptoms it is clearly a mistake to lift a symptom out of its historical context and treat it as some viable thing that has a separate existence. Consider teenage suicide. One can investigate all sorts of current sociological processes to explain the upsurge in the suicide rate, but recent evidence indicates that a difficult childbirth in which these children came very close to death is one of the key indicators of later suicide attempts. The scientific journal, *Lancet*, found 'strong links between teenage suicide and respiratory stress for more than an hour at birth as well as absence of proper antenatal care'.

This kind of research would have been unthinkable a few years back, yet it is exactly what is needed with regard to medical ailments.

I am by no means against treatment of illness. I believe that one can be helped with drug addiction or alcoholism in drying-out centres. Counselling also helps to handle day-to-day problems. One must control one's diet to reduce hypertension, and use drugs to control its fluctuations. But this is an endless task. Beating back history is not the same as resolving it.

More breast cancer patients had divorced parents before the age of sixteen than non-patients. That is a simple statistic, but think of the implications. Something outside the person happened to make her predisposed to a potentially fatal disease. Secondly, that event lingered on in the system as a most unwelcome guest, even though it made no noise and didn't seem to cause any trouble. Thirdly, its stay could be lethal. The question is, 'What is the process by which two parents battling and finally separating becomes translated into a tumour in the breast of their daughter perhaps a decade or two later?'

The first implication is clear. Something that happens outside of us manages to get inside and change our physiology enough to make us sick later on. Not only sick, but sick enough to die. A parents' divorce, in short, can kill. Implication number two: a psychological event registers in the cells (as well as in the brain) which are eventually transformed into malignancy by that memory.

The need for stability, trust, and safety has been shattered in the young girl. The girl may try to 'get over it' but no matter how much she tries and no matter how much she believes she is over it, the body *never* gets over it. One day she finds a lump in her breast. Try to convince her that her mother's divorce ten years ago is the cause.

The Pressure of the Imprint

The neurotic is under siege; the attack is by a painful, alien, memory trying to enter consciousness. In a strange paradox, consciousness, the highest achievement of mankind, becomes the enemy. The neurotic's whole life is spent trying to keep himself unconscious, even while he is expanding his awareness. Some of the most erudite people are the most unconscious. All their widespread knowledge is used in the service of repression. The body's panoply of resources is used to keep us unconscious. It is no wonder that as consciousness approaches patients develop a fever and high blood pressure. It is an attempt to combat the disease of feeling. In infection, the fever aids in sending white blood cells to the site. In neurosis the body treats consciousness as if it were a virus. It treats consciousness as the enemy because in childhood it was.

Consciousness, therefore, is the specific medicine for a wide variety of ailments, while unconsciousness is the essential element for disease. From cardiac distress to hypertension, from haemorrhoids to diabetes, from colitis to migraine, disease responds to consciousness and is effectively treated through it.

Feeling feelings brings the unconsciousness forward, unlocks memory, and broadens awareness. Riding feelings through the vehicle of time back to the past unlocks the present and opens gates of access to the unconscious. I seriously doubt that a significant proportion of most major diseases would be manifest without a substratum of repressed feelings. There is no substitute for consciousness.

When one suffers, it is tempting to want to get well at once. So one tries hypnosis (the antithesis of consciousness) as a cure for smoking, drinking, or physical illness. We have come to accept relief as the same as cure, when it clearly is not. We seek magic – this pill or that, this instant cure or that, this vitamin or that, this seminar or weekend retreat, that lecture or confrontation group, this massage or those vapours, for immediate transformation. We take lithium as a panacea for our depression without ever asking ourselves, 'Why am I depressed?' or, 'What is depression?' Since the answer is so remote, most people prefer not even to ask the question. Out of a basic hopelessness hope springs eternal and forces us to find something to put our faith in, whether it is a macrobiotic diet or a guru.

To be sure, it is a long leap between a father who leaves home when a child is two and the emergence of arthritis three decades later in that same person. The lacunae between chain-smoking at forty and being locked in one's room repeatedly at age four are so great as to invite scoffing if such a connection is merely implied.

Fortunately, however, experts don't have to make the connection; patients will do it for them, given the right circumstances. When enough patients with the same or similar ailments relive specific traumas and recover from that ailment, the connection between past history and current symptom becomes evident.

The Silent Conspiracy about our Pain

There seems to be a silent conspiracy about our neurosis. Half the ads on television are selling painkillers. No one dares say to the public 'You are in pain'. It is just assumed, implicit, announced *sotto voce*. The painkillers are for head-aches, stomach distress, or backaches, but the simple fact is that many of us are hurting. And we don't know what to call our hurt. There isn't even a name for it. What do you call the hurt inflicted by a mother who was depressed all the time or a father who was impatient and demanding?

Pain is a kind of given these days. Our deep-lying pains are rising to the surface, and though they find different chan-nels for their expression – from anxiety and phobias, from obsessions to migraine and stomach distress – treatment is often identical: painkillers. Tranquillizers, from alcohol to valium, are all ultimately painkillers. Because the pain is part of the body, we are slowly killing our selves. We are treating 'dis-ease', but not the disease.

The Role of Primal Therapy

Does everyone need therapy? Can only Primal Therapy undo all of this? Clearly I have made the point that pain is at the basis of neurosis which, in turn, feeds into a multitude of ailments. Any effective therapy must therefore address itself to the basis of this widespread affliction, and it must do so in a systematic way, pain by pain, in reverse order from the way in which the original pain was laid down. The most recent and easily experienced first, the most remote and catastro-phic last.

Not everyone can do Primal Therapy. Not everyone needs to or even wants to. There is a vast population that is 'making it'. They are healthy and can adjust to their surroundings. Crying with a close friend when the need arises is important. Having a warm shoulder to lean on is essential. We all need to express how we feel from time to time, even if we are not reliving an old event or writhing on the floor in pain. We need to talk out our sentiments, resentments, hurts and humiliations. If we isolate ourselves so that we have no friends to talk to we are worse off. Unfortunately, those in need of all this are usually the ones who are emotionally removed from others and have few friends.

It is important to let go from time to time. If one cannot cry, just screaming may bring up buried tears. The neurotic really has only two choices: one is to feel and connect with his past imprints; the second is to discharge the energy of those feelings without proper connection. The first is resolving; the second is ameliorating. Both are better than continued repression.

Primal Therapy is a way of recapturing feelings. There are natural ways as well, namely, to feel the traumas of one's life when they occur. When the trauma is too great, or when society makes feeling opprobrious, then my therapy can be useful.

People can feel without the therapy, and no doubt did so long before the therapy existed. We have been forced to invent techniques to root out feelings only because defence systems have become labyrinthine. If they weren't, any friend could do the same. We are supposed to cry when we're sad and act on the fact when we're angry. We are equipped for that.

The repressive system is the backup system which takes over when we cannot act naturally. It is charged with holding back our natural feelings. We don't just act unnaturally or in an unreal way; we are unnatural on the most fundamental level. Being unnatural and acting against our biologic nature leads to disease. Restoring tears restores the system's ability to be itself.

There is no shortcut, no easy way, as much as I'd like to offer such a thing. I believe that the unique contribution of Primal Therapy is to offer access to the deepest layers of the unconscious that were heretofore unreachable. While Freud posited unconscious forces, he could neither specify what they were nor find a method of penetrating down to their deeper levels. This was partly because he believed in a timeless, immutable unconscious that did not derive from life experience, but from some subterranean genetic cavern. He felt, therefore, it was best left alone, suppressed or controlled.

Thus, for Freud and his followers, the most liberating of factors, the unconscious, became an anathema to be avoided lest the person disintegrate or somehow lose his personal cohesion. Back a half century ago they had no idea about how to integrate shattering unconscious forces, because they thought they were some sort of psychologic demons that could never be understood. Now we know that, in dialectic fashion, when the unconscious is made conscious, we set the stage for cure. Even though consciousness is the antidote for serious illness, unconsciousness was an antidote also, early in our lives, when too much pain could have been lethal.

Nature Versus Nurture: The Role of Heredity in Illness

The legacy of repression is that we shall die from our own survival mechanisms. This is because these mechanisms are designed for the survival of the *species* not the individual.

The argument over what is nature or genetic and what is caused by our social conditions has raged on from time immemorial, mostly from a philosophical perspective. Having access to events in the womb, however, allows us to clarify, for the first time, some of this dilemma from a biological perspective. Until recently, we thought life's shaping events began when we were born, and we attributed all the rest to heredity. Now we see that life's most critical and powerful shaping events take place before we are born, and what we used to think was heredity may, indeed, be the result of those events in the womb.

Thus, if a child is short for his age, (something we used to explain by looking back at the grandparents or great grandparents) we now know that this may be the result of a smoking mother. A hyperkinetic child may be acting like his father did when he was a child, leading to the assumption that he is a 'chip off the old block'. In reality, however, the birth trauma itself may have galvanized the boy's system into hyperkinesis.

This is not to deny the effects of heredity. The mere fact that we look like our mother or father, that we have the same nose, eyes or hair colour, is clear evidence. And there is no reason why nature should stop there. We may also inherit tendencies towards heart disease, hypothyroidism, migraine, or high blood pressure. Whether or not disease tendencies become manifest often depends on the imprint. It is clear that even with inherited tendencies we may not be afflicted with the disease if life is not too harsh. When the body is under stress, however, it is going to react where it is most vulnerable. Thus, a hereditary tendency towards stomach distress will lead to stomach ulcers in a person who is under continual stress.

In general, we can say from our experience of having reversed a number of diseases through the reliving processes of therapy, that some diseases thought to be hereditary may not be strictly so, but stem from events that we never before considered tributaries, such as womb life. This would include mental illness such as schizophrenia and manic-depression.

A number of studies have found strong correlations between birth trauma and later psychosis. A recent study by Wilcox and Nasallah found that in those schizophrenics with a poor treatment prognosis there was a significant history of perinatal trauma.

Migraines are manifested regularly with the rise of very early pain in our therapy. The symptom becomes acute as pain approaches consciousness and is eliminated when pain actually enters consciousness for resolution. We see the migraine patient turning blue from lack of oxygen, gasping for breath for minutes, seemingly in danger of dying from lack of air. It is an event that cannot be faked, and it happens with such regularity to migraine patients as to make reasonable hypotheses such as those we have advanced. In fact, we don't really have to hypothesize. We are looking at the unconscious and seeing what it contains. Migraine can be triggered by any situation in which the adult feels he can't breathe – a job that keeps him down and 'suffocates' him; a relationship that gives a person 'no room to breathe'. For women, it can be the time just before their period when their hormonal changes resemble the same changes that took place just before birth. The trigger can be almost any stress that 'reminds' the body of the original trauma.

Migraine headaches are very different from tension headaches, which generally have a later origin. Migraines deal with the vascular system and are less involved with the muscular system. There are times when so-called tension headaches stem from early trauma. For example, severe rotation of the neck at birth. Generally they have a strong second-line component. These headaches are not like migraines, which feel like a hot rod in the temple or behind the eyes. Tension headaches involve the neck and the head in a more global way – a tight band around the head for example. They are less likely to lead to later cerebral stroke than the migraine, because the pressure is muscular rather than vascular.

What survives in humans are those qualities which have helped the species survive in the past. Since our present is going to be someone else's past, what happens to us eventually has the ability to eventually be passed on.

In the most general sense, neurosis occur because it is compatible with life's overall aim – to perpetuate itself. Under stress, the brain and body scan the past, both the personal and the species' past, to see what worked before. The system then digs into its archives and retrieves the behaviour again. It retrieves the prototype. If we want to understand symptoms we must understand the prototype.

Gaining Access to the Silent Scream

Without access to remote origins of development, we are

forced to deal with what is known as phenotypes or appear-ances. That is why phenotypic therapies – either psychoth-erapy or physical therapy – couch their results in appearances rather than in profound physiological states.

The more limited the access, the less likely the cure. Remission of symptoms, yes. Temporary amelioration, yes. Relief, yes. But cure, no. So many months off drugs, so many weeks symptom free, is not the same as cure.

This is just a reminder that trauma is not registered simply as an idea, but as an *experience*, and must be dealt with as *ex-perience* – not simply discussed.

Conclusion

Neurosis is not a perversion of man, it is a necessary ingre-dient for his development. The human structure of today is the product of the recorded (imprinted) memory of mankind. A person's genetic progression throughout life reflects the unfolding of the history of mankind. This recapitulation of the species allows us to understand our phylogenetic past by looking closely at individual development. The minute exam-ination of an individual is to observe ancient history, as well.

To see how excess pain causes humans to flee to their cortex and defend with ideation is to get an idea of how and why the cortex developed in the first place. We have only to look at those who have taken a good deal of LSD which undoes lower level gates to see what great adversity does. It does what it did in history; forces the person to recruit high level cortical neurons, conjuring up mystical ideas as a way of dealing with the onrush.

It is a powerful notion that one can travel back decades to recapture one's personal history and undo aspects of that history. But it is so. It is possible to release the suffering component of early trauma into consciousness along with the specific memory, and to discharge the energy and the pressure of that memory forever. When this has been done, as we have seen, there are significant permanent changes in important physiologic parameters including growth, stress and sex hormones, cholesterol levels, and immune functioning. The same thing that makes us sick – *pain* – makes us well. The difference is only a matter of integration. No integration means illness; integration means health.

Finally, it must be recognized that neurosis is a biologic disease. It is not caused by purely biological agents, but it is manifested biologically and psychologically at the same time. You can die of despair and hopelessness. And you can die of trying to suppress those feelings.

Hope abandoned becomes despair, and hope is essential to survival. Even unreal hope. Hence the cults and myriad schools of psychotherapy. It is not possible to live in a constant state of hopelessness, as so many depressives will testify. So many people search for 'the answer' – not because of the content of the answers, but because the search involves hope. That is why some psychotherapies tend to be endless. The patient doesn't want it to end. So long as he has not explored the depths of hopelessness he is determined to keep hope alive.

Secrets Keep You Sick

I believe there is an effective treatment for catastrophic illness. It involves dealing with those forces strong enough to disrupt natural evolution, producing bitter, broken and sickly adults out of the healthy, lively children they once were. So let me end with a few 'Janovian laws', if you will:

1. Keeping secrets from yourself makes you sick. (The problem is that no act of will can help divulge those secrets that lie hidden away.)
2. Suffering is healing as long as it is at a level that can be integrated.
3. Salvation lies in pain. (Where have we heard that before?)

4. He who acts it out, lasts it out; he who acts it in, caves in.

The No 1 killer in the world today is not cancer or heart disease. It is *repression*. Unconsciousness is the real danger, and neurosis the real killer. In order to lie, you need to know the truth. The body always tells the truth and overwhelming truths force the mind to lie.

The ability to have access to the earliest events of birth and infancy, I believe, is crucial to the ultimate explanation of the intensity, quality and direction of many catastrophic diseases. We can pinpoint origins and deal with impelling sources rather than abstractly theorizing. Finally, *symptoms do not have to be a mystery*; they can be a precise map leading back to precise causes.

Illness is often a silent scream. The cure is to give it voice.

13

Sex, Sensuality and Sexuality

A sex problem isn't a sex problem unless it's a sex problem. That seems like a contradiction, or just semantics. It is not. Sex problems reflect what we are as total human beings and reflect our neuroses. To extract the sex problem out of the human condition is to consider a person no more than a bunch of parts that need fixing here and there – a most mechanical view.

Problems in sex are very much like our dreams – a condensation of our entire lives, circumscribed, and yet reflecting and symbolizing deep unconscious processes. A sex problem is rarely just a sex problem. The neurotic, no matter how fixated on sex he or she may be, can't be truly sexual because neurosis, with its repression of feeling, desexualizes. For the feeling person, each sexual act is a sexual act. For the neurotic, the sex act is burdened with old neurotic needs which can never be satisfied and thus basically a discharge of tension eroticized.

Frigidity in Two Women

Let me describe two women I recently saw. Both were in Primal Therapy. The first woman could not have an orgasm. She was considered frigid. She had gone to sex therapists to learn sexual techniques, but to no avail. The techniques did not change her feeling state. She would get excited and simply shut down. As her therapy progressed, things changed. After eight months, she could become somewhat aroused in sex, but then would have coughing jags and often feel she was going to suffocate. After one year and two months of therapy, she could get more aroused and then found out something strange: at a certain point of excitement she was thrown into a birth primal. She hunched, arched, writhed and slithered; finally she convulsed while remaining conscious.

She realized that her frigidity came from deep trauma at birth which produced massive repression and the subsequent inability to feel anything. That included sex. It was such an early, hence deep, repression that it blocked all full feeling experiences. It was as though the repressed birth trauma sat on top of any other feeling experience and during sex that trauma and its repression presented itself before any other feeling could occur. There was no way she could experience convulsive orgasm while holding down convulsive trauma from the start of her life.

At the two-year mark in her therapy, she began to have birth primals. One day, after two and a half years and some fifty brain primals, she found that she lubricated heavily after one of her reliving episodes – an episode that was not directly related to sex. Yet it was liberating and continued to be so. By the three-year mark, her frigidity was radically diminished and she could have orgasms. She had relived a convulsive, capped trauma and she could then convulse for pleasure. It was a monumental achievement which occurred without the patient's attacking the sex problem directly.

If one could have seen the hundreds of hours of agony that went into her primals, one would have realized the amount of pain and repression that can block sexual experience. One would have realized what a minor dent sex therapy makes in those situations. The second woman learned in therapy that she had a mountain of sadness inside of her. Whenever she had an orgasm she cried. Every time she tried to experience sexual feelings, other feelings came up as well. These feelings were all of *one piece*. When she felt aroused it excited the sadness; she felt it all at once.

The only real sex problems are those which are a result of a lack of education and experience. In such cases a sex problem is a sex problem. Those cases are rare. It is true, however, that for those who cannot feel and have had limited experience, education and technique are a great help. However, feeling people manage to learn by themselves to do what is instinctive and natural.

Does this discount the experience of so many of us, in which the atmosphere at home ranged from nonsexual to antisexual? No, it does not. Feeling parents are also pro-sex. They allow the child all her feelings, and have not suppressed her from the time she could crawl. On the other hand, the non-feeling parent is suppressive in all spheres, as one might expect. A parent who demands obedience and respect, who doesn't allow the child to get angry or jealous or demanding or excited and enthusiastic, will transmit that suppression to the sexual area without one word about sex being spoken.

Later on, as adults, we find that friendly grandma, Dr Ruth, speaking openly about sex and giving permission for it. In her own way, she is helping change the atmosphere around sex as best she can. However, she can change very little of what we learned in childhood; one's sex life can be ruined just by a general atmosphere about feeling in the home. If every time you got loud and enthusiastic you were shushed by parents, when it later becomes time to give way to total abandon, it won't be possible. Early memories which shaped you will intrude.

One girl was very attached to her father. The only sane one of her parents. She was devastatingly traumatized at the age of six by his death, and 'learned' never to get too involved emotionally after that. She kept her emotional distance and could not get into sex fully. The minute she got too attached to someone and too excited, she shut down; the old wound intruded. When her body felt good and anticipated love, it remembered the leaving by her father and the agony. This stopped her feeling, and no conscious will to do otherwise could surmount it. Clearly, she didn't remember her father's leaving when she was having trouble with sexual excitement, but her body did. That memory in the body is what produced the problem with her body in sex. She had to travel down a trail of history and find that specific memory in order to undo the physical problem. There could be no other substitutes, for in that physical memory lay the problem and the solution.

Sexuality radiates from someone in the same way that lack of it also radiates. One senses its presence or its absence in others. The feeling person has an aura about her or him which has nothing to do with trying to be sexy. You either are or you are not.

Sex Problems Are Human Problems

So if a sex problem is not really a sex problem, what is it? It is a human problem. We need to talk about that human condition before getting to the so-called 'sex problem'. What does the term 'human condition' mean? It means, among other things, that events happen to us early in our lives which warp us. The central condition for this warping process is what we had to do to get love, how we had to twist our natural and spontaneous selves out of shape to get what at least looked like love. I say, 'what looked like', because true love requires no effort. The minute you make an effort, conscious or not, what you get is not real love but an unsatisfactory substitute. Once we are warped, we are warped completely, not in one part of ourselves or another.

This, then, is reflected in our sex life, which I remind you, is like our dreams – condensations of our total past experience. It is therefore, the hub of us – the central kernel which can tell us what we really are and how we have been warped. There is, in fact, a strong equivalence between dreams and sex. Both deal with feeling, both involve condensations of our whole lives, both operate on a level where feelings are transformed into images.

Feelings, Symbols and Perversion

When one is sexually aroused there is a general arousal of the entire system. Sexual arousal means arousal of all feelings: old feelings ascend and provoke the creation of symbols. In certain perversions, feelings can be triggered off and then immediately transformed into sexual rituals. Primal pain is then eroticized so that the pain is never felt for what it is. For some, it is sex, for others it can be food. The impulse for sex or to eat is equal to the strength of the pain. If one cannot act-out, one begins to suffer, not from lack of sex or food, but from the real pain that the ritual masks. In exhibitionism, for example, a number of individuals report that when they were in the throes of their particular sexual ritual they felt as if they were in some other world. The exhibition was a symbol of their lives in which an old feeling from childhood predominated. This gave the person the feeling of being in another world – the old world of childhood feelings.

One exhibitionist I treated had to flash in parking lots next to women who were loading their cars. Was he trying to prove his manhood, as psychoanalysis would have it? No. He was trying to shock these women into showing simple emotion. He had to exaggerate everything with his mother, because she was so 'dead' that simple emotion aroused nothing in her. He needed to have an emotional woman respond to him. Because of other warping events in his life, having to do with sex, there was a combination of motives and a focus for his problem in the sex area.

Another man with the same kind of mother became a pornographic magazine freak. This chief executive officer of a major corporation was embarrassed at having to frequent porno parlours, yet his intellect couldn't stop him. What was he after? He wanted to see pleasure on a woman's face. It was as simple as that. The women in these magazines enjoyed sex. They even showed ecstasy, which might be one reason why these magazines are often outlawed. Our culture, in its grandiose mercy, manages to repress sex magazines wherever it can, perhaps because women in them simulate great joy while having sex. It certainly goes with the old cultural norm that a 'good' woman is only a passive participant in the act for her man, never enjoying sex or seeking it on her own.

This patient bought these magazines and masturbated continuously while watching the women's faces, not their genitalia or breasts. It was really an unsexual act done with his sex organ. It brought relief – relief for his basic need.

Sex is one of the most effective ways deprived individuals can make themselves feel good, since the people who were charged with the task – their parents – could not. If one could release tension as effectively in some other way that act-out, rather than sex, would become the problem.

We see from the above that a pervert is someone who has been perverted, not sexually, but in every way, particularly in his search for love. As a young child, he was warped by his environment and became sexually perverted only when he became sexually mature. It is not possible that someone is just a little weird in sex, but perfectly normal in every other respect. He may seem normal, but like all neurotics, he has a secret inner life that is not so apparent. It is only when you get emotionally involved with him that you can discover that facet of his or her personality, often as well hidden as the sexual perversion.

The Split Self and Sexuality

What is key about neurosis? It is the split self – a feeling self which is sealed away from an understanding self. It often happens that a person will start to feel, but then 'splits'. He observes the self, rather than reacting. It is the real self which begins to feel, but the neurotic self which splits away, aborts the feeling process, and takes behaviour down the symbolic channel.

All kinds of complications arise from the neurotic split. I am reminded of one of my patients who is a dramatic example of the split in neurosis. He was a well-known sports broadcaster, the picture of elegance, but he would find himself cruising parks after dark in search of young boys for sex. Not only was his homosexuality well hidden, but it was the kind of homosexuality which indicated he had the emotional level of a ten-year-old. (Sex, incidentally, also brings out the emotional level we are on.)

This sports broadcaster was married to a mature woman, but his unfulfilled needs predominated and drove him to his sex acts. His father was cold and distant. His older brother, to whom he was deeply attached, left home when the patient was only ten. That great trauma arrested his emotional development and left a gaping hole, a need he never got over. He sought symbolic fulfilment. He continued his act-out until he felt his agonizing need in its early context.

Life's circumstances perverted him and his sexual orientation. He was the best athlete in school, and because of his macho image could never act out his needs. In addition, there was no one in the home he could go to with his feelings. The pressure mounted until he could no longer contain himself. He then began his secret life. Because he felt compelled to keep up his image, the split was unbearable and his tension level was high. He drank and smoked to ease the tension. These self-destructive habits he used to ease his burden were going to put him in an early grave. This is the real meaning of dying from a lack of love.

The latent homosexuals I have seen, both men and women, are often heavy drinkers and drug users. Constantly denying an overwhelming need forces them to turn to something for relief. The person then becomes an alcoholic and is treated for alcoholism as if it were the problem, when in reality it is the attempted *solution*. Trying to kill pain is normal when you're suffering; it is not an aberration.

In some respects, the homosexual is a lot straighter than some heterosexuals. He or she has needs and goes about trying to fulfil them, warped or not. At least the homosexual is pursuing love. A heterosexual who is a latent homosexual (who denies his real needs) is further removed from solving the basic problem because he or she is no longer even trying to find love in most cases, and may deny that such a need exists.

An alcoholic football player came to me because of fears that he might be homosexual. Only after a year of constant treatment did he become aware that he had been deprived of his father's love. He wasn't afraid of being homosexual as much as he was frightened by his desperate need to act out the need for male love. He became worried when he had those 'funny' feelings when he tackled and held an opposing player. He was being pressed by this need for love, and as an adult converted it into fears of homosexuality.

When he felt that need for what it was, when he screamed out time after time with his arms outstretched, 'Hold me, daddy, hold me!' the fears were no longer there. Needless to say, his drinking diminished radically.

The act-out gets complicated. I treated one man who 'dressed up'. His father died when he was very young and his older brother took over the leadership of the family. The older brother was closer in age to his sisters, whom he seemed to favour, and somehow the young boy began to think, not entirely consciously, that to be a girl meant to be loved. He was so crushed and so full of need after the death of his father, that the slightest hints in his environment changed his attitude and behaviour.

Another patient dressed up in women's panties while masturbating. He wanted to live with a woman but couldn't because he was afraid she would learn about his secret compulsion. His mother worked and had left him alone during most of his childhood. When he was six, he began holding the only remnant of his mother – her panties, which she left on the bedroom floor. Later, he began to sniff the panties to emotionally remind himself of her scent. In his teens, he took to wearing them. The habit took on a life of its own and he had long ago forgotten why he did it. It had its own force and he was helpless before its power. Panties excited him because need excites and agitates towards fulfillment. The basis of his act-out was still his need for his mother – something he never got over. There was a hole in his upbringing that wasn't sick. It was real. It had to be felt. There was nothing more that could be done.

The ways to act-out sex symbolically are innumerable. Many men relate only to women's breasts because, whether they know it or not, they were deprived of adequate breast feeding in the earliest weeks of their lives. I saw a homosexual who could only feel great relief when sucking his partner's penis while his partner came. In his imagination it was, (not to be too Freudian) mother's milk.

A woman patient of mine became homosexual for the most obvious of reasons – her mother was cold and hard and never touched her. She needed a woman's love, and further, she wanted it in one position, the 'spoons' position with her holding her partner from behind. It was only after months of therapy that she relived a trauma of holding her mother like that at the age of two and being thrown out of bed and told she was too big to sleep with mommy any more. The memory of that trauma shocked her, because she realized that what comforted her most (her father was a violent alcoholic) was holding mommy like that, and that was never to be again. She had spent her whole adult life looking for it.

Let's suppose we call her problem a perversion. In my analytic days, I was taught that any sexual proclivity to the exclusion of all others was a perversion, and that we must try to recondition that 'bad' habit. Can you see how silly and vain that would be? It would be a useless exercise for just about any ingrained sexual behaviour, including lack of behaviour, such as frigidity.

I remember seeing a woman who was deathly afraid of

men. Her father was terribly domineering. She was comfort-able and could arrive at a partial orgasm only when she rode on top – a position in which she dominated. Is that simple habit to be treated with sex therapy? It reflected thousands of experiences with her father, day in and day out, and her terror of him.

Fear of men was part of her general personality. She married a wimp just so she wouldn't have to be so afraid – all done unconsciously, of course. She was never aware of this fear, however, or how it dictated her choice of marital part-ners.

The same principles apply when considering why some women can achieve orgasm while masturbating but not in sex with a partner. There are many reasons, not the least of which is that they know themselves better than anyone else does. They can massage the clitoris directly, which a partner doesn't always do. More importantly, with a sexual partner there is necessarily a relationship, one which reflects every-thing that went on before in key relationships with one's parents. Masturbation eliminates the relationship and the complications inherent in it. The masturbating woman is not being judged, no one is watching to see if she is sexual, if she comes, if she performs well, etc. All this is most reassuring and anxiety avoiding.

In neurosis, the lover is only a stand-in for the real thing, a situation which is one of the major causes of infidelity. The stand-in always leaves one wanting because she or he is not the real thing the person is searching for; so there are other lovers and other sexual encounters because of a massive need for a mother which may not be satisfied by just one wife or husband. The neurotic person in this pattern has to have many, many partners, all in a futile attempt to fill this vacuum inside of him. It is called infidelity, but in reality it is just a young child looking for a mother's love.

Treating Sex Problems Without Sex

For the neurotic, pleasure is confused with release of tension. Whenever there is release, as in orgasm, it is release of tension. This tension is sexualized so that it feels like sexuality.

The more global the repression, the more diminished the sex drive. That is why, in deep depression, the sex drive is almost non-existent. The more anxiety-ridden a person is – where repression is faulty – the more the sex drive is increased. Not surprisingly, it has been found that when senior citizens drink several cups of coffee per day their sex drive increases. Obviously, coffee had nothing directly to do with the sex drive; it merely activates the system against repression.

To a certain extent, psychology seems to follow anatomy where sex is concerned. A woman's problems are internal – errors of omission. A man's problems, such as premature ejaculation, are external – errors of commission. In orgasm, when the neurotic's body tries to hold back old feelings and not let go, the man complains of painful ejaculation and the woman talks about frigidity. She suffers inside, he suffers outside.

I had one male patient whose mother was a terror. She was unpredictable, violent and volatile. Consequently, he was afraid of women. This fear showed itself quickly in his sexual life (he ejaculated the minute he was sexually aroused), but was also reflected in the fact that he was loaded with very early mid-line pain. When he let go, everything pushed up and out at the same time. All of his impulses came surging forth and spilled out. In childhood, he was a bedwetter, a frequent forerunner of the adult sex problem. The penis became the focus for the discharge of tension.

Generally, problems to do with sex are the most difficult to treat and the last to go. Because they are at the centre of one's being, because they directly involved love and affection, their amelioration requires the prior resolution of many other problems. When a person has dealt with all manner of nonsexual traumas, the sex problem begins to fade away.

There is no way to ignore a lifetime of lack of love, abuse and neglect, and expect to treat sexual problems. The resolution of sex difficulties means the resolution of one's traumatic history.

In Primal Therapy, we encourage patients to face their fantasies and then help guide them into their feelings. They are never encouraged to change their fantasies. Everyone has a right to his fantasies. Besides, they are only the symbol of need.

Incest

I have treated a great number of incest victims. The first thing to know about incest is that it is by and large psychosis-making. Its effects are hardly confined to later sex problems, although these are present as well. Indeed, incest warps the general psyche enormously, almost irrevocably.

The earlier the incest, the more likely it is to produce severe mental problems. In my decades of practice I have observed that it is the most psychotogenic event in the life of a young girl or boy. The only thing that can come close is being sent away to an orphanage or foster home before the age of eight. In our measurements of the vital signs and brain waves, we found that the only event that moves the needle off the edge of the graph is incest – the equal of a birth trauma. That correlation, among other things, explains why when pre-psychotics enter therapy they begin reliving their birth right away.

Many of the psychotic women I have seen were incest cases, and many were not aware of the incest until after a year or two of primal therapy, at which point they suddenly began reliving strange events.

A year after she left therapy one woman I had seen began hallucinating and talking to herself. She had enough lucid moments to know she was going crazy, but didn't know why. She re-entered therapy and began a series of primals as follows: first, she felt a dark shadow, a presence in her bedroom when she was six. She felt this for two weeks and suffered a nameless dread, a terror that was inexplicable. Then the shadow turned into a person – someone standing by the door. She relived this for several weeks and was puzzled and afraid. Then she heard footsteps coming down the corridor and the door squeaking ajar. More weeks went by and then she relived, with convulsive upheaval, the realization that the presence, the shadow, the person, was her father. She relived his getting into bed with her and his fondling her and trying to penetrate her in spite of her quiet terror. He warned her not to scream or tell anyone or God would punish her.

For weeks and months she relived his almost daily footsteps late at night and his entering her room. Her life had become a sleepless nightmare. Her mother seemed not to want to know – as happens with sickening regularity in these cases. She had no one to turn to. Finally, he stopped. (He had started on her sister.) She repressed the experience out of existence. The clue that such an experience was about to surface in her reliving episodes lay in the symptoms of psychosis, which foreshadow heavy-valence pains on the march.

There are always sexual complications in incest. I have never seen a woman whose sex life wasn't ruined by it. Because her self-esteem has been destroyed, she either becomes sexually promiscuous and treats herself as a whore or becomes an actual prostitute. Many prostitutes endured incest as children. The other avenue for incest victims is that of utter and complete frigidity. Also, we should not neglect homosexuality as a possible outcome – the complete turning away from any relationship with a member of the opposite sex.

There are rare incest cases in which sexual functioning isn't impaired. A girl over the age of twelve might enjoy the excitement involved, but has great guilt about this enjoyment and therefore suffers from other mental aberrations. Her resulting relationship to men is generally askew.

We see from incest that frigidity is a survival mechanism, and will remain until the person is ready to feel the traumas completely as they happened. Imagine the difficulty involved in encouraging a frigid woman who was a victim of incest out of her condition. Especially when the incest is unknown to therapist and patient.

The lack in one's life can't be made up for. Therapists can't give back the love that someone never got. Need isn't sick. That which need drives you to do is. Even then it is not true. It is simply the only avenue available to express a need that should have been fulfilled naturally.

Research on Sexual Deviation

Our own observations and research, as well as current research on intrauterine life, indicate that sexual problems may begin while we are in the womb. Research on animals indicates that certain stressors on the pregnant mother can alter sex hormones in her, and later in her offspring. These sex hormones can be altered by chemical manipulation, before birth or just after, and this alteration endures.

In West Germany, Dorner discovered that manipulation of sex hormones in the womb could render an animal homosexual. Further, he found that animals deprived of maternal contact, or social contact in general, very early in life, can also become homosexual.

In our research, we found that sex hormones were permanently altered or normalized after the elimination of imprinted pain. Our hypothesis was that if the elimination of pain could stabilize sex hormones, the original trauma could alter or skew them in the same fashion. In some people, the levels of the sex hormones changed by fifty per cent, which gives us an idea of what early pain can do to our sex lives.

These hormonal changes are one reason why sexual problems are so difficult to treat, particularly through sexual techniques alone.

I am not saying that sex problems are necessarily hormonally caused. However, given certain life experiences – a distant mother or tyrannical father – I believe hormonal changes may help to direct the patient's response to experience in certain directions A distant mother may not make a woman into a homosexual later on, but a distant mother combined with hormonal changes seem strong enough to alter sexual orientation.

We have measured the testosterone levels in a patient who had relived the strangling at birth, and discovered that after the reliving experience the levels were raised. These changes seemed to have made the person more aggressive and sexually active.

Sex problems, like many neurotic disorders, offer a window into a situation of great complexity. They involve all of the things we have discussed thus far: needs, pain, the repression of pain, imprints, birth and its consequences, anxiety and stress, and symbolic acting out. Many sex problems can be treated without once mentioning sex. That is why we say that consideration of sex problems leads directly into the core of the human condition.

Reproduction, sex, seems to be the purpose of life. It is the way that we pass on encoded memories of survival. We not only need to keep the seed going, but we must also ensure that the seed contains the mechanisms to continue itself. Almost everything else is extraneous. The species, after all, has the same survival instinct as the individual members of the species. The absence of sex can be a threat to that survival. What a strange twist, that so-called moral behaviour is anti-survival.

PART THREE
How We Get Well

14

On the Nature of Normal

Are you normal if you think you are? Not necessarily. Are you normal if others think you are? Not necessarily. So how do you know if you're normal? If you are normal, chances are you won't think about it. If you're not normal, chances are you will. If you think you're normal, you're probably not. It all seems so Catch-22. Can normality ever be determined?

Behaviour Only Part of Being Normal

We must rid ourselves of the notion that 'normal' and 'neurotic' describe only behaviour. Behaviour is just one part of it. Psychology should not simply be the science of behaviour or the study of appearances, any more than navigation and oceanography should be the study of tips of icebergs. If oceanography were confined to studying the tips of icebergs, there would be a lot more shipwrecks around. If we continue to regard psychology as the science of behaviour, there are going to be a lot more human wrecks around.

Determining What is Normal

Is there something one can point to as proof that one is normal? Can people do normal things? Is there a gauge that

309

indicates when you have said something normal?

Each of us is different, and therefore what is normal for one is not necessarily normal for another. Standards are individual. You can only do what is normal for you.

What generally happens is that an average is calculated for the group, and that is called normal. Deviations from the norm, therefore, being abnormal. But being average is not the same as being normal. The developers of psychological tests might not agree, since they are among those who take a group's response to certain questions and decide on normal by averaging the result. Normal means that all systems are functioning as they were intended. A normal blood pressure might be 110/70. Someone with a blood pressure of 180/110 is not normal. We know this empirically because consistently high blood pressure leads to disease such as stroke. But now we come to our first contradiction. Is the average blood pressure 'normal?' It may be that the blood pressure of the general population from which we establish our norms is too high.

Similarly, in our studies of body temperature, we have found that after a period of Primal Therapy there was a consistent drop in body temperature of about one degree. There were many whose norm after therapy was below the standard 98.6 The old averages were no longer valid. They did not reflect normal.

The Context of Normal

What was normal for the group in therapy changed, and the change occurred only after we managed to remove a certain level of pain from their systems.

'Do you cry often?' is a question designed to measure neurosis on many psychological tests. Most people do not cry often. The norm is therefore 'no'. But suppose one discovers, as we have, that normal people do have easy access to their tears, and it is the culture that has established a behaviour of holding back which is, in reality, not normal.

Most of us become warped by pain by the time we are born, so we think our peculiar deviation is normal. We came into the world that way. Our behaviour is then shaped by our culture, and that culture determines what behaviour is normal. Going to school and sitting in classes for many hours a day, for example, is considered well adjusted and normal. Not going to school is definitely considered abnormal. A child who doesn't want to sit still for six hours a day is thought to have something wrong with him. What's wrong may be that he is normal.

Neurosis is designed to make us feel comfortable and normal. When neurosis works, we feel normal. When neurosis doesn't work, we feel abnormal. So, as we approach normalcy, having access to ourselves (and to our pain) we begin to feel abnormal, and may come to psychotherapy to get better in order to regain the neurosis so we can feel our old normal selves again.

One Man's Meat ...

Unless we are dealing with mental illness, it is not for one person to judge the normalcy of another, nor to establish private criteria for what is normal. No therapist can know what is going on in someone else's body and brain. Abraham Maslow tried establishing criteria for normal two decades ago. He topped his list with the need for self-realization and for peak states – the existence of which are dubious, but very much a possibility for Maslow's liberal mind. In fact, many of us elevate personal problems, drives, values, and deficits to the level of a principle, and call these normal.

For example, Freudians believe that the ability to defer pleasure is one sign of normality. But many neurotics can defer pleasure. In fact, they are afraid of it and believe that if they enjoy too much something bad can happen. Some holistic schools believe that it is normal to 'go for it!'. But 'going for it' can be either a sign of spontaneity or neurotic impulsiveness.

What further aggravates the problem of normality is that each therapeutic system has its own criteria for normal. For some, it is the ability to analyze one's dreams, for others it is the facility of insight. For still others it is social adjustment – remaining married, keeping a job, staying in one place. It is a dictatorship of therapy. Therapists decide what is normal for someone else. How and what they decide may depend on their own psychophysiological deviations. What I have noticed is that people's thoughts and beliefs follow who they are. A neurotic therapist who doesn't acknowledge her own feelings isn't going to make feeling a condition for normal.

What normal means, then, is that all systems are working normally. That seems like circular logic, but imprinted pain tends to dislocate functioning on every level of the human organism. The system then compensates, body and mind, in an effort to be normal, or establish equilibrium. This compensation can take the form of an elaborate theory about what is normal and what is deviate.

Nearly all neurotic behaviour is an attempt to normalize or 'right' the system. A person might drink five cups of coffee a day because his early imprints have produced a 'down' system with low energy and a tendency to depression. Coffee helps. It seems normal. He feels better after a lot of coffee. He feels like 'himself'. He only begins to discover the abnormality of his practice after he has felt his early parasympathetic prototype. Drinking five cups of coffee is not normal, because no normal system can tolerate that much artificial stimulation. Chronic artificial stimulation in the form of things like coffee, whisky and cigarettes is not abnormal just because someone decides it is so. It is abnormal because a wholesome system will not permit such abuse.

Whisky drinkers decide that marijuana is abnormal and pass laws against it. Which is normal? Their vice or the one they condemn? Those who take LSD have 'seen the light', and believe that the rest of us are poor, benighted souls. They feel quite normal and believe it is normal to feel a cosmologic consciousness or that they are in touch with past lives. Those who have felt their pain never have such notions. Those who abreact and remain disconnected do.

Origins of the Abnormal

Abnormality starts in the womb when mother is stressed and transmits this stress to the foetus, which then gears up to handle the input, changes functions, and increases its stress hormone levels. There is altered thyroid function, immune efficiency, etc. Thus, the stage is set for abnormality. The baby is already abnormal before it has seen the light of day. Much later when he has seen a lot of light of a lot of days he will develop abnormal ideas which will accommodate the original warping. He is not going to develop ideational systems which run counter to his own biology. Someone full of rage isn't going to believe in gentleness. Thus, the Cold Warrior, full of fear and rage must have an enemy in order to justify what is going on inside. He can develop complex rationales for why this enemy is to be feared but the danger is really inside.

Physiologic changes are the way the foetus 'behaves'. The imprint has high level, cortical representations so that, eventually, this dislocation will find its way into affecting psychological behaviour. The psyche merely follows the imprints.

Statistically, the child of a smoking mother is shorter than it should be according to its genetic program. It is abnormal. The child does not feel abnormal, however, and doesn't know it is shorter than genetics dictate. The baby of a heavily drinking mother is more apt to get cancer. He may seem to be a well-adjusted child, but suddenly, at age twenty-five, he is struck down. His system was always abnormal, but there was no way to find out. There may have been changes in blood platelets, lymphocytes, and kidney function, all unseen and undetected, all subclinical abnormalities.

Babies reared in orphanages often do not grow properly. Placed in loving private homes, they suddenly begin to grow in a natural manner. Then they discover what normal height is for them.

Being loved is normal, because it allows the system to be normal. Being unloved is abnormal, because it does not.

The Psychological View of Normal

You cannot be sick and well (or normal) at the same time. Although this sounds obvious, many mental health professionals take the opposite view. They discount the body in considering normality. They think it is only the mind that becomes neurotic. You can't have an altered physiology and be normal, no matter how normal you act.

Being normal or neurotic both present a wide spectrum of possible behaviours. The same behaviour in a person with pain can be neurotic, but normal after the removal of repressed pain. A high sex drive can be considered neurotic in those who have eroticized pain, while a high sex drive can be considered normal in those with relatively little pain.

The neurotic does not spend in accordance with what he has. Money is the way he deals with his pain. It has great symbolic significance. He often spends too freely, or more often cannot spend at all because money means security. It is no longer what it is. It is now a symbol of need fulfilment. A great deal of money in the bank spells safety and makes the neurotic feel comfortable and reassured. 'Nothing bad can happen when you have money', is the underlying formula. It soothes the insecurity of the past, either because there was never enough money, or because the neurotic's parents left him feeling afraid and insecure all the time. Money fills the emptiness.

Is it normal to want to save? Yes, for the normal, and no for the neurotic.

One of my patients gave up trying to communicate with

others and seemed to be stupid. Not saying anything was protective against feeling that she could not communicate with her parents. Thus her non-communication was neurotic. The great discovery she made in therapy, which seems quite simple, is that her need to communicate was abandoned almost from the time she learned to talk. To try to communicate would be to feel how hopeless it was. Feeling the impossibility of it all allowed her to communicate again. Being reticent for her was not normal.

It might be said that being helpful is normal. And yet there are some patients who use being helpful neurotically. They learn in the presence of their parents to be quiet, to stay out of the way, and to be completely helpful to avoid their wrath. Being helpful in this case is neurotic. A person without pain could be helpful as well, and this would not be neurotic.

Curiosity, to cite another example, is and should be a normal trait. There are neurotics, however, who use curiosity as a means of survival by knowing exactly who people are and by knowing their motivations. This would come from living with parents whom one senses to be dangerous, and against whom one must know everything in order to avoid the danger. In this sense an intense curiosity and perceptiveness would be neurotic.

But what does it all mean? These are just words: normal and neurotic. What matters is that they describe a condition which can get in the way of an adjustment to life. The term neurotic indicates a person not in control of herself, dominated by unseen powers. That is not the best thing in the world. Fortunately, or unfortunately, most people don't feel dominated by inner forces; they just act it out. Being neurotic is the ultimate obsessive-compulsive condition, because one is condemned to repeat patterns over and over again throughout one's life.

Neurosis as Corruption and Dissatisfaction

A neurotic can be transformed by the illusion of reward, because that was what happened in childhood. Dangling security, love, or understanding and protection will corrupt because it anchors into unfulfilled need, the same need that allowed for the corruption in the first place. A normal person cannot be so easily swayed and corrupted because there are no free-floating unfulfilled needs to hook into. He is not overly tempted because temptation doesn't trigger a mountain of needs that he imagines are going to be fulfilled.

The neurotic leads an exaggerated life. Need forces too much smoking, drinking, gambling, or risk taking. He either overreacts or underreacts, because straight reactions cannot be felt and measured. When one is out of touch with one's self, one's reactions are not in harmony, so one tries to act interested, excited and loving. But it is an act.

When one's feelings are blocked away one doesn't get much out of life. The gifts are meaningless, the trips disappointing, because 'you' are always there when you travel. Nothing is as it should be. If the neurotic could take stock, he would know that he is uncomfortable, ill at ease, and dissatisfied. But so long as his neurosis works, he doesn't take stock. He just keeps on going, working, moving around, keeping busy. That releases some of the tension and makes him feel comfortable. When he breaks a leg and cannot move around, he begins to hurt. It may be the first inkling that he is not so normal after all.

Criteria for Normal

I have seen thousands of patients who have relived their pain. They have some facets in common which I would call normal. I shall describe this composite.

The hallmark of normality is the ability to be satisfied. The neurotic is often dissatisfied with almost everything. He is missing something, something crucial, so there is never enough money, security, love, sex, power, prestige, or fame. Just feeling satisfied with one's life is an enormous achievement. For the neurotic, no matter what the gift, no matter what the achievement, it won't make an unloved person feel loved. Being completely loved as a child is what makes someone feel satisfied. It is the most relaxing thing on earth.

To be ambitious is a cultural norm in our society. Yet, after the removal of imprinted pain, my patients are less ambitious and they have less drive, not because they have been convinced that less ambition is normal, but because their system seems to dictate new values and behaviours. They no longer work twelve hours a day.

It is always up to the patient to choose his own values. His system knows what these values should be a lot better than anyone else. Too often, what is known as ambition is simply transformed tension. High energy levels based on pain activation has been diverted into the goal-seeking conduct we call ambition. A person wants to 'get ahead'. Yet getting ahead may be an analogue to trying to get ahead in the birth canal. This seeming 'stretch' of the imagination is often reported by patients who have relived trying to get out of the canal during a difficult birth. The problem with high-energy neurotics is that they usually feel the energy but not the pain behind it.

I believe that there are some clear criteria which can be used in a general way to define and assess normality. One is the absence of struggle. The neurotic has learned to get love through struggle, since love wasn't given initially without effort. The neurotic, male or female, has learned that certain ways of behaving bring approval, and others bring disapproval. So the person struggles to be good, modest, quiet, unassuming, and non-sassy. These are not natural behaviours, but ones learned as a way of getting along with parents.

Struggle is the symbolic way the neurotic goes about getting fulfilled. The neurotic rarely goes straight for love. On the contrary, the pattern is first to find a neurotic like your parent, then *struggle* to get love. You find a cold woman and try to make her warm. You find a critical, unsatisfied man and try to make him accepting. The struggle for love is what is ingrained, not the getting of it. Getting apparent love often makes the neurotic feel worse because the underlying feeling is of being unloved.

Sometimes neuroses mesh, and then there seems to be a normal relationship. Both parties feel satisfied. The woman who had a tyrannical father, who needs a weak man she won't be afraid of, marries such a man. He in turn is looking for a strong mommy. It is a marriage made in neurotic heaven. Each of their choices is symbolic, acting out in the present in attempt to master the past.

Another factor in being normal is the absence of neurotic tension, the tension that keeps someone constantly on the move, talking a lot, tapping the fingers and the feet, eyes darting, head moving, posture rigid, trembling, seemingly bubbly and effervescent or face impassive and 'frozen'. Normal people give off a relaxed air. They can be talked to easily, and because they are not blocked inside their warmth is apparent. There is a give-and-take about them. There is a tone of feeling in their speech.

A normal person cares because he or she has access to feelings and can truly emphasize and sympathize. Normal people are able to care. Unlike the neurotic, the normal person can rejoice in the achievements of others. The neurotic has a problem with that. The normal is not naturally self-aggrandizing, selfish, aggressive, uncooperative, self-centred and defensive. Being repressed is to be not totally human, no matter how humanistic and/or altruistic one believes one is. When part of one's humanity is locked away one can do insensitive, cruel things without knowing the effects of one's acts.

The neurotic is by definition self-centred. He usually must relate every conversation only to himself; a person with constant self-reference. He cannot really listen. His pain and need keep him from seeing others and from focusing unreservedly outside of himself. During each social occasion he is trying to add to himself.

Thus, narcissism is a key factor in differentiating the normal from the abnormal. Is there a healthy narcissism? No. That is an oxymoron – a contradiction in terms. Is self-love normal? Normal people don't love themselves; they just live and don't consider whether they love themselves or not. It is not a question in their repertoire. A loved person who is shaped by parental love doesn't think about it. It is a given, like the colour of his eyes. It is not a debatable issue.

The normal can also take criticism because his whole world isn't going to collapse if someone disapproves. He is not going to feel devastated if someone doesn't like what he does. The neurotic defends against that kind of criticism because he has been made to feel bad about himself in the first place. 'I must be bad to be so unloved', is the unconscious equation. He is therefore not open to suggestion or new ideas, or anything that smacks of a challenge to what he has done. The normal is open to what others say and can accept it. Defensive behaviour is not normal.

Is being in politics normal? I haven't seen any post-graduate patients from Primal Therapy hankering to be in politics. On the contrary, they can't imagine wanting to run anyone's life but their own. That in itself is a full-time job. Those who have been unloved need to be wanted and respected by millions. They will always need more. Their reality is that they feel unfulfilled, and remember, we always respond to our primary internal reality first.

Normal is whatever normal people do. The trick is to find out who and what is normal. If you have been accepted and loved for exactly what you are, chances are you are normal. Normality radiates, just as neurosis does.

Because there is no therapeutic dictatorship that determines what and who is normal, we each have to find out for ourselves. It is a discovery of relief. Can an insight into one's neurosis make one normal? A mental gyration known as an insight is not going to change an altered psychophysiology.

The normal is intelligent without necessarily being intellectual. He knows what is right and good for him. He leads the life he needs to live. He doesn't raise false goals and then struggle to achieve them. His needs are modest and within reason. He doesn't live in his head. Neurotic intellect serves to keep the person detached from himself. Wide-ranging ideas, broad knowledge rarely help a person establish and keep a relationship or stop compulsive smoking and drinking. The intellect was originally designed to guide our instincts and feelings in order to solve our needs. Neurotic intellect works against need.

The normal person is an historic being. He is conscious of his past, has access to remote memories. He senses the continuum of his life. Normal for him is to be whole and integrated, past and present. To be neurotic means to be cut off from one's history – an ahistorical being.

A normal's dreams are as clear and realistic as he is. Lower level memories are no longer blocked and directed into bizarre dream symbols. The memory is what it is. He has no nightmares, and he knows what his dreams mean, just as he knows why he has a symptom. His body, in short, is no longer a mystery to him.

The normal person is guileless. He has no façade, nothing to hide, nothing to pretend about. He is what he is. He will therefore, by his presence, allow others to be themselves. He isn't someone so removed that he can only relate to suppressed, remote, emotionless people. He isn't so domineering that he can only relate to weak, passive souls. A normal woman isn't so fearful that she can't leave the house. Being afraid is normal when there is reason. Being afraid when there is no apparent reason is neurotic.

The neurotic is, in a sense, incomplete. He is looking for the rest of himself; in search for the other half of his nervous system. The very tight person finds the loose one to relate to. The wild, uncontrolled hysteric finds the controlling partner.

Being warped early in life means that neurotic parents who placed a condition on love, the condition that you be what they need instead of what you are. As long as a parent needs, that will always be true. Neurotics avoid normals. They won't be your drinking buddy and they won't gamble alongside you. They won't flatter your ego, nor build your self-esteem. You cannot use the normal to construct your own personality.

The principle is as follows: reality surrounds itself with reality, just as unreality is attracted to unreality. The normal person does not need or appreciate flattery. The neurotic lives for it. The normal can accept healthy praise; the neurotic searches for it constantly.

The mystical neurotic is not going to relate well to those who do not believe. If he seeks out a guru-protector, he isn't going to remain with those who feel that his search is ridiculous. His unreal ideas need reinforcement, not challenge. The idea is not to stick with those who do adhere to reality because that, too, might lead to painful realizations.

The normal person is characterized by his stability. Stability, incidentally, is not a synonym for 'dullness'. The normal person may not sound as exciting as the unstable person who needs to travel, seek adventure, and take risks with his life. The normal's life may not make as good reading as that of an out-of-control neurotic who does the bizarre and unusual, but that does not mean that a normal is not interesting. His is an internal state of conveying feeling, of access to the zone of the interior. His meaning is not in pyrotechnics but in inner experience.

Who is the Judge of Normality?

Is running ten miles every day normal? It can be if that is what a normal person wants to do. But there are many obsessives out there who must run every day. They are working off tension and so feel good doing it. But it is not normal.

Is talking a lot normal? There are many who have a lot to say. There are others who have to say a lot. It feels good.

They are neurotic-normal. They do normal things neurotically. One of my former colleagues ran around the country delivering talks. He elevated his neurosis into an art form; 'delivering talks' is really what he was about.

Is the normal energetic? Yes. He is because his energy is not being exhausted in the battle of repression. Hyperenergetic, however, is not normal. How can you tell the difference? The hyperenergetic is tiring to be around.

Can one imagine a normal person's taking a cigarette from a package that says, 'This is injurious to your health'? It is not normal to be irrational. When you smoke, knowing that you have a high risk of cancer, it is not rational. But pain forces people to be irrational. Smoking and drinking are neurotic behaviours in an attempt to be normal – to bring pain down to manageable proportions.

The normal tries to make his life easy. Not so the neurotic, who often complicates his life. He often cannot be organized enough to be on time. He may be late because he cannot stand waiting for others. Unconsciously, he arranges it so they wait for him. He must function under pressure, (re-creating over and over the pressure from within) so he waits until the last second to get ready and then is invariably late. 'I'll be there at eight', means something else. He won't be there at eight. He may be so distracted that he forgets his appointments.

The normal can love. He can give. He can be affectionate, something a neurotic has difficulty with. The neurotic mother is too often trying to get the love from her children that she didn't get as a child. The normal can let his children be, because they don't have to fill his old needs.

There is always some kind of emotional barrier between the neurotic and others. The closer he gets to himself and his feelings the closer he can get to others. Those who are emotionally removed are first removed from themselves.

The normal is unusually healthy, physically. His system is functioning without all the old painful baggage that eventually wears down the body of the neurotic. The normal isn't rushing off to doctors for this or that ailment. Almost every neurotic has something – headaches, stomach distress, muscle tension, tendonitis, backaches, etc. The normal is not wasting money and time in the constant pursuit of health.

The neurotic creates a cocoon in which he feels safe. The newspaper he reads, the people he relates to, the music he listens to, all help to reinforce his beliefs and view of the world. He re-creates his world every day so as to stay neurotic. The normal continually rediscovers his world in order to expand his horizons. What the neurotic enjoys most is a chance to be neurotic; to express his neurosis fully.

For many, the belief in God is considered normal. Here is where the average and the norms meet. For ninety per cent of Americans believe in God; clearly they consider their beliefs normal. If one is in the church, the belief that God is talking to you and sending you a message is also considered normal by church members. But on the street, to believe that you hear God's voice sending you that same message might be considered psychotic. This also depends upon the content of the message. If one hears God saying, 'The devil's is going to punish you', one is considered less crazy than if one hears God say, 'The devil says to punish your next door neighbour'.

Is normal the same as being happy? I'm not sure about 'happy'. I think that normal is content.

Many neurotics try to do things to make themselves happy. Having plenty of sex makes some happy, while having plenty of money satisfies others. They are happy only because they have reduced tension. Reduction of tension, however, is not happiness. Feeling good, therefore, is not always equated with being normal – unless you're normal to begin with.

Can you Feel Normal?

Is 'normal' a feeling? Can you feel normal? Unfortunately

not. There is no label that stands out that reads 'normal'. If one can experience all of one's self, one is normal. If one cannot, one is not normal. If you think you feel normal you are in trouble.

If you feel content, relaxed, undriven, and comfortable, you are normal. The key phrase here is, 'if you feel'. If you don't, your imagination goes to work to make you believe you are normal. The mystical neurotic never feels just good. He feels just 'wonderful'.

Are there, then, really no objective criteria for normal? Our studies of hormone levels after the removal of the patient's pain helps answer the question. After pain was lowered, our patients all had hormonal changes but some men found their testosterone elevated and some lowered. Normal wasn't a matter of opinion or consensual validation. It was different for different people.

Many mental health professionals don't see neurosis as biological so, of course, their concept of normal is confined to the mind. You act normal, *ergo*, you are normal. What is diabolic about normality is that the better defended we are, the more we can pass for normal. We have no apparent hurts. We function and we get along.

The very term 'mental health professional' indicates the limits of psychotherapy. Freud saw it more clearly. He talked about the 'organ neuroses' and postulated that organs manifested neurosis. That observation was cloaked in Freudian mumbo-jumbo about the id and the superego but still, he saw neurosis in our biology.

Can a psychotherapy make one normal? No. A psychotherapy can alter your mind, but it will not make you normal. Only an experiential therapy, encompassing both body and mind, can do that. And in reality, no therapy can make you 'normal', it can only make you an ex-neurotic.

A psychotherapy can teach you to act in ways thought of as normal. You can learn to control your impulses, lessen your obsessive-compulsiveness. But you won't be normal.

By trying to modify behaviour, modern day psychotherapy

tries to produce a normal façade. This drives the pain deeper into the body and makes it more inaccessible. Then the patient is pronounced 'better', whereas there is nothing like 'better' to shoot for. The most we can achieve is for someone to be himself. You can never be better than yourself.

There are any number of professionals who believe that a certain amount of tension is normal and necessary. They argue that one needs anxiety to galvanize the system. They believe that there would be no drive to succeed if not for tension. They take a neurotic state and make its quest for neurotic goals into a virtue. I still believe that next to neurosis one of the great afflictions of mankind is the treatment for it.

Those with little tension, in my observation, still have motivation, still produce, and often succeed, but not because they are driven. The normal's brain is not as busy as others'. That is why he can focus, concentrate, and have a long attention span.

The concept of normal is an important one because most psychotherapies, consciously or not, aim for a state that they consider to be normal. How they define normal determines their methods of therapy and their goals for the patient. If the patient is striving towards unreal goals, even if he achieves them, he will still not be real.

For example, biofeedback therapy decides you should have a certain brainwave pattern that indicates relaxation. Normal is tied into those waves. However, normal doesn't mean controlling your brainwaves. It means having certain patterns of waves without effort or control.

Other therapies are content to see symptoms disappear. They think that what you can't see indicates normality. We know that driving a symptom away is not a necessary indicator of normality. If the symptom disappears with the resolution of pain, that is one thing, but to attempt to manipulate it into disappearing is quite another.

We need to trust the patient – not just what he says, but what his body is saying as well. There is no higher judge in the universe than the body. No expert will ever know more.

This means that each of us holds within us the absolute criteria for normal within us, and the means for our own cure. Therapists no longer have to be 'the doctor', making pronouncements about patients; and patients no longer have to act brilliant or adjusted. They, too, can trust themselves, because the body is the doctor. The body makes its own diagnosis. That seems to be a miracle, but it is only normal.

15

The Role of Weeping in Psychotherapy

Tears from the depths of divine despair
Rise to the heart and gather to the eyes
In gazing on the happy autumn fields
In thinking of the days that are no more

Lord Tennyson

Primal Therapy has been likened to a 'weeping fit'. Patients weep on a regular basis. It has been called self-indulgence, pampering of the ego, weakness and hysteria. I don't think it is any of these. On the contrary, crying is a biological necessity, an attempt at healing, an effort to re-stabilize the organism and restore an essential natural function. In fact, I do not believe that anyone can get well in psychotherapy without it. *Too little* of this kind of so-called self-indulgence can keep you sick, psychologically and physically.

Crying and Need

The original purpose of crying for a baby is to be comforted, to have her needs fulfilled; long before the infant has a sense of tragedy, it has raw need. That need even supersedes the ability to tear, which isn't evident until some time after birth. For the infant, crying is a signal of discomfort, a signal to be protected and loved. She isn't able to articulate what she needs specifically, so she cries to express lack or hurt in a general way.

We scream before we cry, cry before we speak, and speak before we can organize conceptions about what we have and don't have. Each of these stages of expression forms part of the skill of communication. *Crying is a language* – a primitive one, but nevertheless a very human one. The history of neurosis is the history of misery and the need to cry out this misery. Crying is not only an expression of general hurt; it is also a vehicle that carries us back through time to those specific traumas that were buried long ago by the processes of repression. It is tears that break down those barriers and help us on that voyage through time when we were hurt and could not cry. *Tears wash away our pain and unmask the unconscious.* This is not a metaphor but a biological fact.

Primal Tears and Repressed Pain

Tears of early loss are the solution that dissolves the walls of the unconscious and liberates encapsulated pain. The neurological origins of crying are in the hypothalamus. There, the neural circuits stretch from the lacrimal nuclei, the crying centres, up into the cortex.

Deep weeping as we see in our therapy is not hysteria but a unique new category that involves healing. It is the first convulsive phenomenon to be related to the healing process. Here, the adult brain gives way to the child's brain, travelling back to an exact feeling, an exact moment and scene where crying should have taken place but did not – tears suspended in time by the agony of the experience. The regression from the adult brain to the emotional brain and then to the 'pretear' perinatal brain is the exact reverse of cerebral development.

Tears Are Uniquely Human

Tears, by and large, are uniquely human. We differ from animals in our ability to cry and tear. *Crying is a curative process.* I do not believe that one can cure either mental illness or a host of serious physical ailments without it. For some reason, however, this natural function has become opprobrious. We shush our children and deride them as 'crybabies', consider it grown-up *not* to cry, and believe that it is a sign of weakness to give in to tears. So we block out this innate, biological process and then pay the price, because along with that blockage goes a host of other suppressions and dislocations. It is not just wispy tears that are blocked, *but basic biologic functioning.* That is why when we restore this function, the whole system (including hormones and brain waves) seems to normalize.

It seems likely that the physiological effects would be analogous if we weren't allowed to laugh. As it turns out, those who are inhibited seem to inhibit both their laughter and their tears. It is ultimately their entire spectrum of emotionality that is trampled by repression.

If a baby is left to cry it out in the crib because the parents do not believe in indulging him or her, sooner or later the baby will stop crying because the cry for help has gone unheeded. The *need* to cry, the many hours of weeping held in check, however, still remains and will come gushing forth decades later when those scenes are relived.

And it isn't simply tears that are suppressed; there is also a sense of despair and helplessness as the baby's cries are ignored. The amount of tranquillizers necessary in adult life will depend, by and large, on the amount of crying *not done.* The optimistic part of all this is that the amount of crying needing to be done is *finite,* so that after you cry for a certain amount of time you feel good again, because you have done something that the body needed to do.

When, in therapy, one scans one's history and focuses on past scenes, tears well up that were never before expressed.

The injustice and the tragedy of it all strikes one, and in those tears are the agony, the pleading, the urgency and the demand. The flood of tears lays bare the entire traumatic scene, including details that were previously forgotten. Tears are the agent of memory. They are the most eloquent expression of that past. Remember, some feelings are evident long before we have words and concepts to describe them. A return to the past, a return to tears, *is the memory*. Often, there is nothing more to do than cry.

The Repression of Tears

Sometimes repression has gone on for so long that tears are no longer recoverable. Those in this state are the candidates for serious disease, because those tears are somewhere. *Somewhere*, the body is crying out. I recall seeing one patient who had an eye condition that involved constant tearing. The disease had a fancy name, but when she cried her heart out in therapy we didn't need a name for it any longer.

In addition to forbidding tears in their children, parents simply may not 'be there' for the child. The fact that there is no shoulder to cry on, no sense of empathy or human kindness and softness, is enough to dry up the tears. A young child gets the message very quickly that crying is useless; he turns to other languages – anger, tantrums, psychosomatic ailments, and learning disabilities. He cries for help in ways that cannot make him well. He's got to re-enter the 'place' where his physiology was stopped in its tracks. Otherwise be becomes a whiner or a complainer. As one patient, put it, 'I complained about everything in my life because I never knew what was wrong. Now that I have felt what I should have complained about, I don't have to do that any more'. The child whose nose is constantly running is crying through the nostrils. We have seen a number of allergies disappear when the person achieves access to his tears again. We don't have to theorize about the relationship between crying and healing. We see it in action.

When we watch a film in which two struggling people finally embrace, why do we cry? Because it represents a deep longing in us that is finally realized. We cry for our own needs on the screen.

Tears and the Sense of Loss

Tears not only signal a need or desire but also a loss, which is the other side of the same coin. They are the attempt to regain contact, to re-establish a relationship that means survival. They are, as Browning noted, 'the silent language of grief'. When grief is too profound, there often are no tears. One is simply numb. When one enters the realm of depression, one is usually beyond crying.

For those who grieve, there is a therapy. In 'bereavement therapy', the person is simply encouraged to discuss the loss over and over again and to cry about it. Crying, it seems, is a specific antidote for depression, first, because depression is really an elevated state of repression where there is little specific access to past memories, and second, because the psychological state of the depressive is one of massive inhibition with global repression of all feelings.

In Freudian theory, depression is hostility turned inwards. Psychoanalytic patients encouraged to let out their anger may get better – for a time. But we have also found that depressive people get much better when they cry, even without the release of anger. And, indeed, anger alone will not release certain repressive biochemicals as tears do. Tears are the expression of need; anger is the expression of *frustration* and of need. The release of any feelings helps depression.

Abreacting

It is important to understand the difference between deep

weeping and *abreacting* or *catharsing*. Abreacting or catharsing means the diffuse or amorphous release of the energy of disconnected pain. The focus is on one level while the real feeling is on another. For example, crying during the movie *E.T.*, when E.T. leaves Elliott, is abreacting or catharsing. Crying about the time your father left you is crying in context. We have done research on patients who were abreacting or catharsing versus those who were weeping in context. The biological differences were profound. In the crying group, there was a change in hormones, brain function and personality; this was not the case with the others.

One clear sign of the global effects of recaptured tears is the fact that some women become truly sexual for the first time in their lives after recovering their ability to cry. The release of tears seems to be the cause of this change – not always and not in every woman – but enough for us to see a connection. And, since deep weeping triggers changes in the stress and sex hormones, one might expect such changes.

Crying and Stress

There is little doubt that crying releases stress, since stress hormones are found in tears. In our own research on tears by Dr Barry Bernfeld, together with Dr William Frey of St Paul-Ramsey Medical Center in Minnesota, we found the release of ACTH, a stress hormone triggered by the pituitary gland in the brain. These same tears also release the endorphines. We need to think about this: *hormones dealing with pain and stress processed in the central nervous system are found in tears.* Indeed, they are found in almost every fluid released by the body. They literally wash away pain. They help remove the biochemical aspect of stress and are therefore a biological necessity.

The research conducted in conjunction with Dr Frey involved studying both emotionally triggered tears and tears that resulted from breathing onion fumes. This research demonstrated that both kinds of tears are an attempt to remove toxins – one external, the other internal.

It is no accident that the centre for the release of tears, the lacrimal gland, is triggered by the same brain structure that organizes pain, and is packed with endorphine receptors.

Other research was done with our patients in 1978. Thirty consecutive patients who were admitted for Primal Therapy were classified as their therapy proceeded into (1) no crying, (2) mild suffusion of the eyes, and (3) infant-like postures with deep weeping. Blood pressure and heart rate were measured.

Eighteen of the patients arrived at the deep weeping level within six months of therapy. They showed significant changes in the levels of various hormones including those mediating sex, growth and stress. After the twenty-sixth week, there was an important rise in growth hormone levels for the deep weeping group.

The level of male hormone, testosterone, also showed major changes with deep weeping. Six men with testosterone levels above 600 were shown to have a decline between fifteen and thirty-five per cent after six months. Contrarily, those with very low levels of testosterone showed a significant increase (twenty to thirty-five per cent) as a result of deep weeping. This indicates that those who were high dropped, while those were below normal levels came up – both shifts indicative of a normalization process. Stress hormone levels were reduced in the majority of deep weepers.

Patients who could feel a bit but did not reach deep weeping levels did not make the changes indicated above. Control groups made no changes. Those who acted 'as though' they were feeling, who thrashed, pounded and screamed – also showed no significant changes.

The Necessity of Weeping

For tears to heal it must not be 'crying about'. It must not be adult cries but rather baby tears of the frightened, lonely, unprotected and unloved child; that is what heals. Those tears are always accompanied by truly infantile wails. Adult tears don't heal, they relieve. We see all this clearly when patients have difficulty crying until they actually reach up with outstretched arms for their mommies. With that movement of the arms, the tears pour forth as never before as if the screams and cries were coded into the arms that needed to reach out for comfort. Others cannot cry until they actually make the sound 'mommy'.

Why is it necessary to cry now? Because it *was* necessary to cry then. The toxins that come from a system abusing itself – from all those stress chemicals – now are swept away. No system can be clean when it is shutting away part of itself. When major subsystems are dislocated, the body is toxic. One can see this in the stress hormones. Patients who relive major traumas report that they have never felt so pure, so clear, so clean and relaxed as just after a feeling.

It is not enough to talk about one's sadness; talking, in itself, cannot influence overall homeostasis. To understand what one's parents did, to forgive, rationalize, or decide to forget won't change anything.

It is no accident that after several months of reliving and weeping, there are also major changes in the relationship between the two brain hemispheres, which seem to equalize or normalize, as well. Every major system is involved in feeling or in its blockage. Nothing escapes.

One of the reasons why children are suppressed in their crying is that parents don't want any reminders of their own hidden pain. So one hears, 'You stop crying or I'll give you something to cry about!' The child already has something to cry about. It may not be exactly in response to the current situation, but he is crying *for a reason*. No one cries because it's fun. A child cries to express some kind of misery, unhappiness or sadness. Neurotic parents want it suppressed. As long as he snivels, he will be smacked again until he finally chokes back his tears. Then he is considered mature. In the parents' eyes, he is growing up – growing up and *growing into neurosis*.

One of the scientists associated with the research surveyed the medical literature regarding weeping going back 100 years. There were some 400 relevant articles, including those from *The American Journal of Insanity*, 1844, and the *British Journal of Psychiatry*, beginning in 1856. In more than one century of writing, there were no more than a handful of articles even mildly related to weeping, and practically none which related it to cure. Something so obvious had been completely overlooked.

The way a society treats tears is indicative of its degree of humanity. I also believe, based on our observations and research for the past twenty years, that tears increase longevity. A study of the sickness ratio and longevity of various tribes and societies in relation to their treatment of tears would be fascinating.

Deep weeping, in our therapy, has affected colitis and ulcers. These charges show clearly the relationship between repressed tears and physical ailments. The skin 'cries', the lungs 'cry', all in their own way.

Another important benefit of weeping is its calming effect. We see this in the average twenty-four-point drop in blood pressure in our hypertensive patients, and in a ten-beat drop per minute in heart rate. We find it also in the subjective reports of patients. Patients who weep need progressively less tranquillizers. Since a Congressional task force recently found that over two million women are addicted to legalized tranquillizers, we can see how important weeping is.

Another change we see in our patients concerns their respiration. We have discovered that breathing is one automatic way tears are kept down. Shallow breathing doesn't dip into the body where feelings are stored. It aids repression. Crying seems to change the shallow breathers to deep breathers. There is more 'body' in the breathing, and this has an effect on physical development as well, particularly in the chest area. We found out long ago that simply encouraging deep breathing in some patients would bring them to tears – a technique we no longer need to use. In fact, we find it potentially dangerous to encourage deep breathing among those who are overwhelmed by pain. Any extraneous, mechanical method often brings up pain before its proper time, an out-of-sequence trauma that simply overwhelms rather than integrates. But the relationship between crying and breathing is unmistakable. Patients will arrive at deep breathing and deep weeping in small steps as they can integrate more and more pain. As they feel deeper, the breathing takes care of itself.

Weeping as Healing

The question is, why does healing only take place with weeping and feeling? The answer is, because active *suffering* and *healing* occur simultaneously. The reason that we did not heal in the first place is because we did not feel the totality of an early series of traumas. If one could have felt one's early traumas originally, there would be no biological motive to re-experience them.

When repression sets in, it also blocks the healing processes. The wound becomes hidden. One can experience only so much pain at one time, and beyond that there is a fail-safe mechanism which sets an upper limit to our ability to respond to pain. Such a mechanism determines the outer boundary of feeling. When we are driven beyond that boundary, we are beyond full reactivity, we stop crying, and are therefore beyond healing. Healing ceases when reactivity ceases. When a person is cut off from the experience of suffering, he is stripped of the necessary condition for healing, and prepared instead for disease. Just as pain and repression form a dialectic unity, so do active suffering and healing.

Ordinarily, neural information about hurt is relayed to the thalamus. When the pain is not overwhelming, information is then sent to the hypothalamus which initiates a variety of responses; including crying, that make up the healing process.

When repression exists, information and tears are rerouted away from the hypothalamus. If this did not occur, the excesses of hypothalamic activity in blood pressure, pulse and temperature, for example, would be lethal. It is therefore important that the hypothalamus not accept all of the input. *The excess neural energy of the pain is rerouted and finds its neurotic destination in the limbic system, and it is because of this bifurcation that full healing cannot take place.*

The Dialectic of Suffering and Healing

Because the reactivity to pain has an upper limit beyond which the system cannot go, there is simultaneously imposed an upper limit beyond which healing is prevented. In this sense, early trauma is a wound that never closes. Inasmuch as all of us have a built in analgesic factory in the form of the endorphines, it is clear that neurotics do not heal as fast as they should.

The clearest example of my point is the fact that patients, just before entering into the reliving sequence, develop a fever; the same fever that exists when one is acutely infected with a bacteria. It is the approach of the feeling that causes the fever, and hence the healing process, for the fever signals a host of curative reactions.

All of this is well illustrated in a prisoner who, as a heroin addict, was put on methadone (a pain killer) for several months to ameliorate the addiction. During this time he was given a TB test that showed no reaction. Many months later when methadone was removed, he was tested again. This time there was a large red mark and swelling indicating an allergic reaction and possible exposure to TB. He did have a previous history of TB which did not show up on the test so long as he was under the effects of chemical repression of pain. When repression was lifted there was a large red wheel, as the area became swollen with lymphocytes carrying antibodies against the antigen which was injected. As long as he was repressed, all reactions *and healing* were suspended. The body could not react as it was intended to.

The cure of the wound called neurosis involves full reactivity of all that is repressed. Each deep feeling is one more step towards healing. Reactivity is crucial. When children are able to cry about hurting themselves they will heal faster. A patient's six-year-old son had a car trunk door accidentally close on two of his fingers. The fingers were badly bruised and the child cried for a few minutes after the accident. After that he stopped crying and tried to forget about it.

Two days later, in the morning, he seemed to be agitated and irritable. He sat down at a table with a pencil and paper, held the pencil in his traumatized hand and tried to draw various shapes. His hand hurt more as he did this until he became so frustrated that he screamed out, 'I can't draw, I can't draw.' Then he fell off the chair, clutching his right wrist and started screaming and crying, 'My hand, my hand.' He was soon writhing on the floor in agony. This went on for about a half an hour. Afterwards he was calm, exhausted and, to his surprise, said, 'I'm okay; my hand doesn't hurt any more'. Thereafter, the wound on his fingers healed with unusual speed.

During Primal Therapy, history is asserting itself. That is why patients will relive the emotional and physical suffering of times gone by. It is not uncommon for them to relive a surgery, for example, in which they were unconscious, (anaesthetized). The longer patients are in my therapy, the deeper the access to lower levels of consciousness, the more likely it is to occur. Science has discovered that those who are less profoundly anaesthetized during surgery seem to heal faster, and those who have hypnotic anaesthesia, rather than drug anaesthesia, heal the fastest of all. So, clearly, the level of repression and anaesthesia has something to do with healing, and the level of unconsciousness due to anaesthesia will give us some idea about how rapidly one can heal. That is why it is not possible to heal a neurosis on an unconscious level, such as with drugs or hypnosis. Consciousness is crucial for the healing process.

Weeping is healing. Feeling is healing. Repression is anti-healing. Every process of our brain and bodies has an evolutionary rationale. To block weeping is to run against the sweep of evolution. That is why those who weep deeply seem to 'restart' the evolutionary process – beards begin to grow at age forty, wisdom teeth develop at forty-five, breasts begin to grow at age thirty-five. The genetic code can now proceed to its destination; that destination is growth, healing and health. Not a bad job for minuscule droplets of moisture. Imagine! Tears have the power to transform our physiology, change our personality, and refire the evolutionary engine. What has seemed like weakness to so many of us turns out to be one of the most powerful forces on earth.

16

Why Do You Have to Relive Your Childhood to Get Well?

One may wonder why it is that patients have to relive their past rather than simply discussing it. Why do I make so much of reliving? After all, isn't talking about it or even crying about one's life enough? What is the crucial difference?

Reliving Old Emotions

It is not necessarily the scene and its recall that one must relive; rather, it is the emotional content. I have seen patients who have been in psychoanalysis and have discussed certain memories in minute detail. In Primal Therapy they have been put in contact with the emotional component of these same memories, and that is an entirely different experience. The suffering component has a different storage site from cognitive recall. Reliving opens the gates to emotional storage areas; the agony that was never felt is now experienced; the tears never shed are now flowing; the sadness and/or rage held back is all encompassing. Blocked energy has found its outlet.

In discussion, the energy aspect of a memory is still blocked. The difference between crying about and reliving the intense early agony of the four year old sent to his room is like the difference between two universes. One is an adult

340

remembering a childhood with his cortical apparatus; the other is a child immersed in that memory, body and soul.

There is a memory of a feeling – the talking about and the feeling of a memory – the experience itself. One needs the latter for resolution. You do not get hypothalamic normalization without feeling. If a child was repeatedly sent to his room and made to feel bad or stupid it does no good for him to intellectualize about it. He has got to express his rage in context. It certainly won't help for him to understand his parents and why they acted the way they did. Understanding can only cover it up. The fury and the agony over feeling belittled time after time is there. Putting a person back in time and letting that old feeling wash over him reawakens all of the memory and its feeling. What happens from there on is a natural progression that requires no interference from anyone. If the feeling is rage, as it often is, and hurt, which nearly always lies below the rage, then that is what will come out. And it surges forth with a force that is ineffable. It is a force that accompanies unfulfilled need. The kicking, screaming, pounding the walls for hours are essential. They are not forced to do this. It simply pours forth when the context is relived.

Levels of Consciousness in Reliving

As previously discussed, memory is represented on all three levels of consciousness, the thinking, feeling, and self-regulating or visceral, levels. When one sees each level at work one sees immediately why one must relive. No brain structure or level of consciousness can do the job of another. To see patients coughing up copious amounts of fluid during birth primals, together with releasing tremendous energy in convulsive movements, is to understand the difference between discussing and reliving. During these reliving episodes there are never any words, and no tears.

As the patient moves ahead in time to his earlier years

there will be words and tears. Those words are often baby talk and the sobs of a young child. Patients cannot fake that, nor can they even duplicate those sounds afterwards when requested. If a patient uses words or moves his arms during a birth episode we know immediately that it is not real. The best they can do is grunt. All explanation lies in the reliving.

The levels of consciousness are discrete and viable, and have separate functions from one another. The birth trauma, for example, is stored deeper and lower than events which occur at age ten. There are then layers of experience over-laying that early trauma, which is why we usually do not get to early material until months of therapy.

To relive the suffocation of a birth episode which resolves migraine is something that could not happen in any other way. It is dealing with generating sources on its own level. Migraine is a first level symptom. Trying to discuss the event is a contradiction in terms, since there were and are no words for it. The minute one uses words, the experience is over and has been left unresolved. Even if one cries about it, the experience is fake. A newborn wail, however, is what we do hear. That sound is unmistakable.

Artificial Reproduction of the Levels of Consciousness

I recall participating in experiments with hypnosis where we would take individuals back to the age of five and have them talk about their lives. Often they would hit upon a key event – 'Mommy gave away my dog', and the tears would gush forth. When they were out of hypnosis they had no recall of the early memory nor of the fact that they cried about it.

Age regression in hypnosis is dramatic evidence of the permanent existence of memories, as well as repressed tears. One had only to gain access to that memory to find the tears again.

There is a tendency to think of reliving as some kind of play acting. But reliving is neither an act nor a game; it is a neurologic happening. Patients are not acting 'as though' they were children. They are in the grips of a child brain with the entire panoply of associations that go with it. Only during reliving does one find a discharge of the full force of the pent up reverberating energy through the crying, and screaming.

The Infant Always Exists

It is tempting to think of grown men and women talking baby talk or sucking their thumbs like the newborn as 'regressed'. The fact is that the infant exists in the brain and body at all times. It is constantly trying to come to consciousness. What we do in our therapy is allow for a 'release' phenomenon of the kind we noted in our discussion of weeping. It is then that the infant surges forth and allows the adult to see what has been there all the time. This same kind of release of cortical inhibition occurs in certain kinds of brain damage to control centres. What one sees, again, is foetal-like, subcortical behaviour. This is not because the damage made the person a child, but because it undid inhibition, allowing for the expression of what is already there.

Reliving as a Process

A reliving is a slow process. It has to be titrated in such a way that the pain is manageable and is able to be integrated. It usually happens in an ordered sequence going from the most minor, recent events, to the remote past. Usually what happens is that a person will feel for months about something in childhood, for example, 'They never helped me out'. The patient will recall scenes and cry about how they were never there for him when he needed them. Then, at a certain point, the body sends a signal that it is ready for a deeper-lying aspect of the same feeling and the person will drop down to a birth feeling, 'No one was there to help me out'. He relives the painful birth, the attempt to get out, the struggle to make it, and the feeling of no one to help. This is part of what I call a compounded feeling – the second-line, childhood feeling compounding an earlier engraved aspect of the same feeling.

The ordered sequence of reliving allows history to be our guide and the pain to determine in what order events will be relived. It is what I call, 'the chain of pain'. One link of a feeling hooks into another more painful and more remote link until the whole feeling is relived.

A full feeling is a three-tiered event encompassing all levels of consciousness. Remember that very deep, early pain has its representations on higher centres of the brain with each level adding its bit to the feeling – from the heart rate, to the emotional tone to the images and context. Despite the fact that nerve circuits are gated from each other there seems to be a coding mechanism that allows one aspect of a blocked circuit to 'recognize' chemically its counterpart when connections are made.

The Meaning of What is Relived

The trauma which the patient relives in the first three weeks of therapy tells us about her general neurosis and defence system. To plunge into very early material right away (and this is done without any suggestion from the therapist) means a faulty defence structure. It means that consciousness is constantly disrupted by major early traumas, which in turn means a rather fragile system. We take care, therefore, that this kind of shattering reliving process is well controlled so that flooding does not occur.

Reliving is really neurosis in reverse. We begin with the most recently acquired brain and its memories and work backwards. It is a journey from the neocortex back eventually to the reptilian or primitive brain. The journey extends back through the limbic system where in some structures such as the hippocampus one can literally slice away memories in sequence. For example, we might see a patient feeling about his girlfriend who left him. Some time later the feeling brings him to the past which involves rejection or abandonment by his mother. Then, perhaps months or years later, he arrives at a reliving of total abandonment just after being born. It is usually only when a major segment of the feeling has been relived that symtoms begin to disappear. One feeling does not undo a neurosis. It takes many reliving episodes to make a full connection and integration to consciousness.

Timing

The sequence of reliving cannot be rushed. I liken it to those pop-up plates in a restaurant. You take one plate and the next pops up for use. Memory is laid down like that. You relive one part and the next part arises for its turn. It is not always as neat as that, but in general that is the way it works.

There are times in therapy when reliving would not be encouraged. If there is such tumult going on in the present life of the individual that it would be disintegrating to do so, the present life and its problems have priority. The person must sort out his present problems; otherwise reliving the past can become a defence against dealing with present reality.

I often look at patients reliving their birth and wonder why it is necessary to go over pain like that. Why do they have to relive it perhaps hundreds of times over many years? To go back to that same agony, the suffocation at birth? It is because the force of it shapes one's life forever. It is eventually lethal. It takes a mature adult with some semblance of a defence system to feel it, and even then it is horrific. Luckily, it is pain that 'feels good'. It is such a wonderful feeling to let it out and get rid of that aspect of the feeling forever. That is why patients rush to the clinic to feel. They know what lies on the other side. Not to feel the pain is to live in hell. To paraphrase Santayana, 'He who does not relive the past is doomed to repeat it'.

Reliving means recapturing history. This is quite an astonishing idea – to go back decades by travelling down the brain and reproduce an exact environment with its smells and colours. And then to undo that history. It is not undone by suggesting a different ending. That flies in the face of reality. It is undone by experiencing all of it so that one can finally be done with it. It is astounding in the most profound sense. But the human system is just that – miraculous.

17

Primal Therapy Today

I am aware that the techniques employed in Primal Therapy used to induce patients into primals have not yet been discussed in this book in any detail. This has been so for two reasons. First, any mention of technique in my previous books was utilized by charlatans to the detriment of their patients. Second, contrary to holistic, touchy-feely, altruistic therapies, Primal Therapy utilizes a precise scientific methodology which requires years of training for its correct employment. The techniques involved are complex. Another book would be required to explain them. It is, I believe, the first systematic, scientific psychotherapy extant.

In this chapter I would, however, like to discuss a number of important aspects of the therapy, and note some of the common kinds of mistakes made by untrained, would-be practitioners.

Primal Therapy Uses Rigorous Scientific Methodology

This therapy works, not because of the liberal, good intentions of those who practice it. It works because, aside from the qualities of human warmth and empathy necessary for its correct application, it is a rigorous and systematic procedure that allows for predictability, and most important, testability. Over the years it has become more and more precise.

347

By and large, people need help to get into feelings, at least initially. This is primarily due to the defence systems we all carry around. Just as important, the journey into feelings cannot be accomplished by a mere act of will. Indeed, an act of conscious, deliberate will defeats getting into feelings because it means the utilization of the logical, methodical cortex by the patient; the use of a different brain, if you will. Thus, the more one tries, the less one succeeds; this is another one of those diabolic dialectical facts that are everywhere in Primal Therapy.

The entire format of our therapy is different from other therapies practiced in the past hundred years. Our demarche has not changed. The patient still has three weeks of individual therapy, almost every day. The idea is to get the defence system open. That is done in one of two ways. First, by identifying the defence and blocking it, and secondly, by helping the patient go to a feeling which unlocks the defence. We must remember that each heavy feeling provokes its own counterpart – the defence against it. So feeling, in and of itself, goes a long way to dismantle the defence system. Even a certain position a patient takes just before a feeling comes up can be an effective defence. For others, that same position may help them get into a feeling. In any case, we are not after defences as such; we want the feeling underneath them.

The Primal Style

It is in the first three weeks of therapy that the patient learns a 'Primal Style', the way he or she characteristically gets into feeling. For each person this is different. Patients soon learn for themselves what to do to help themselves feel.

After the third week the patient enters a group in which he feels, along with thirty or forty other patients. He can do this just as if he were all by himself. Some patients need more individual treatment; we try to give them that while they are attending the group, usually about once a week for six months to one year. After six months there is another individual week of therapy in which the patient is monitored again to determine where he is, what feelings he is into, and how well he is integrating. Some patients do feel broken down to this point, and feelings come flooding forth. In some cases, tranquillizers are used to soften the blow of feelings and to allow them to be integrated more easily. The aim is not to keep the patient on drugs permanently, but to remove the need for them.

During the sessions, one of two things happens. Sometimes something has happened to the person beforehand, a relationship gone bad, for example, which he begins to talk about until the deep feeling is apparent. He then may dip into that old feeling and feel it for one hour or so. At other times, the patient is more fragmented and comes in totally anxious, with no current focus, and is swept into an old feeling right away. He immediately falls into that feeling because he is constantly inundated with feelings all of the time.

The pre-psychotic is that way precisely because, in all the intervening years between the very early trauma and adulthood, he has never developed an adequate defence. So you have a troubled patient immediately reliving events which occurred at the age of six months or one year.

Falling Into Feeling

I realize that 'falling into a feeling' doesn't mean much to non-primal people. Generally, a patient will talk for perhaps ten to twenty minutes until he makes a 'primal statement', such as 'My Grandfather was the only decent person in my life', or 'My dog was my only friend', or 'My girlfriend drives me crazy when she refuses to help me out'.

There are thousands of such primal statements. Often they are accompanied by the beginning of a feeling. There may be a tightening of the stomach, a wobble in the voice, a tear, or a tensing of the hands. These are telltale signs of feelings on the move.

When this happens, a therapist will slow the patient down and focus on the feeling. If there are signs of defence we try to stop it. If the patient goes on talking over the feeling we might say, 'Whoa, you're travelling over the feeling. It's right there.' 'What is it?' The patient invariably says, 'I don't know.' But he will stop and let his body take over. The feeling mounts, and at a certain point we ask him to say it like the child or to talk to his dog. He'll say, 'Heidi, you were my only friend', then cry and cry, first about the dog, and then about all the deprivation and lack of warmth that made him seek out the dog for comfort. The final feeling might be, 'Hold me, momma, touch me!' This is where the agony lies because the need always means pain. Obviously, this is a vastly oversimplified idea of a primal session. The defences often are most subtle.

The Crying Has to Be Done

If a child never cried at his father's funeral, either because he was the 'brave soldier' or because he wasn't allowed to attend, he has all of those tears that need to come out. When the patient has put himself back into the scene, and he looked at the cemetery, the casket, and all the friends, his sobs begin and tears flow. When he can finally say goodbye to his father he is writhing in agony. He never said it before, and he may begin screaming, 'Come back, daddy, I need you.' His post-session insights afterwards are filled with the ways he tried to bring his father back by seeking out a father in the men he associated with, or his boss or teacher.

Too often the child is never talked to about the death of a loved one. He is given a fantasy, that 'Daddy is in heaven', but he never cries or screams out his loss. The screams are still there in the tight belly and the knots in the stomach. It takes a good deal of tension to hold back those needs.

In order to feel the need again one has to risk feeling the pain of deprivation, because to ask for love means to feel that it isn't going to be there. How many of our patients, when asked to call for mommy say, 'What's the point? She's incapable of affection.' They are encouraged to try, then comes the pain. It is easier to forget about it and pretend one doesn't need it. If only the body could forget. It grinds itself into a nub trying to obliterate the memory. But need cannot be erased any more than any organ can be exorcised.

Fitting the Feeling into Current Life

After the feeling is felt, the patients sit up and discuss the feeling and its insights, and how it drove their behaviour. They also discuss their current life and how the feeling fits into it. This can take as much time as the feeling itself. It is a time of integration of the feeling and a chance to discuss current problems. But it is necessary to remember that neurosis is not made up of current problems. Problems exist because of neurosis. Our task is to get old feelings out of the way. Then a person can deal with what is going on in the present. It isn't a mystery to him or her. The woman who can feel past needs is no longer misperceiving, projecting and symbolizing. She isn't demanding too much of her man because she wants a daddy to take total care of her. She has felt that need and knows the difference between that and real present needs. She separates the past from the present, which is what the discussion period, the post-feeling part of the therapy accomplishes.

The same is true of groups. Half of the group time is spent in post-group where patients recount their feelings and their insights, confront other patients and the therapists, ask questions, and try to get information from others. Patients learn from each other, from their act-outs, and from what feelings helped overcome what kind of problems. They learn from each other's insights and from their own changes. They learn how each treats their mate, their parents, and themselves. They make statements like the following: 'I could never be good to myself.' 'I could never buy myself a gift.' 'I spent a lifetime feeling I never deserved anything.' 'My parents reinforced this by treating me as someone who was in the way, not worthwhile.' 'I never got any love, and so of course I felt it was my fault.' Another patient can take off from statements like this and use them to describe her state and what her feelings of inferiority did to her.

No one moralizes, no one judges, and no one tries to cheer someone up to get them out of a feeling. It is what it is. But these patients have literally gone through psychological hell together. Thus, they are extremely tolerant of each other. They wait patiently while someone is stumbling around trying to explain himself. All along the way we teach patients the reason for specific techniques and how to help themselves into feeling so that nothing about the therapy is a mystery to them. They are, in a way, being educated as therapists – their own. Because they know the techniques of getting into feelings they often help each other out with feelings in the group. A patient will see another struggling and go over and sit beside him and try to help him out. The authority of the group is decentralized. Patients learn independence not by exhortation but by experience. They are not sitting before the all-knowing therapist, but instead participate in their own cure.

After one year we have follow up interviews with patients to monitor their progress and to be sure that their therapy is progressing. Sometimes, more individual therapy is again indicated. If we have the personnel it is done. Sometimes there are not enough therapists – one of our chronic problems.

Primal Therapy is Systematic

Above all, the therapy is systematic. Part of its predictability is that there seems to be an inherent order to what patients go through. The timing of that order is different for each patient. Some come in with ironclad defences and do not begin feeling for several months. Others start feeling on the first day. What is important is to treat each patient individually, and not to force this timetable.

Some patients will use past feelings to keep from focusing on the present. They will start out with birth primals until they are awash in feelings and completely inundated. They do not connect, and stay fragmented – a most dangerous situation. There are others who become suicidal, not a rare occurrence. Why? Because the feeling of despair is an old feeling that predates words and concepts. When the patient is back in that feeling he cannot separate past and present; everything seems hopeless.

It is crucial for the therapist to know that the patient is experiencing an old precise feeling of despair, and where that feeling is coming from. It signals a very real feeling on the rise. To focus only on the present in this case would be life-endangering.

I recall one patient feeling terror on the street, imagining 'mean eyes' on him all of the time. He could no longer look people in the eye. He had been previously diagnosed as someone with paranoid tendencies. In the primal session he went with that feeling back to the past where he looked up from his crib when he was one and a half and saw the angry eyes of his father. He stopped crying and felt terror. He didn't know what he did wrong. He sensed his parents' anger. They didn't want him to cry any more. The defenceless child felt terror when he tried to express his needs. As a consequence he soon shut down these needs.

We've all forgotten how defenceless and helpless we were back then, and how utterly dependent we were on our parents' moods. It didn't take many 'angry eyes' for us to stop crying. It didn't take many kicks or spankings for us to stop trying to crawl onto mommy's lap. This is called one-trial learning, and it happens early to all animal forms when the punishment is severe enough and the dependency absolute.

There are a number of ways that the therapy can go wrong, which is what makes it so difficult. There are those who remain in the present, what we call third-line, to avoid getting into painful feelings. This must be spotted as a defence so that the person may travel back into older feelings. There are those who only focus on childhood feelings as a defence against dealing with current reality. It is crucial to know when this is a defence and when it is not. I have had to spend many months on the training of therapists to help them discern the difference between feeling and abreaction, between connected and unconnected experience. There are specific criteria for telling the difference. To allow the patient to continually abreact is to invite fragmentation and disintegration – one of the common mistakes made in mock Primal Therapy.

Mistakes in Primal Therapy

What happens with incorrect Primal Therapy is that a patient may have deep unconscious pain which goes unrecognized. The therapist will then deal with current life and problems, leaving a giant pool of pain untouched. Or the reverse is often true: the therapist ignores the present and plunges the patient again and again into the past, even when there are serious problems in the present that must be resolved. Someone with too much present anguish can rarely move to the past. It really depends on the skill of the therapist as to where to focus with the patient. Sometimes the source of the pain is first-line – the birth trauma or a trauma during the first year of life, yet the therapist, blocked from his own early pain, automatically avoids this and focuses on later events.

One of the great mistakes a novice therapist can make is talking to the patient and keeping him in the present with too much discussion when the patient and his feeling are in the past. The patient never gets to go where he must. Therapy then becomes a verbal exercise, when the problem lies elsewhere.

Silence is truly golden in Primal Therapy; it allows a patient time to slip into a feeling and be taken by that feeling into the past.

Many therapists read *The Primal Scream* and decided to try the therapy without any further training. This is tantamount, in my opinion, to setting up heart surgery in your garage. They isolate even the most disturbed patients, keeping them alone and out of any social contact for weeks at a time, with the result that we see a number of psychotics coming to us from their offices. They adopt isolated techniques from *The Primal Scream*, almost none of which are used in the present-day therapy. Deep breathing, for example, is something rarely used and only in special circumstances. Yet charlatan after charlatan (I call them 'mock therapists') deep-breathe their patients. They make them go through exercises such as yelling this or that, calling their momma, punching pillows, etc. They have them do anything but feel because they cannot recognize a feeling when they see one, and have no idea at all about how to get a patient into old feelings. They rely on mechanics.

Connection to memory is what is important. That is what is curative, not the screaming and flailing by itself. Going through the motions of feeling without the memory is to have a literally devitalized experience.

Confusing Abreaction with Feeling

In abreaction a patient acts out a memory or an emotion, and virtually 'pretends' to be experiencing something from the past, rather than actually experiencing the upsurge of the feeling. This is not necessarily intentional, but it is not real.

Abreaction looks so dramatic that it can fool the therapist, particularly when the patient feels better afterwards because he has discharged tension. We have measured the difference electronically and have found that in feeling, the vital signs move as a unit (pulse, blood and body temperature), whereas in abreaction, they move erratically and out of phase. Going through the motions of feeling or doing exercises directed by the therapist, is quite different than feeling, and it is never resolving.

In abreaction there is a release of the energy of feeling without connection. There is an abrupt and sudden plunge into the co-called feelings rather than a slow descent. There is also a sudden shift from one level of consciousness to the other, with a ring of phoniness about the experience. That is because there is a lack of proper contact. It seems like crying for its own sake or screaming for no apparent reason. It is amazing how many mock therapists elicit abreaction and believe it to be feeling. The hallmark of mock therapy is the absolute lack of early context for whatever is going on in the therapeutic situation.

There are distinct telltale or pathognomonic signs that accompany each source of pain. If they are wrongly read, you get a discharge of the energy of feeling on a level other than the correct one. Patients will be crying about something at the age of eight but will cough and gag or arch because of what I call 'first-line intrusion'. This is material from early on that is bursting through the feeling on a higher level. So one gets a mélange, but this mélange foreshadows where the patient is and what feelings he is now near. Great attention must be paid to these pathognomonic signs. If they are too strong and foretell of disintegration, they must be avoided for a time.

Retreats and Primal Therapy

I recall some years ago a patient saying, 'Why is it we always come to you? (Fifty per cent of the patients came from Europe.) Why don't you come to us?' I said, 'Find a place in your country and we'll come.' They did, and thus began a tradition of retreats. Every six months the patients would find a place in another country and all of the patients would go there to stay for one week of intensive group and individual follow-up therapy. We would rent a Swiss chalet, a French monastery, or a Norwegian hotel, for example. All of the staff would go there and the intensity of the therapy was beyond imagination. Marriages and lifelong friendships came out of these retreats, plus a chance to see the world and encounter other cultures. It was always a partnership between patient and therapist. Patients would simply take charge of their own therapy, organize the place, food, side trips and the like. Just because they felt bad did not mean they were incompetent. They were usually more than competent. The encounters I had with the people I met at these retreats, (speaking among them ten to fifteen languages) were among the best encounters of my life. I wouldn't have traded those experiences for anything.

The format for the retreats changed over time, but basically it remained a group four times a week plus individual therapy during the day. Originally we all pitched in with the cooking and cleaning. Later, the cooking was done by the school, convent, or whatever. The worst food ever was that prepared by the monastery. There, existence was frugal in every way possible, but the patients always made the best of it. The experience itself was too valuable to grumble about minor details. Each of us learned about other cultures personally, about habits, preferences, language, tradition, dress, etc. It was a learning experience that none of us could have otherwise had.

Patients organized talent shows at all of the retreats, and in the clinic as well. They also made costumes which expressed their culture or their feelings. We had bands, jazz singers and rock stars. What a wonder to see our worst depressive act the comic in one of these shows, to hear the marvellous poetry composed by working class people who had never tried anything like that before, or to see the artwork done by people who, when they discovered their real selves, also discovered the artist inside. No matter if the singer broke down and cried, or the comic could not contain his tears from time to time, the audience of patients was always kind, patient and understanding.

This was nothing like those so-called encounter groups I used to attend (and run, as a matter of fact) with the phoney hugs and kisses the so-called 'loving' people would give each other. There was something ineffably real about what went on among patients at our retreats. Above all there was no shame about feeling. We were all in it together and I mean that literally, since therapists too would experience their feelings in front of patients.

Therapists

One of the reasons there is a shortage of therapists is burnout. It is just not humanly possible to go on forever dealing with pain day in and day out. That is why training is so essential. Yet it is the most difficult problem, since all therapists must be patients first. They must undergo the therapy to know their own feelings and to learn the therapy from the point of view of a patient. I cannot imagine doing this therapy without undergoing it first, followed by at least two to three years of training. It is nothing like the psychoanalytic training I had, which was largely intellectual. Here it is feelings that count. They can't be hurried or presented superficially. A therapist could never really know the difference between catharsis and a feeling without undergoing the therapy.

Unique Aspects of Primal Therapy

After having spent a lifetime waiting in doctors' offices, I decided no patient would wait in mine. And they don't. Each patient is taken at the time appointed. I have made sure of that because it is just one of the many ways respect for the patient can be shown. Another is not to limit the time of the sessions. Patients stay until it is appropriate to leave. Their feelings dictate how long they remain, not some artificial schedule based on the therapist's need to see so many patients per day. I couldn't imagine cutting a session short while a patient was crying.

Even the structure of Primal Therapy lends itself to feeling. A darkened room, padded floors and walls, sound-proofing, no worry about screaming. Contrast that with the brightly lit therapist's office with its antique desk and tables. We already know in what kind of surroundings the patient will be able to feel.

When I first started working as a Primal Therapist, I had those antiques. But six weeks of Primal Therapy saw every stick of it smashed. I learned a little slowly, but I learned. I saved on furniture thereafter. It is not easy for the ordinary therapist to get out of his suit and roll on the floor with the patient. It is all a bit messy, in any case. Feelings aren't neat and ordered, and they don't stop at the fifty minute mark. They get unruly, and the patient's anger can get wild.

I remember when my centre had walls. Within a month, there were holes all through them. I never saw the unchained furies before, despite the fact that I had practiced psychoan-alytic therapy for seventeen years. Those furies have to be understood. If they are understood and handled well, there is never any danger to the therapist. If they are not, we find murder. Yes, a mock therapist was beaten to death by a patient. Primal Therapy is not another holistic therapy. Neurosis is deadly serious business.

Pain and Therapy

If imprinted pain, something we've seen in every single neurotic over decades of time, is not recognized or acknow-ledged, then it follows that the patient can be kept in the here-and-now to the exclusion of his past. Patients being treated by a therapy which does not recognize pain are going to get well only in their heads. They will adjust better to their current life. They will try harder. Pain will never be the goal of such therapies because it is assumed it is not there. If you do not think that the pain of circumcision, of surgery, of birth, or of early neglect live on, then of course you can and will ignore pain.

The elapsed time before a patient is relatively well is longer than we originally supposed, but the specific time spent at the clinic is not. After one year to a year and a half patients are largely on their own, with only sporadic follow-up necessary. We give them the tools to feel. As we go along, we teach them about their defences and how to get to feeling. There is a lot they can do on their own. Other things they need help with. Therein lies our problem. We never have enough personnel to give everyone all the time they need. Groups help, but there are those who need more individual therapy. It is then that matters become expensive because we practically need a therapist for every patient – a patent impossibility.

Sometimes after two years the patient will get into very deep material and need constant therapy. It is not always possible to provide a therapist; that is why we instituted the buddy system through which we teach patients the fundamentals of Primal Therapy so that they can sit with each other and help each other into feelings. We leave the clinic open for that all of the time.

Having said that, I must reiterate that in the best of all worlds patients need much more individual therapy than we have been able to give them. When they are in deep pain, something that may arise after two or three years of their starting time, they need to be seen two or three times a week. We have never had enough therapists for that, and economics will not permit it. What we do need is government subsidy for treatment and training. Certainly, this would be most economical in terms of the later disease we could prevent.

Patients make great changes after the first year, but major

changes go on for five to eight years. This doesn't mean constant pain throughout. On the contrary, each feeling is its own reward. Between sessions patients often feel better than they ever have before. I think that after five years most of the work is done. It seems like a long time. But remember, we are undoing a lifetime, and a thirty-year-old still has most of his life ahead of him. One doesn't feel constantly during that time. One feeling per month is average. These feelings take far less time (thirty minutes on average), and are quickly integrated.

Is Primal Therapy for the rich? Most of our patients have never been rich. They have saved. Social class and economic status has little to do with pain. We have treated royalty, industrialists, professionals and workers. We have also taken a number of welfare cases. It is all the same. Pain doesn't recognize class. What happens, however, is that the rich have more chances for diversion. They can rent yachts and travel, buy escorts, get a new car or new clothes – all things that delay the day or reckoning. I have seen rock stars who received adulation every day of their adult lives – thousands applauding and clamouring. Nothing changed their pain or made them feel loved. You don't feel loved when you have been unloved. That is certainly a law.

Primal Therapy Now

Is Primal Therapy for a special kind of person? I don't think so. We have seen depressives, literally hundreds of suicide attempts, assassins, migraine and cancer patients, rapists, those riddled with anxiety, psychotics taken out of mental hospitals, a welfare case who threatened to kill his children if he was not accepted, incest cases, colitis sufferers, exhibitionists, and just about everything one can imagine. It is still about pain and need. The psychotics share something with the movie and rock stars – the most incredible load of pain imaginable. To need to be loved by the whole world takes some kind of pain and drive. What is hopeful is that they are all treatable. The absolutely insane man who was about to kill his children is fine today. The suicidals who were saving pills or buying dynamite and guns, wouldn't think of anything like that now. They cherish life and cannot even imagine what they were like before, only that their despair was devastating.

Is the therapy disintegrating for those who are treated? Are patients just feeling machines who leave each session in pieces? I'd say that might be true of mock Primal Therapy. Our job is to see to it that each day one aspect of a feeling is felt and then integrated with one's current life. If that is not done, Primal flooding will result. Obviously, each complete feeling takes months and even years to feel in its entirety. It cannot be felt to completion in one or two sessions. Thus, the therapist must be on the lookout for this flooding and stop it before the patient is overwhelmed. We must keep in mind that the reason the feeling is repressed is that it was too much to feel originally. We don't want to throw open the neural gates prematurely.

The patient must come out of each feeling knowing what it means and placing it within the context of his current life. In short, each level of consciousness must be engaged in the curative process. Otherwise it is feeling for feeling's sake, a necessary but not sufficient condition for getting well.

Primal Therapy has been treated with suspicion because emotions are treated with suspicion. The cool intellect is most appreciated. Yet someone who is in touch with his or her emotions is rational. One who is not is irrational, because he is controlled by unconscious feelings that drive him beyond his control. That is what irrational is – the logical, reasonable mind distorted by hidden forces. Much better to be emotional – not hysterical, but reactive and feelingful. I trust those kinds of people. You always know that you are going to get a reasonable reaction from them.

The job of neurosis is to keep us from being real. For the neurotic, 'real' means pain. Instead of repression we liberate. Instead of symbolization we take symbols to their correct home in feelings. Instead of constructing a defence we dismantle one. Instead of a system which is progressively closing down we are engaged in opening it up. It liberates the warmth we are all born with. We all have the capacity to be that child who is open, warm, curious, engaging, unafraid, daring and alive. That is not just the capacity of children. It is a *human* quality we must try to recapture.

Defences: Case Study

I will follow this chapter with an important case history, an account by a patient in which a long period of therapy and growth is summarized. Particularly noteworthy is the some- what chilling manner in which this patient came to recognize how she had used elaborate defences to survive, and that because of these defences it was extremely difficult for her to give and receive love.

18

Nadine

Lots of feelings about my father's death. Painful scenes in which longings and hopes so twisted at the time that they had made me into a violent, hysterical, possessive and withdrawn child unable as an adult to feel comfortable with a man because I could not share myself with them. I interpreted his death as leaving me because I had done something wrong.

When my therapist made me talk about my father's death I was holding back a terrible urge to go to the bathroom which indicates in me a need to let go. Then I started to describe my grandmother's house. I was surprised to see my grandmother, because I thought she would still be with my mother at the hospital. And my sisters were there too. One of them said that mother is coming in the morning. 'What about Papa,' I said, 'is he coming too?' My sister looked at me in a queer way and said, 'No, your Daddy will not suffer any more.' My sisters asked more questions I couldn't hear, they started to cry, and I heard someone screaming like an animal before I passed out.

In the next scene my sisters and I are in a field with poppies and wheat all around, and in the far distance we can hear the bells of the church signalling a mass for my father. We are too young to attend, my mother had said. So they brought us to the cemetery afterwards ... it's strange, but today I could feel myself walking towards that cemetery; I could hear the gravel crunching under my shoes, I could smell the flowers all around me and really see all those people around as I walked towards the grave. And I saw the box inside, and I am supposed to believe that my father is there. 'Yes,' my therapist, Rick, said. 'Your father is in that box.' I scream that it can't be. I scream for my father to come back to me. For the first time since his death I cry for him, and feel that he is really dead.

One day in therapy I was crying my heart out in a small room, my whole body in some kind of expectation my mind didn't yet know about. The door opened, my body tensed, and as the door closed I knew where I was. I was in an incubator, a bubble-like shape, and I was waiting for the hand to come and touch me and bring me out of my pain. It was really about being all alone. Once in a while a hand would caress my forehead, ease my pain, and stay there for a while. It was sheer agony when it left, agony when it was on my head too, because the hand couldn't understand that I wanted it to stay there. So my body went into spasms. I sucked my thumb and yelled for the hand. The insight I had was like the therapist had predicted a few months earlier. 'You don't want to be loved because you felt something like love once and it was taken away.'

More scenes are familiar to me. One is me sitting at the dinner table with my mother and sisters (papa was away a lot), listening to my mother trying to find out who had been responsible for the latest mistakes, broken the pencils, etc. I would sit there smiling because I knew it would all come down to me somehow. Through it all I wore a smirk on my face, I never cried. I looked straight into her face to show her that she wasn't getting to me. I was getting under her skin all right, the only way I knew how to, and she would lose control and hit me and hit me again and again, with that glazed look in her eyes, until she felt exhausted and sent me to my room.

Feelings about my mother help me realize just how scared of closeness I am, and of women in particular, how much I have rejected my femininity and how ugly and inadequate I feel all the time competing with other women. The first time I felt I wanted to hold another woman in my arms I started clutching at her and soon I was writhing on the floor because the feeling was so heavy inside. I realize now that it makes me crazy, this feeling. I act out sexually in so many ways, wanting to be held and touched by my mother. For the first time also I am able to talk in group about needing to be accepted and loved by the therapist. The therapist says that I should say 'please' but I am not ready yet. I know that all my life lies behind this 'please', this need to say 'touch me, love me'. It terrifies me to ask. So I act it out sexually with quite a few men, one-night stands.

Towards the end of the first year of therapy I stop making love for three months and start to feel that I don't know how to go about it any more. Somehow I feel that emotions should be involved in love-making, not just my body, and this is something new for me. I've learned how to please in order to get what I want, but never to let go. I am terribly afraid of someone 'touching me inside', whatever that means, but the thing I know for sure is that I am scared of being hurt. My cold façade is just a façade now.

I have constant fears with my lovers of being rejected because I am not a nice person, because I am too strong, or not pretty enough. All my concern is really about what they think of me. I never think about what it would be like to be accepted or liked. I believe that if a man likes me it is surely because he finds me sexually attractive and because I am nice to him. Inside I feel that nobody could really understand or accept me. About six months into therapy I go into a large room at the new institute and for about a week scream, 'Arthur Janov, go to hell', because now I feel the pain when it hurts, and I can hear people when they say they dislike me. It seems that the process of therapy has finally broken down the walls that made me function without really feeling.

One morning, walking out of the Institute after a very deep feeling about losing my father, I stopped in my tracks and looked at the world outside. For the first time in my life I could see that the colours were not as shiny as before, that things around me didn't bring about the same intense sensations that I had needed in order to feel that life was worth living. Things were different somehow, not so vibrant or sensational, but there was a more balanced feel to it. Even lovemaking started to be different. I used to faint when I had an orgasm, sensual feelings were really strong. I used to lose myself in mindless passion with my lover of the time. But when he started to care for me, I became cold and usually frigid. I usually left then because I felt suffocated. About seven months into therapy I had lots of feelings about my religion. I had been brought up Catholic, but somehow had lost the faith a few months after papa had died. Still, some hope lingered inside. That hope related to God was that if he really existed one day I would be united with my father. I believed very strongly too that there was really no death, just transition. I spent countless hours screaming to God about all the lies I had believed in because of the hope of seeing my father again.

About six months into therapy I finally felt and understood why all my life I had been a compulsive nailbiter (and that included chewing on my toenails as well, and making myself bleed). The insight I had was very simple, but it showed me the extent of my neurosis. I needed the pain that one gets when doing anything with their hands and having no fingernails. I needed the pain of walking every step in agony from bleeding toenails, because I felt physically so dead that it was my only way to feel (through pain) that I still existed.

About nine months into therapy, living with a guy, I started to have strange fantasies regarding women. I was absolutely fascinated by women's breasts. I felt that I wanted to touch a woman and be touched by her. I told my lover that, and he didn't mind my going out to lesbian clubs. So, for a while I acted out my fantasies but couldn't bring myself to make a sexual move. I danced with women, and let them pick me up, but I couldn't bring myself to go home with one of them. It drove me insane and my body was literally on fire all day long. Finally, one evening at the Institute in group, I told the therapists about what was going on. 'I really feel that only a woman can satisfy another woman,' I said, 'because we know each other's bodies much better than men do.' Fred, one of the therapists said, 'Really, Nadine, you are sure that you are not having feelings about your mother....'

'No, I haven't felt anything about my mother yet. It is all about my father.'

'All right. If it's a woman you want, a woman you shall get ... someone, please get me Alice.'

They brought in this curvy new therapist, and Fred said, 'You really have two options, Nadine. Either you act out the feeling now and get to it, or else you act it out later tonight and you won't get to it.'

In front of all these people staring at me I felt cold and detached, but I knew that he might be right, so I stood up facing Alice, who was waiting against the wall.

'Are you sure you don't mind. I mean, you know what I want to do?'

She assured me that she didn't mind, and I could hear that Fred had continued the group in order to divert some of the attention from me. So I started to touch her face, still not feeling anything, down her neck, and as I started to touch her breast there was no more noise around me, something incredible was tightening my body. I felt like I was in another space or time, and it only took a minute before I crashed on the floor screaming for my mother for the first time since my therapy had started. The feelings about my mother started from sorrow, not having a mother really. About the same time I started having lots of angry feelings toward my Dad for not protecting me from her, for never being there when needed; then understanding and compassion came and I stopped feeling about papa for a very long time. Years.

About the same time I realized that when someone is too interested in me my mind goes blank and it gets even worse when I think about needing someone. My relationships with men since I started therapy seem to be with the same kind of men – insecure, looking for someone better, never satisfied with me except in bed, afraid of showing their feelings or needs and accusing me of being the culprit behind many of their negative emotions. I spent most of my time trying to figure out their pain, but still hung on because there was nothing else I felt I could do. I felt for the longest time, years, that maybe if I were better, maybe if I changed enough they would finally accept me. Unconsciously, I really believed that the problem in the relationship was mine. After all, I had heard that all my life, so what they were saying must be true. From that level nothing had changed me for years because deep inside I had no self-esteem, and I was as scared of receiving love as I was of breaking up.

I find that I always have to put myself in a hurting position to find out if people care for me. But they don't because what I do is so out of character nobody really understands it. The connections I made are all connected with my Mom and the devious ways I used to get her attention, to be touched, to show that I was hurting. Like coming back from an outing in the mountains of the south of France with both my legs scorched and bleeding from a fall on the rocks. She was never home, so I bathed my wounds with water and tied as many handkerchiefs around my legs as I could find. I was quite a sight, with the blood all over. When she came, I made sure to be waiting in the hall. Inevitably, after her scream of fear, her fist would come raining down on my head for not being careful. The insult would push down any needs for reassurance I might have had. Eventually, I stopped hurting myself. It really was hopeless anyway, and I really didn't know what I wanted any more.

I never ask for love because I feel that I don't have the right to expect nor to ask for anything. So I bitch. I make demands. I always get what I want. I understand, I compromise, I get cold, and the ultimate satisfaction of closeness for me is to make love. I keep blaming myself for my coldness, my anger, and my inability to connect to any of my needs. I am used to the pain so much that I don't know anything else.

At work people resent my bossiness; some don't like working with me. I know that they talk about me behind my back and in a way I'm proud ... but why? I am always trying to get ahead, to screw people one way or another by being better, to control them, and give only as much as I want to give. I don't want to be fair. It is the same feeling I have with stealing, which I still do here and there, little things like magazines and books. I want to get at people, to get something back that I don't have, as if they owed it to me. I feel that other people have it. My sisters had it, the attention, the love, and I have to steal it, to take something in a devious way.

I am not fair with anyone, I don't give people what is rightly theirs, I want to keep it all for myself because I don't have enough with what I have, and I never will, I fear, because what I want is something from the past. And I do this in countless ways, from stealing to cheating, to getting ahead in lines, to twisting things to suit me so I can have the feeling that I'm ahead, that I have something more than the next person, that I'm not losing. I also feel that I have the right to do this just because it is me. Very few people like me, lots fear me, but to be honest I am more secure with that feeling than any other because at least I know that feeling and how to deal with it.

As an adult, I started bingeing and throwing up just about every day. It was like wanting to feel an empty hole inside, and I felt numb. One day I went to pick up my son at his babysitter, and she said that he was calling her 'Mama'. It brought up some heavy feelings of rejection, not being wanted by my own son. I could understand that. I have had problems playing with him maybe because I never played as a child, never had a playmate except my sisters, and those games ended in a fight with me the loser.

So I have a hard time giving my son what he wants for more than fifteen minutes at a time. Rages build inside me. I want to scream, to hit him, or throw him against the wall, and I just walk away. After a session I realized that I needed to play with him, to get to some of those deeply buried feelings inside instead of avoiding them by smoking. I let him be as aggressive as he wants, because I realized it is his time now to express his feelings and also because I don't want to kill him like my Mom killed me. So he screams that he doesn't want me or love me, doesn't want me to hold him or touch him. And I think of all the times he begged me to play with him, but instead I buried myself in books. Today we both left the beach crying. He, because he wanted to play some more, me, because of his screams of anger and rejection. But I know that I have to bear it and undo the damage I have done.

I went to group tonight and cried about the fact that my mother really wanted me dead. Then I felt really dead, just the way she had wanted it, and realized that I had fought all those years against that knowledge which was lodged in me, and that had been my reality. She filled me with her constant hatred of me, and I fought back hard to pretend that her hatred didn't matter. But as it started to matter now I found myself begging for her to forgive me for being born, for messing up her life, for hanging on tight inside of her despite the fact that she had tried unsuccessfully to get rid of me.

'You were very deeply attached in there,' she had said once when I made her talk when I was sixteen. I needed to know why she had done all those things to me. I feel so guilty now for being alive, preventing her from becoming the nurse she wanted to be, free of her family and past. I really messed you up, Mama, I am sorry. But I feel so mixed up inside. How crazy she made me, so that there is nothing really worthy left in me. I don't know the first thing about myself, don't know the colours I like, the things I want to do. I've always been scared of the world because nobody prepared me for it, except for the pain. I live in a constant defensive mode, ready to attack, to defend myself. I am the perfect survivor.

After a time in therapy my relationship with my son has improved. I feel real love towards him and it makes me more patient. I know now that in trying to avoid my son I was really trying to avoid myself at his age, and I know the pain he feels because I felt it too. In a way, having a boy is easier for me than having a girl ... and I know why. Somehow I grew up with the notion that boys are tougher, less sensitive than girls. If I had a girl it would have been too close for comfort for me, because I would have seen myself in her.

I have connected this to the anger I have towards my mother, not letting me out of her, my feeling that I was trapped and exhausted. No wonder I don't want to work any longer. Trying to be born is exhausting.

When I went back to France, my native land, my first feelings when I finally walked in the streets of Paris were that I felt totally removed from the place. I didn't belong any more. It hit me that I belonged in LA where I had learned about myself. It was the best feeling I had ever had. I finally had a home, a place to go back to.

There I was, facing the shadows of the past, and nothing was the same any more. I went to see my mother who didn't even know I was in the country, and who hadn't heard from me since I was eighteen. We drove to her place and it took lots of courage for me to ring the bell and hear her voice.

'Who is it?' I heard her say. But I didn't answer.

I walked up the stairs, my heart beating hard. I could see someone waiting up on the balcony. I covered my face with my hat, and when I reached her floor I looked straight up at her. There was a strange light in her eyes, not believing what she was seeing, a moment of suspense, a startled expression on her face before she hesitantly said my name. The very first thought that hit me right there and then was that if I was going to hit her now I could kill her. She looked small and frail, an old woman. Gone was the mad woman of the past, the huge monster of my nightmares. In her place was this tiny, old woman, stuttering. She was ill at ease with me, trembling. I couldn't feel a thing. I just stared at her, my mother, fussing about my son, stammering badly with a voice I hardly recognized. My sister had told me that since her last operation she had changed quite a bit, but I didn't expect it to be that bad. We talked a bit about safe things. I couldn't take in all the changes in her. I left telling her I would come back to talk to her, and I saw fear in her eyes for the first time. Memories. I went back to the house where we had lived when my father was alive. There also were a lot of changes. The paint on the house was chipping away. Gone was the beautiful garden my father spent so much time on. The general look was one of total neglect, and the new owner didn't want to let us in.

I insisted on visiting the old lady I used to call 'aunt' Berthe. I had spent two whole weeks with her right after we had learned of my father's accident. She was quite deaf, but we managed to talk quite a bit, and I was happy to go through the rooms where that old lady, for a short period of time, had treated me like a real little girl. And in a way I pushed at her for recognition. Later that day I felt quite intensely about those weeks I had spent with her, the only clue to the existence of a carefree little girl. I was still hanging on to her in order not to become an adult because I never had a childhood.

Back in the States, the realization that for Berthe I had only been one of many children she had taken care of over the years made this pillar of my childhood finally crumble. I was never special for anybody. This was the most devastating feeling I ever had.

My reality seems to change every day, yet I still get submerged under old pain and often can't tell the old feeling from the present. It is a lot like scenes of *déjà vu* with new people and different places. But still thinking about loving someone and being accepted is enough to send my senses reeling crazily towards an exit. My mind always analyzes people's motives, but I am more careful now with the judgement I pass on them. In a way the biggest discovery for me is to realize that the way I operated and used to think, came out of a pure reaction born of defences and pain. When that truth hit me I lost the only sense of protection I had, what I thought was knowledge of myself. In fact, I was learning that I knew nothing of myself, that I had fabricated a whole edifice in order to shield myself from further pain, and that most of my healthy or normal reactions were, in fact, distorted, and that nothing about me was spontaneous or free-flowing. I can't express in words what it feels like when one realizes that one's whole life has been a pack of pretences and make-believe.

I am now shifting gears. It is frightening to have to relearn how to be with people and to realize how wrong I used to be. The main connection was in regard to asking my mother and father to acknowledge my existence. I got down to the feeling that I had never existed in their eyes, but that I was a nuisance, a thing with no name that should have died because it created too many problems for two people who really didn't belong together. The other insight I had at this time was to feel completely that if my father had never acknowledged me it was because he never felt that I was his daughter. Now I don't especially want to be anybody else's daughter. I am no longer hoping to find a better daddy somewhere. The fact that I understand now why my father always looked at me in a questioning way, avoiding me, and treated my sisters in such a different way from the way he treated me all makes sense, and it is enough for me.

Now I have had a nine-month relationship with a Swede and for the first time I feel love towards him. I realized through my lover for the first time that behind all my act-outs with men is a deep need to be reassured by them that I am a real person, and the feeling of wanting to be special emerges for the first time. To this day I still have the same need of wanting to be special for someone, to be everything for them that they never got. In turn, I'd like to feel needed and wanted the way I have always wanted to feel.

Unfortunately, I became a dream woman, a substitute mother who rendered my lovers helpless and needy. It was finally I who broke down under the strain of my efforts, and cut off the relationship. I can't seem to let men do things for me, take care of me without having the most helpless feeling inside. If they really know how to take care of themselves, If they are happy and all right, then they don't need me.

I need to feel needed and in a way in control of the situation in order to feel safe inside. I realized that in order to be taken care of I first try to take care of my lover so I can earn what they will give me. But again the trade off is so heavy for me that once that stage is reached nothing they can do is good enough. I am really terrified of being helpless and needy, because as a child experiencing these feelings ... I can't even remember feeling helpless and needy ... I only remember a dreadful feeling of nothingness in me. Once I broke up with my lover and was sick with fever for a whole day until he came back. I never understood why at the time.

With my lover I learned about my real sexuality. I learned to accept his touch all over my body, and overcame the biggest resistance I had at being kissed on my sexual part. I had never wanted anyone before to kiss me there. With time and patience I was able one night to relax myself enough to accept that intimate touch, and as I started to let the pleasure wash over me I started to cry very deeply. The feeling was very simple. I did not feel worth being given to when I could not give back. Looking back, I see that food is an obsession with me. My whole day is planned around what I will eat or deprive myself of eating. I feel guilty about eating all the time, so I binge and throw up quite a lot, and I don't understand why. So I start the 'Beverly Hills Diet', mostly pineapples throughout the day, and other fruits, quite a regimen. It works the first two days. It is hard, but I only eat pineapple. The third day my lover gives me a bite of his bagel and cream cheese, which I throw up immediately after tasting it. The strangest feeling of deprivation hits me. It was so intense I started to cry in the street. I felt the emptiness inside of me, vivid scenes washed over me ... it is absolutely monstrous. I can see myself as an infant crawling on the floor towards a door that is shut, and screaming because I am hungry. Nobody comes and I cry myself to sleep. Next scene, I am being fed and my tummy hurts because I cannot take in the food because of the pain I feel inside from waiting. I realize, in shock, that my mother starved me. Memories of what she said once came back. 'You were a premature baby, so the doctors said you needed to be fed small amounts of food every two hours ...' I can see her angry face, her impatience. It is so terrifying to be so small and to need so much. In the next scene I am crying on the floor, behind the door, and I try to crawl up. I hear noises, and suddenly the door is jammed open so hard I am thrown against the wall. My mother walks in – so angry and so tall, grabs me and throws me back into the bed ... for the first time I feel fear about my safety. I had to make myself safe as an infant.

I learned very early that attention and affection were not for me. What really drove me crazy was the idea that whatever I did never changed my mother's attitude. Being good, being bad, it was all the same. Ultimately I started to believe that something was wrong with me. For me this is the ultimate feeling summed up in one sentence ... deep inside of me I felt like a real piece of shit.

The next four years of my life contributed greatly towards that feeling in a very strange way. I became an art dealer, flying out of town, meeting serious businessmen, dealing with real hard core people and really acting out the unreal part of myself until it finally died. During those four years I was literally on stage all the time, at galleries, art shows, power meetings, but it finally gave me the confidence in myself I had never felt. I now experienced the realization that I was intelligent and cunning and shrewd in a positive way too. I used most of my defences to my advantage, and finally realised that I could make choices and decisions in my life, a thing I had never thought possible before. I never liked the job, never believed in it. The feeling was so real that for the first time it made me face being a fake just like them. I don't need to play games any more.

19

Conclusions:
Primal Therapy Twenty Years Later

Primal Therapy is a revolution in psychotherapy. It is the end of the fifty minute hour and the end of interminable therapy with twice weekly or more visits to a therapist over many years. It is a new concept in group therapy in which confrontation is only a by-product, and each person is into his own history, despite the fact that he is surrounded by others. It gives patients back their self-determination and their right to make discoveries about themselves by themselves. It returns the power back to where it should be, in the hands of the patient. It means that feelings dictate how long a session will last and not some arbitrary time schedule.

Primal Therapy is also revolutionary because it focuses on generating sources, rather than on manifestations. In an era of superficiality, in which appearances are everything, this is almost heresy. The only way one can focus on sources is if:

1. One believes in early pain as the source of neurosis.
2. One recognizes imprinted memory.
3. One has access to deeper levels of consciousness.

If one does not believe that these propositions are axiomatic to the human condition, despite overwhelming evidence for their existence, one is obviously forced to focus on the present.

Empirical Evidence

Our research approach is unique. For the first time investigators have undertaken systematic empirical research into the biological processes involved in neurosis. Resolving the pain changes personality. It changes brain function, muscle electrical potential (electromyography), blood circulation (our infrared photo studies), hormones, (our stress hormone studies) and blood pressure, heart rate and body temperature. These changes, found in our research, indicate that neurosis is embedded throughout the system.

The fact that the alcoholic is off drink, the addict off drugs, or the pervert sworn to renounce his perversion, does not necessarily constitute a proper index of the absence of neurosis. I repeat this point because relying on such indications is the most common error in the treatment of psychological problems.

Resistance to the Notion of Hidden Pain

Pain from whatever source is measurable. We can demonstrate its force in our laboratory. Memory can be pinpointed with an electrode in the brain. It can be reached with hypnosis. Why then is the notion of hidden pain so difficult to accept? Why then is it so often systematically ignored? Because the pain in each of us elicits repression and unconsciousness. To ignore one's own reality means to be unaware in general.

What a dilemma. We find ourselves talking about something that well-defended people cannot see or relate to. It's like talking about Mars. But if the pain we speak of does exist, the focus should be on it directly, and not just peripherally as some byproduct of a so-called feeling therapy such as Gestalt or psychoanalysis. Yes, people do cry in other therapies. They also talk about their past. What they don't do is what is curative – descend to the past in *orderly fashion* –

and relive it as it is engraved in the nervous system.

There are those who even experience primals occasionally in the feeling therapies. But the process is not systematic, methodical and ordered. It is hit and miss, and therefore dangerous. Patients do not finish a feeling, or stay too long in it. They do not know how or when to get out of it.

The Claim for Primal Therapy

So why do I maintain that there is only one effective therapy for neurosis? Or do I still think that? After all, I'm, twenty years older and I hope wiser by now. But I still think it because I have twenty years and thousands of patients' experiences to draw on. How could there be any other approach if we are talking about an effective therapy for neurosis? If the pain is there, if it is imprinted and endures, if it can be resolved through reliving, then it seems ineluctably logical to pursue it; above all, not to mix it with other so-called holistic psychotherapies in the name of 'improvement'. You can't improve on reality.

It works, not only because it is logical but because wherever we look we find significant changes.

Post-Primal Patients

What are post-Primal patients like? Some twenty years ago it seemed as if they were more homogeneous than they are today. I think the major difference is in their value system. Then, as now they value their time, the preciousness of life, beauty, the environment and the sanctity of living things. By and large they know what they want and try to get it. They do not stay in situations or relationships that are bad for their mental health. They appear more alive now that the deadness has been lifted from their faces.

What a relief to be able to love and be loved. To be able to accept warmth and caring and not have to fend it off to keep the old feeling of not being loved away. What a nice feeling to be able to be nice to oneself. Not to be driven twelve hours a day; to be able to take a vacation without nagging worry about getting back to work. What a relief not to be plagued by obsessions and repetitive thoughts that block out all thinking. How nice that the sexual parts finally work and work with pleasure. How relaxing not to have to prove oneself to everyone and not to feel so devastatingly inferior. That is what the therapy is all about.

Pain is not the ultimate aim of this therapy. We are neither sadists nor masochists. Pain is embraced to get on with living. It is never an end in itself. It is just that pain stands in the way of pleasure. For the neurotic, pleasure is the successful analgesia of pain. For the normal it is a pure, global state of good feeling.

When we become detached from our feelings we lose touch with the meaning of our experience. Since it was the meaning of our early experiences that made them overwhelming, repression was enlisted to render them meaningless. Then we spend the rest of our lives looking for meaning. Feeling not only heals, it gives meaning.

The ultimate truth about neurosis lies on the level of experience. No amount of statistical data is going to help people understand what feelings are; feelings can never be understood in terms of ideas. The more one rationalizes and uses logic the less one understands about feelings. They are a universe unto themselves. Those who cannot feel need proof, yet no proof can help someone feel or understand the nature of feeling. Proof is a 'civilized' invention; feelings antedated that ability by millions of years.

Unlike other diseases, neurosis is a disease of the person, not an organ. It is the ultimate human disease. That is why it is so hard to find. It is everywhere and nowhere; yet it has a force of steel, and creates an explosive pressure that can disrupt the psyche and damage our organs; an invisible, intangible force that creates havoc without our knowing it;

and even when pointed out it is denied. What a dilemma. Neurosis stealthily invades every part of us so disguises itself along the way. When it is channelled into a specific affliction we come to think that 'it' is the real illness.

In my days of doing psychoanalytic therapy I met some great talkers who delivered up masterpieces of insights – and who never got well. 'More insights', we thought, never realizing that the insights were just one more defence. A person sometimes felt better with his insights because they became a protective barrier. But comprehending a sickness doesn't mean it goes away any more than a good diagnosis of high blood pressure will eliminate it. Why on earth did we ever think that it could work in the mental area? Neurosis isn't built through lack of insights, and more insights won't help eradicate it.

Once each aspect of a feeling is integrated it never has to be felt again. That is why one cannot go back and be neurotic again. One would have to put back all those felt pains.

What we all must learn is that there is no easy road, no shortcut to mental health, not after decades of deprivation and neglect. How could it be otherwise? Could anyone really imagine that there will be a magical solution to decades of pain – a solution that can be reached in a few weekends or perhaps months? How could it be a solution reached through a mantra, concentration on a higher force, periodic meditation, pills, etc.? It is simply not possible. Vitamins won't undo a harsh childhood. They will, however, attenuate its effects. There are no 'how to' books that are going to reverse a lifetime of no affection, no matter what the person thinks; unless a person's problems involve a serious lack of knowledge. 'How to' books can't touch major neurosis.

The only way out is the same as the way in: pain and more pain. There is no painless way out of pain as much as we would all desire it. The ones who already suffer sense the truth of hidden pain. They just need a safe place to go and feel.

Our patients consider the therapy to be an incredible

voyage. What a voyage of discovery it is. Everything the patient has to learn already lies inside him. It has only to be discovered. Feeling is like opening a book to one's own history. We become students of ourselves.

Does it last? Yes. It lasts because in giving someone back their tears we are restoring a natural function. Tears seem to right the entire system. Anyone who has had a good cry knows how much better they feel. Imagine crying out all of the misery of one's life. We have done five-year follow-up studies which indicate that the therapy holds. Patients go on feeling long after they leave the clinic, so that the therapy really continues on. It then becomes less of a therapy and more of a style of life. I do not think it possible to eradicate every last vestige of hurt in our systems.

Need as the Generating Source.

Concentration on need is basic and always progressive whether we are talking about a psychotherapy or a socio-economic system. Avoidance of need inevitably leads to reactionary systems, whether psychological or social. It leads to compensatory mechanisms making up for the lack of fulfilment of need; in the personal area, organ systems go awry. In the social sphere there is increased need for mental hospitals and prisons.

A recent survey found that even among men who were not addicts but who were entering prison for other crimes, eighty per cent had drugs in their systems. Doesn't that speak eloquently about the connection between pain and crime?

Primal Therapy has the power to unlock the unconscious. No other therapy thinks that it can or should be unlocked. Most think in quasi-religious terms that we are loaded with demons that must be left quiescent. So they do not rock the boat for fear of bringing about the disintegration of the personality. I have found that disintegration occurs only when too strong a feeling is provoked. If one is very careful in therapy this doesn't happen. Particularly when we make sure that every feeling is thoroughly discussed afterwards and applied to one's current life.

We have found the unconscious to be a friendly place. There are only the needs and pains of childhood all dammed up, trying to become conscious. We have spent a lifetime in tension because we could not let those memories into consciousness.

Consciousness is the cure for neurosis. Feeling is the vehicle to that end. To be conscious of feeling is our goal, no more and no less. Primal Therapy offers an individual a way into the unconscious, and hence a way out of unconsciousness. The feeling mind is a free one. What more can any therapy do?

EPILOGUE

Most of the clinics advertising today, despite their claims, have no connection with me. I recognize the great need for therapeutic help. To that end I have begun a training centre for those who have undergone the therapy and who have professional training. My hope is that all these individuals, who come from many countries of the world, will be able to practice soon, and perhaps by publication date I will have graduates to recommend. We are taking applications now from professionals for our continuous training programme, hoping to expand the Primal network as much as possible. We are also taking a handful of new patients into therapy for training purposes.

I must point out, however, that I did not invent feelings. They have existed throughout the millennia. I have found a way to retrieve them once they have gone underground. In the absence of a formal therapy there is a good deal that can be done. An understanding and sympathetic friend, is no doubt a good place to start. With him or her one can let down, cry, even scream, even if the friend isn't sure what it is all about. A little previous explanation would be helpful. But a good friend isn't going to be judgmental or critical. He or she will be content to 'be there' for you. Just talking to a friend about one's feelings, without screaming or deep crying, is also an important step. Anything on the way to expression is a bonus.

There are those who have no understanding friends. That does not preclude crying and screaming by oneself, at least letting the pressure out. It is, after all, feeling that we are after, and there is no monopoly on that. Of course, the best possible alternative is a skilled therapist. But there are not enough to go around so we shall have to improvise.

Some years ago a number of colleges formed 'Scream' clubs. They all got together and wailed. Of course, this is not therapy, but for some it served a good purpose. It taught them to let it all out, to express rather than repress. There are those who stop their cars when they feel bad, roll up the windows and scream.

It is not a bad thing simply to be aware that there is such a thing as feelings, and hopefully, what those feelings might be. There are many people who still don't realize that it is feelings that propel us, guide us, cause our symptoms, nightmares and physical ailments.

There are those who are concerned because I do not place enough emphasis on value systems, not enough weight to cognitive aspects, nor the spiritual. It is my belief that value systems derive directly out of feeling without having to be taught as such. For example, someone who has felt her childhood needs can sense what her own child needs. The mother doesn't need a list of values of what to do about child rearing. She doesn't need to be taught to pick up a crying child, to hold and soothe a child who has fallen down. She doesn't need to learn about the value of listening to a child's feelings, having already felt the deep need to be listened to.

A spouse doesn't need to learn about the value of tenderness in a marriage – something so absolutely basic. I'm not denying values, nor awareness, nor certain ideologies. What I have found, however, is that they seem a logical evolution in those who feel. I am therefore not advocating a bunch of decorticates roving around, mindless and heedless. On the contrary, teaching values is what is desperately needed for those who do not feel, who cannot sympathize, empathize and understand naturally. Too many of us not only lead lives of quiet desperation, but of broken dreams and secret compromises. We have compromised ourselves to make it through life. We can get back that self which has been compromised.

What could be more spiritual than valuing human life and the human spirit? For those who are deeply repressed, the value of human life is not so evident. No feeling person could travel thousands of miles, while in a special uniform, to kill a stranger based only on some abstraction, such as 'honour'. In the same way, a person who has felt his own nature deeply and has discovered its profound beauty, could not destroy nature around him for the sake of profits. One doesn't have to be educated to respect nature; it is inherent in the respect for one's own nature.

Values are the later development by the cerebral cortex all too often replacing feelings. Feelings came first. Values are inherent in them. We value life and everything associated with making it good and decent because we have felt the life inside of us and it is wonderful.

Primal Therapy is not 'Primal Scream' Therapy

Primal Therapy is not just making people scream. It was the title of a book. It was never 'Primal Scream Therapy'. Those who read the book knew that the scream is what some people do when they hurt. Others simply sob or cry. It was the hurt we were after, not mechanical exercises such as pounding walls and yelling, 'mama'. This therapy has changed what was essentially an art form into a science.

There are many hundreds of professionals practising something they call Primal Therapy without a day's training. Many unsuspecting patients have been seriously damaged thinking that they were getting proper Primal Therapy. I must emphasize that this therapy is dangerous in untrained hands. It is important to verify by contacting us.

Of the hundreds of clinics in the world using my name and falsely claiming to have been trained by me, I have never seen the therapy practised correctly. We spend about a third of our time treating patients who come from mock primal therapists.

For years a good part of our budget went for research. I was hopeful that other clinical centres would continue Primal research but such has not been the case.

I cannot honestly recommend any centre doing Primal Therapy now as I am no longer associated with any of them. What has compounded the problem is that some therapists have had a smattering of training by me and gone on to practice.

I'd like to offer Primal Therapy to the world. In every clinic we have established throughout the world we have been inundated with requests for therapy. It works. The patients know it. And I hope by this book to make it known to suffering humanity.

The Primal Training Center in Venice, California, is now accepting patients for Primal Therapy. We are looking forward to opening the Arthur Janov Center for Primal Therapy in Europe in the summer of 1993. Applications for both Centers should be addressed to the California clinic:

Primal Training and Treatment Center
1205 Abbot Kinney
Venice
CA 90291
USA

INDEX

To find out more about our books and to read about
more about Abacus and other Little, Brown authors
and titles, as well as events and book clubs,
visit our website

www.littlebrown.co.uk

and follow us on Twitter

@AbacusBooks
@LittleBrownUK

To order any of our titles direct to you in the UK,
please contact our mail order supplier on:

+44 (0)1832 737525

Customers not based in the UK should contact
the same number for appropriate postage
and packing costs.

To buy any of our books and to find out
more about Abacus and Little, Brown, our authors
and titles, as well as events and book clubs,
visit our website

www.littlebrown.co.uk

and follow us on Twitter

**@AbacusBooks
@LittleBrownUK**

To order any Abacus titles p & p free in the UK,
please contact our mail order supplier on:

+ 44 (0)1832 737525

Customers not based in the UK should contact
the same number for appropriate postage
and packing costs.